AUTHORS' NOTES

The authors would like to express their gratitude and appreciation to a number of people who gave of their time and assistance to help produce this book.

Joe Mullins and Ken Harrell of the *Globe* provided valuable insight and cooperation. We would like to offer a special thanks to them and *Globe* editor Tony Frost for graciously providing us with many of the photographs reproduced in this book. We also owe thanks to the Zuma Photo Agency for its assistance with other photos.

The book would not have been possible, however, without the time and assistance provided by those who agreed to give the authors the benefit of their knowledge, experiences, and information about this tragic case. Those sources include retired FBI agent Gregg McCrary, Marilyn Van Derbur Atler, Judith Phillips, Peter Boyles of KHOW Radio, Joe Barnhill, Jeff Merrick, Jane Stobie, Jim Marino, Frank Coffman, Boulder Director of Communications Leslie Aaholm, and former Mayor Leslie Durgin.

We also owe a debt of gratitude to our editor, Michaela Hamilton, and her staff at Penguin Putnam Inc. for their guidance throughout this project, and their continuing efforts to make this the best book it could be.

PROLOGUE

She turns slowly with her weight on one foot and the other leg cocked coquettishly at the knee. She glances back over her shoulder with a knowing smile as her hip swings around in just the right way to catch the eyes of those watching closely from the dark. She smoothly opens the clasp at the waist of her skirt, and it glides away from her body in a seductive flourish, revealing the high-cut bottom to the tight outfit she wears so well. She flips her blond hair and bats the made-up eyelids that accentuate her green eyes above her bright, ruby lips. She's drop-dead gorgeous—she knows it and so does everyone in the audience. She struts across the stage again as the MC booms out her name and pumps the crowd for more applause. She flashes what someday will be a million-dollar smile, and she knows that she is already the winner on this night. No one else can touch her.

Welcome to the world of JonBenet Ramsey. She is six years old.

CHAPTER 1

The night-shattering scream awoke the woman in the 700 block of 15th Street just after midnight on what had seemed to be a peaceful end to Christmas evening of 1996. Even in the haze of abruptly interrupted sleep, the woman was absolutely sure the piercing cry had come from the little girl in the house across the street—the Tudor mansion that would soon become the most famous, and haunting, house in the world. The woman awoke her husband, but by then the screaming had ended. He heard nothing at first. But then there was a sound—perhaps the clashing of metal against concrete a hundred or so feet across the street. The woman gave thought to calling 911, but decided against it. After all, the little girl's parents were home. Surely they would attend to whatever nightmare had brought such a terrifying shriek from their daughter. But the woman and her husband still had trouble falling back to sleep as those unsettling sounds echoed in their ears in the holiday darkness.

Unknown to them, another neighbor was also wondering about the events in that mansion with the high-peaked gables. Some strange, dim lights in the kitchen had caught the eye of the man who lived next door—just to the north on the street framed magnificently by the Flatirons and the front range of the Colorado Rockies, the majestic backdrop to the city of Boulder. In the several years he had lived there, he'd had a clear view into that side of the mansion but had never seen such eerie lights. They suggested to him that someone was moving stealthily about inside the house, perhaps trying not to awake anyone else.

Six hours later, these startled neighbors would begin to see unmistakable clues that they had indeed been witnesses to something so sinister, so bizarre, and so tragic that the rest of the world would soon focus on that house in this enchanted town in a way no one could have imagined.

The little girl whose scream had ripped through the cold winter night was gone, and she would never return. When the police arrived about six o'clock that morning, they were met with what surely seemed to be a kidnapping. The girl was missing, and an ominous, threatening note was all that was left behind. Had this little girl—an impish beauty queen with titles and trophies and tiaras—been spirited away from her bed by unknown intruders?

But then, as the hours passed with no word from these abductors, even more disturbing possibilities arose. In another, more careful search of the huge house, the little girl's father retrieved her abused, broken body from a basement room that had become her sepulcher. He carried her upstairs to a new resting place in front of the regally decorated Christmas tree. As her family and their friends knelt around her body and the police looked on solemnly, it seemed apparent that this beautiful, innocent child had been murdered.

JonBenet Ramsey was dead at six years old. And the death of this little girl with the unique name was about to be etched on the hearts of the world like few before her.

Amid the most bizarre investigation anyone had ever seen, the case would drag on through controversy and turmoil and conflict and accusations—but without solution. Dr. Cyril Wecht, a forensic pathologist a half continent away, would be the first to develop a coherent analysis of how and why JonBenet had died. From the publicly available materials, he would draw disturbing inferences about what might have happened that night. He would unlock secrets that others were unable or reluctant to face.

The eyes of the world would remain on Boulder, this New Age college town described as "Plan Boulder, twenty square miles surrounded by reality." Everyone would await the answer to the question:

Who killed JonBenet Ramsey?

Almost a year later, the police would turn to a new lead detective, Commander Mark Beckner. On December 5, 1997, Beckner would tell reporters assembled for his first news conference that the little girl's wealthy and prominent parents, John and Patsy Ramsey, remained "under an umbrella of suspicion." Others had come and gone under that same umbrella, but the Ramseys remained in its shadow.

But what Commander Beckner's well-turned phrase did not acknowledge was that there were many umbrellas of doubt over the case of the little beauty queen who screamed in the night. Many people remained under that skepticism in unique and extraordinary ways. And everyone wanted to know when those shadows would give way to the light.

* * *

The darkest umbrella covered John and Patsy Ramsey.

In the glare of television lights from around the world, their behavior had struck almost everyone as peculiar and troubling. Before their daughter's body was cold, the Ramseys assembled a slick, powerful defense team that built a seemingly impenetrable wall around them. When the Ramseys ventured carefully outside that wall, their words and appearances gave critics plenty of fuel to power suspicions that something about this handsome, wealthy, seemingly perfect couple was just not right. Their insistence that some deranged intruder had killed JonBenet seemed to many to be too preposterous to believe. As the details of the Ramseys' lives slowly emerged, critics continued to find copious reasons for suspicion. Defenders pointed to years of good conduct, hard work, and family togetherness. Was John Ramsey a driven, ruthless businessman or a gentle, loving father and dependable friend? Was Patsy Ramsey a fading beauty queen given to financial excesses and emotional obsessions? Or was she a dedicated mother, a courageous survivor of cancer, a generous and loyal friend?

There is, of course, no one proper, appropriate way to mourn when a precious daughter has been savagely abused and killed. But many were uncomfortable with the way the Ramseys responded. His cool, controlled calm. Her edgy emotion. Their uneasy silence, broken only by carefully orchestrated comments.

Were they the grieving parents of a hideously murdered daughter—or a sexual pervert and accomplice who abused their daughter's innocence, ended her life horribly, and then constructed a masterful cover-up?

* * *

After the Ramseys, the widest shadow covered the team they assembled to protect them. The effort was led by influential Denver attorney Hal Haddon, who had managed former U.S. Senator Gary Hart's first political campaigns. He was viewed as one of the most powerful lawyers in Colorado, with deep connections to the Democratic power structure that controlled state politics. Before long, some would marvel at his ability to hold the police and prosecutors at bay. The Ramseys' first official spokesman was a champion of right-wing heroes, a public-relations expert from Washington, D.C., named Patrick Korten. He was known for his outspoken defenses of Iran-Contra figure Oliver North and the embattled former attorney general Edwin Meese. In addition to a phalanx of lawyers and private detectives, the Ramseys would retain retired FBI agent John Douglas, often described as the father of the bureau's unit that produces psychological profiles of serial killers and other master criminals.

The Ramseys' team would wage months of battles over police requests for formal interviews with John and Patsy. The team would issue terse, angry criticisms of the cops and their suspicions of the Ramseys. Some would call those statements and other actions— like the full-page newspaper ads and the offered reward—little more than cynical spin doctoring aimed at deflecting suspicion. Others would counter that Haddon's team was doing exactly what it should— protecting its clients from a muddled, misdirected, and wrong-headed police investigation.

Soon after the investigation started, criticism of the Boulder police began to pile up. Over the ensuing months many pundits would conclude that the investigation had been botched from the outset. An avalanche of questions was raised about police performances at the Ramsey house on December 26. How many basic steps had been missed? How many opportunities had been frittered away? How many wrong turns had been followed? How many errors in judgment had accumulated? How much evidence had been destroyed, tainted, or simply overlooked? In this college town—this New Age mecca of liberal thinkers—there had been few murders and, therefore, there were few experienced murder investigators. JonBenet's death at the end of December was the first homicide of 1996. Despite that the Boulder police turned away offers of assistance from more experienced cops in Denver and the Colorado State Police. Chief Tom Koby would become—rightly or wrongly—a symbol of police arrogance. His own officers had no confidence in him. Detectives would be removed and replaced. Within the investigative team would be accusations of misconduct and even threats of lawsuits, officer against officer. After a year Commander Mark Beckner would become the new leader. But by then, many wondered, was it too late to track down JonBenet's killer?

Months would pass before doubts fell on the office of District Attorney Alex Hunter. A career prosecutor serving his seventh term in office, Hunter seemed to be a seasoned professional. He quickly drafted a team of experts, securing the formidable services of renowned forensic scientist Dr. Henry Lee and famed lawyer and DNA expert Barry Scheck—both of them fresh from their roles on the victorious defense team for O. J. Simpson. But as the months passed, questions would arise about Hunter's approach to the case. By the end of 1997, calls for appointment of a special prosecutor or intervention by the Colorado governor and attorney general were growing.

There were many—too many—questions haunting the case. But they all boiled down to a few that captured the essence of this uniquely American tragedy.

How did it happen?

Why did it happen?

Would anyone ever expose her killer?

Was her death being covered up and, if so, why?

Would there ever be justice for JonBenet?

Who killed JonBenet Ramsey?

CHAPTER 2

"Send help! Send help!"

The woman's panicked 911 call to the boulder Police Department at 5:52 A.M. shattered the calm of the morning after Christmas. Within minutes of the call on Thursday, December 26, 1996, patrol officers arrived at 755 15th Street—a sprawling three-story mansion in the neighborhood that abuts Chautauqua Park at the foot of the jagged Flatirons.

Another 911 call from the same house just three days earlier had turned out to be a false alarm. It had been phoned in during a big Christmas party, and an officer had been sent out to check. Everyone assumed a tipsy guest had been to blame.

But on this morning officers were met by the panicked residents of the charming Tudor-style house—John Bennett Ramsey and his wife, Patricia "Patsy" Ramsey, a socially prominent couple who had lived there for five years. The distressed Ramseys told the officers that Patsy—an attractive thirty-nine-year-old brunette—had awakened before dawn and gone downstairs to make coffee. As she descended the circular stairway from their third-floor bedroom, she discovered a three-page, hand-printed note on the bottom steps. As she began to read, she realized something was horribly wrong. Although the full text of the incredible note would not be seen by the public for some nine months, the police knew they had something extraordinary on their hands.

Written on white lined paper with a black felt-tipped pen, the note read:

"Mr. Ramsey,

Listen carefully! We are a group of individuals that represent a small foreign faction. We respect your bussiness [*sic*] but not the country that it serves. At this time we have your daughter in our posession [*sic*]. She is safe and unharmed and if you want her to see 1997, you must follow our instructions to the letter.

You will withdraw $118,000.00 from your account. $100,000 will be in $100 bills and the remaining $18,000 in $20 bills. Make sure that you bring an adequate size attache to the bank. When you get home you will put the money in a brown paper bag. I will call you between 8 and 10 am tomorrow to instruct you on delivery. The delivery will be exhausting so I advise you to be rested. If we monitor you getting the money early, we might call you early to arrange an earlier delivery of the money and hence a earlier pick-up of your daughter.

Any deviation of my instructions will result in the immediate execution of your daughter. You will also be denied her remains for proper burial. The two gentlemen watching over your daughter do not particularly like you so I advise you not to provoke them. Speaking to anyone about your situation, such as the police, F.B.I., etc., will result in your daughter being beheaded. If we catch you talking to a stray dog, she dies. If you alert bank authorities, she dies. If the money is in any way marked or tampered with, she dies. You will be scanned for electronic devices and if any are found, she dies. You can try to deceive us but be warned that we are familiar with law enforcement countermeasures and tactics. You stand a 99% chance of killing your daughter if you try to out smart us. Follow our instructions and you stand a 100% chance of getting her back. You and your family are under constant scrutiny as well as the authorities. Don't try to grow a brain John. You are not the only fat cat around so don't think that killing will be difficult. Don't underestimate us John. Use that good southern common sense of yours. It is up to you now John!

Victory!
S.B.T.C.

An incredible document.

Patsy told the police that as soon as she read that the note writer had her daughter, she screamed and rushed to JonBenet's second-floor bedroom. Her worst fears were realized when she discovered JonBenet missing. The Ramseys' nine-year-old son, Burke, was safe—still sleeping in his room at the other end of the hall. John Ramsey's two older children from his first marriage were not in Boulder at the time. John Andrew Ramsey, twenty, lived at a frat house on campus while attending the University of Colorado, just blocks from the Ramsey home. Melinda Ramsey, twenty-four, was a nurse in Marietta, Georgia.

Only John, Patsy, JonBenet, and Burke had been in the house that night.

From all appearances, JonBenet Ramsey had been kidnapped from the home of her wealthy parents by abductors who claimed to be international terrorists and had left a note promising a ransom call in two to three hours. A dramatic kidnap scenario, something right from the movies. The patrol officers called the station to ask for detectives to be dispatched to the house.

But the officers then conducted a superficial search of the house, making no effort to push open the apparently stuck door of a small basement room.

They compounded that with another error. They allowed the Ramseys to admit their pastor and four friends into the house, people that John or Patsy had called about the same time she called the police. Instead of securing the scene of an apparent kidnapping to protect vital clues—fingerprints, footprints, hairs, fibers, etc.—the officers started down a path that would contaminate the obvious crime scene—perhaps beyond salvation. No one but the police should have been permitted in the house, and certainly no one else should have been roaming the premises, treading heavily on the evidence that should have been carefully preserved. The whole house was a crime scene—even if this was a kidnapping—and it should have been secured and protected as the first order of business.

Around six o'clock that morning, the Ramseys had called Fleet White—an oil company executive and close friend who lived barely a mile away. White arrived a few minutes later with his wife, Priscilla, a dear friend of Patsy's. The Ramseys also had called John and Barbara Fernie—perhaps the Ramseys' closest friends in Boulder. Sometime after those couples arrived, the Ramseys' Episcopal priest, the Reverend Rol Hoverstock, also joined the growing support group that was contaminating the crime scene inside the mansion.

Detectives would not arrive until 8:10, two hours after the patrol officers. The conduct of those in the house before that would remain among the many mysteries in the case until September 1997, when writer Ann Louise Bardach would disclose in *Vanity Fair* magazine that she had gained exclusive access to some of the police reports. She quoted Officer Richard French, the first uniformed patrolman on the scene, as he described very odd behavior by Patsy and John Ramsey. According to Bardach, French said Patsy sobbed as she sat in an overstuffed chair in the sunroom, and a cool and collected John—ever the distinguished, graying executive of fifty-three—paced continuously and explained the sequence of events. He told the police that the family had spent Christmas evening at the Whites' home, returning about ten o'clock. JonBenet had fallen asleep in the car, and they had put her to bed in her clothes as soon as they got home. That was the last they had seen of her. They said they had heard nothing in the night.

French went on to state that Patsy sounded as if she were crying, but he saw no tears in her eyes. He was struck—haunted, in fact—by the way she kept staring at him, even peeking awkwardly from between her fingers when they covered her eyes. French added that he had seen no physical contact between the Ramseys, not a single touch of consolation or grieving affection. They barely spoke or even looked at each other.

French also noted that Patsy gave him two slightly different versions of how she discovered that JonBenet was missing. First she said she had gone to her daughter's room to wake her up about 5:45, found her gone, and then discovered the ransom note as she went down the stairs. That account later changed to the one Patsy would tell thereafter, in which she was on her way to the kitchen to make coffee and found the note on the stairs.

According to many published reports, the police errors continued when the detectives arrived. Detective Linda Arndt was in command until her supervisor, Sergeant Larry Mason, arrived later that day. Arndt, recent winner of the district attorney's award for advocates for crime victims, reportedly concentrated on "bonding" with the Ramseys, whom she saw as the victims of a terrible kidnapping. Law enforcement studies have shown that crimes in the home most often are committed by family members—in a 12 to 1 ratio. Also, she and the other detectives never split up the Ramseys and took detailed statements from each of them that day—another error. Detailed and independent statements were demanded by the most basic police procedure.

Officers were seen taking photographs of the melting snow in the front yard, but reports would insist that police had found no footprints in the snow around entry points to the house. Nor did they find evidence of forced entry, although one officer noted what could have been pry marks on a kitchen door that appeared to be less weathered than other marks nearby. John Ramsey told them that all of the doors had been locked when they went to bed the night before, and still locked when they discovered JonBenet missing that morning. The police also noted a small broken window in the basement—explained innocently by John—and a blue suitcase that rested just below it. Could that have been the way an intruder had squeezed into the house? It was deemed unlikely by the cops.

The police called the FBI and attached tape recorders to the phones to record the ransom call that was to come between eight and ten o'clock—

according to the bizarre note. Reports said FBI agents arrived later, sometime around one o'clock. Meanwhile, John Ramsey made phone calls to arrange the cash that had been demanded in the curiously specific amount of $118,000.

When no ransom call came, *Vanity Fair* quoted Arndt as writing in her report, John Ramsey left the house for about an hour—alone—between ten-thirty and noon to pick up the family's mail; she saw him open and read it later. That revelation has disturbed observers as much as anything else in the troubled investigation. How could the police let the father of a kidnapped girl, a man awaiting a ransom call that could decide his daughter's fate, leave the house in the middle of an investigation—without a police escort? And would a father be likely to leave and risk missing the call his daughter's life depended on?

The fate of a heavy black flashlight that looked out of place on a kitchen counter also became fodder for criticism of the investigators. Media reports said an officer suggested bagging it as evidence, but a detective was uninterested. When it was mentioned later and a detective decided to have it examined, it could not be found, the story went. That tale would be retold with a flourish much later, but new information from officials would suggest it was nothing more than a mistaken media report.

But perhaps the worst error occurred about one when Linda Arndt took John Ramsey, Fleet White, and John Fernie into the kitchen and asked them to search the house again, top to bottom, to see if they could find any sign of JonBenet or anything of hers that was missing. Here is an unnamed investigator's account to Bardach of what happened after that:

John Ramsey bolted from the kitchen and headed down to the basement. Fleet White told us that Ramsey went directly to a small, broken window in the north side of the house and paused. Fleet said to Ramsey, "Hey, John, look at this." And John said, "Yeah, I broke it last summer." He wanted Fleet to see the window to set up the intruder theory, but no one but a small child or a midget could have crawled through that space. While Fleet is looking at the window, John disappears down the hall, directly to the little room. . . . It's a huge basement with a lot of rooms and corridors, but Ramsey went directly to that room. He screamed, and Fleet ran to him.

Although the investigator said Fleet White had looked into that dark windowless room earlier and seen nothing, John Ramsey now had found his daughter's body in this tiny space intended as a future wine cellar. It was nothing now but bare concrete walls and floor and a single light bulb hanging from a cord; it was used to store Christmas decorations and to hide some of the children's presents. Bardach would report that Officer French was startled by the revelation later that the room, on the front corner of the basement, was directly under the chair where Patsy had sat as she watched him so intently.

Ramsey ran to JonBenet's blanket-wrapped body, pulled back the cover, and saw her ashen face. Her mouth was covered by duct tape, which he immediately ripped away. Her lips were blue and her body—stiff from rigor mortis—was cool to the touch. Her hands were thrown back above her head. She was dressed in a white knit top with a silver, sequined star on the front, and white long underwear.

A garrote of white cord was wrapped tightly around her neck and had furrowed into her skin. The cord was knotted to a wooden stick that had been used as a handle, allowing the garrote to be tightened by degrees. Strands of JonBenet's beautiful golden hair were caught in the cord and its knots. Another loop of the white cord loosely circled her right wrist, outside the cuff of her shirt.

According to a police affidavit released ten months later, "Fleet White came running upstairs, grabbed the telephone in the back office, located on the first floor, and yelled for someone to call an ambulance."

Back in the little concrete room, John scooped up JonBenet's body and dashed upstairs, where he laid her on the living room floor near the front door. Bardach's source for the *Vanity Fair* piece described John as carrying his daughter's stiffened body by placing his hands around her waist, the way one would carry a large doll. He never cried, but began to moan as he hovered over her body in the living room. Reminiscent of his wife's staring at Officer French, John looked around the room to see if anyone was watching him.

According to the source, Detective Arndt moved JonBenet's body to a location in front of the Christmas tree and covered the child with a blanket (Arndt would later deny that in a lawsuit she would bring against the city). Her description of the body in the affidavit released later was painfully frank: "The girl's lips were blue . . . she had rigor mortis; she was not breathing . . . her body was cool to the touch . . . there was a red circular mark in the front of her neck, about the size of a quarter, at the base of her throat; she had an odor of decay to her; she had dried mucus from one of her nostrils." Arndt concluded JonBenet had been dead for some time.

Patsy collapsed on top of her daughter. "And then she got on her knees," the Bardach source said, "and screamed, 'Jesus, you raised Lazarus from the dead. Raise my baby!' " At Arndt's request, the Reverend Hoverstock gathered everyone in a circle and led them in a grieving recitation of the Lord's Prayer.

Not long after that the Ramseys were whisked away to a secret location, never to return to the beautiful mansion that was about to become the most recognized house in the country.

In this sequence the police errors had grown immeasurably. Not only had they allowed the crime scene to be contaminated by the Ramseys' guests, but now John Ramsey had irretrievably corrupted both the location of his daughter's body and the body itself. He had disturbed and perhaps destroyed any evidence to be gathered from the area around her body in that little room, and then he had adulterated any evidence that could have been gleaned from the body. He had torn the tape from her mouth, picked her up, and carried her from the basement to the living room, all the while losing evidence—hairs, fibers, fingerprints, saliva, tears, and other bodily fluids—that may have been left on her body by her killer. During all this John was depositing on her that same kind of evidence from him. His actions would lead everyone to wonder whether he had reacted naturally as a horrified father finding his daughter's body, or he had intentionally polluted the scene and the body to make evidence collected after that worthless.

If JonBenet's body was covered with a blanket, that may have been damaging. Later reports stated that a spot of dried fluid on the body had disappeared by the time the blanket was removed. If that had been saliva, semen, a tear, or some other bodily fluid left behind by the killer, the hope of an incriminating link using DNA analysis had been lost forever.

In the seven hours since the police had arrived at the Ramsey house, the errors in the investigation had been almost too many to count.

At 10:45 that night, the day's final chapter was written. In a black body bag, JonBenet's body was wheeled from her home for the last time on a coroner's gurney and loaded into a station wagon. As cops and reporters watched silently, the sound of the slamming door echoed through the chill night.

CHAPTER 3

The first newspaper reports on Friday, December 27, about the death of JonBenet Ramsey were thin and barely hinted at the mystery and fascination with the case that would follow.

A six-year-old girl, at first reported kidnapped, had been found dead in the basement of her Boulder home. No details about a cause of death were released; an autopsy was scheduled for that day. The police said the Ramseys were grief-stricken but cooperating as best they could with investigators.

Family friends and neighbors began offering tidbits that soon would become the focus of this incredible story. JonBenet, a kindergarten student at High Peaks Elementary School, not only was excelling in the advanced program there, but had also been a multi-titled beauty pageant winner, including Little Miss Colorado of 1995 and America Royale Tiny Miss. She had even boasted her own float in the Colorado Parade of Lights a year earlier; her mother had walked alongside the float. JonBenet was following, it seemed, in her mother's footsteps. Patsy Ramsey had won the Miss West Virginia title in 1977 and had gone on to compete in the Miss America pageant. JonBenet's father was a respected executive, president of Access

Graphics, a high-tech subsidiary of the Lockheed Martin Corporation. Access Graphics sold computer systems, with sales for the year placed at $1 billion.

Joe Barnhill—a gentle, good-humored elderly fellow who lived directly across the street from the Ramseys and had developed a close relationship with them—told reporters they were a happy and congenial family. "The best neighbors." JonBenet was a polite, well-mannered little girl, and her mother traveled around the country to attend the beauty pageants with her.

Neighbor Nelson Schneider told the *Denver Post*, "They were so serious about this beauty queen stuff, but they never put any pressure on her."

The *Rocky Mountain News* printed perhaps the most telling detail of all in its first story that Friday. Bill Wise, an assistant district attorney for Boulder County, noted that it was unusual for the body of a kidnapping victim to be found at home.

"It's not adding up," Wise said.

And that was the first tiny crack in the delicate, short-lived Ramseys-as-victims scenario.

The house at 755 15th Street quickly became a local attraction. Television stations repeatedly aired the videotape that captured the startling contradictions on the tree-lined street. The beautiful mansion was still brightened by Christmas decorations, big candy canes along the sidewalk, and a lighted Santa Claus. But it was still chillingly foreboding under the dark cloud of JonBenet's death and the yellow crime-scene tape that still marked it.

Soon a different kind of videotape would hit the air waves—the images of a miniature showgirl, strutting without inhibition across a stage and belting out a song at these extraordinary children's beauty pageants.

No longer was this just the sad loss of some child somewhere. As viewers sat transfixed by these oddly beautiful and disturbingly erotic scenes, they began to wonder just who this little girl was. She was just six, but she was a troubling picture of sexuality and tease. Were these performances cute and sassy and talented? Or were they dark and distressing, tipping the scale of juvenile morality? Many parents shuddered as they watched and wondered what it all meant.

JonBenet could no longer be just a six-year-old girl who was killed in her home. What role, everyone began to wonder, had the teased hair and the makeup and the swiveling hips and the pouting lips played in her death?

The mystery of JonBenet Ramsey's corrupted, stolen innocence was about to replace the disillusionment with O. J. Simpson's bloody fall from grace in America's hearts, and in its powered-by-television quest for justice.

CHAPTER 4

Even though Dr. Cyril Wecht was enjoying his traditional two-week holiday out of the country with his extended family, he still began Friday, December 27, 1996, with his daily ritual of poring over the *New York Times*.

The Wechts were staying this year at Montego Bay in Jamaica, marking the twenty-fifth year of such gatherings in the Caribbean or Mexico, a tradition that had successfully survived four kids in college and graduate schools, and the assorted other distractions of life that sometimes keep families apart. This year they were enjoying a stay in a terrific house by the bay—for the first week. They would have to move to other quarters the next week because the house had been promised once again to the rather notable tenants who had rented it for a dozen years in a row—Paul and Linda McCartney.

As Cyril Wecht relaxed and read the *Times*, however, he had no idea that he was about to be introduced to one of the most mystifying and frustrating cases he had ever seen.

Wecht, the elected coroner of Allegheny County in Pittsburgh, was a world-renowned forensic pathologist whose extraordinary experience as a doctor and medical detective was supplemented with the unusual additions of a law degree and experience as an assistant district attorney. Among the 13,000 autopsies he had conducted and the 30,000 more on which he had served as a consultant are many of the most famous murder mysteries of modern times.

Most recently Wecht had been a consultant in the "trial of the century." His friends and colleagues— defense attorney F. Lee Bailey and forensic criminologist Dr. Henry Lee and Dr. Michael Baden—had turned to him for assistance in the case against O. J. Simpson. Wecht concluded that there was substantial, damaging evidence linking Simpson directly to the murders of his former wife, Nicole Brown Simpson, and her friend, Ronald Goldman. But the evidence also proved to Wecht that more than one assailant had inflicted those heinous injuries on two healthy young adults who would have fought like tigers. The savage slashing that ended those lives would have caused their blood to spatter over several feet, coating the assailants. There was not enough blood found at Simpson's home, on his clothing, or on his body to name him as the sole attacker.

Such high-profile cases were not new to Cyril Wecht. He had become well known for his study of the assassination of President John F. Kennedy, an analysis that led to the inescapable conclusion that Lee Harvey Oswald had not acted alone; the evidence clearly contradicted the "single-bullet" theory beyond any scientific doubt. In fact, it had been Wecht who disclosed to the world in 1972 that Kennedy's brain was missing from the assassination evidence in the National Archives.

Nor, Wecht had determined, was Sirhan Sirhan the

lone assassin of Senator Robert F. Kennedy. Called in to consult on the case—after deciding not to grant a request from Sirhan's mother to serve as his defense attorney—Wecht learned the senator had been felled by a shot that struck an inch behind his right ear and two that hit him near the right armpit. The fatal shot was fired from a pistol that had been within inches, perhaps less than two inches, from the right side or back of the senator's head. But Wecht's study and interviews with witnesses proved that Sirhan had been no closer than two to seven feet from Kennedy—and always in front of him. There had to have been another assassin who escaped into the crowd, and out of history.

Wecht's links to the Kennedy tragedies had continued. He had served as a consultant on the investigation into the death of Mary Jo Kopechne in Senator Edward Kennedy's car at Chappaquiddick, and had called for her body to be exhumed for an autopsy Wecht believed was necessary to establish a cause of death. His request was denied by a judge. Wecht did not maintain that her death was anything other than an accidental drowning, but the lack of an autopsy made an official and final verdict on the death impossible.

Wecht's consultation in the case of the murders of Dr. Jeffrey MacDonald's family—made famous by the book *Fatal Vision*—failed to lead to a definite conclusion about the Green Beret doctor's innocence or guilt, and that left Wecht deeply troubled. He interviewed MacDonald for hours and found his sincerity and candor impressive as he denied killing his pregnant wife and two young daughters in 1970. Wecht also found the evidence supporting MacDonald's claim of murder by four "hippie" intruders credible, despite the jury's decision to convict him of murder. In the end, Wecht's instincts told him Jeffrey MacDonald was innocent, but that was no consolation to the imprisoned MacDonald or the frustrated Wecht.

The untimely death of the King—Elvis Presley—offered a more definitive case study, and Wecht found evidence that Elvis did not die at forty-two of a heart attack, as the medical examiner in Memphis had announced in 1977. No, Elvis had been killed by the accidental combined effects of a number of drugs—principally codeine and a quantity of sedatives including Valium, Valmid, Placidyl, phenobarbital, and butabarbital. The amount of codeine in his system could have been fatal by itself. When a judge ordered the release of the autopsy report after Wecht's announcement, the doctor's conclusions were verified. A federal grand jury later indicted Elvis's personal physician on charges of overprescribing drugs, but he was acquitted.

Wecht was actively involved as a forensic pathologist and medical detective in other famous cases as well. He believes Claus von Bulow to be innocent of the charges that he injected his wife with drugs that caused her permanent coma, and that Jean Harris's shooting of her lover—Scarsdale diet doctor Herman Tarnower—was indeed accidental. Wecht has also studied the apparent suicide of White House counsel Vincent Foster and the fiery demise of the Branch Davidians with David Koresh at Waco.

With his unquestionable qualifications, his professional expertise, his articulate conclusions, and his brutal candor, Wecht had become a popular medico-legal analyst for television networks and many leading journalists, as well as a noted author, lecturer, and teacher. Defense attorney Alan Dershowitz had called Wecht "the Sherlock Holmes of forensic medicine," and F. Lee Bailey termed him "the best medical-research expert witness in the country."

But nothing in his forty-year career had prepared him for what he would read in the *Times* on this Friday. His attention was naturally attracted to a story about the murder of a beauty queen in Boulder, Colorado. But as he studied the photograph that accompanied the story, he found himself confused. There he saw what seemed a little girl. But she was a beauty queen? The more he studied, the more confused he became. There was this tiny figure, bedecked in teased blond hair and heavy makeup, wearing some kind of glitzy showgirl costume—but still childlike. Was she a midget or a child or what? He finally shrugged off the grotesque contradiction and dismissed the story with a shake of his head. He returned to his holiday reading with little more thought to this sad, odd event so far away.

CHAPTER 5

Asphyxia by strangulation.

The clinical term—the cold, hard fact—could barely describe the horror of the way JonBenet Ramsey had died. But it was as much as the public would get that Friday, when Boulder County coroner John Meyer announced the results of his autopsy. Someone had strangled JonBenet, and that made her death a homicide, he said. But he would disclose none of the sordid details—nothing about the garrote that had been tightened around her throat or the other salacious facts that would leak out to the public over the ensuing months.

On this day the *Denver Post* could report only that JonBenet had died in "a killer's stranglehold"—not exactly an accurate description, but all the newspaper knew at that time. The rest remained a mystery.

Police Commander John Eller, head of the Boulder detective division, stood somberly before a large photograph of a smiling, ponytailed JonBenet that had been thumbtacked to a bulletin board when he held the first news conference on the case that Friday. He was among the leadership in the department and on the Ramsey team, including Chief Tom Koby, who had never headed a homicide investigation.

The investigation remained "delicate and sensitive,"

Eller explained rather abruptly, and he could not reveal much about it. The police had treated the incident
as an apparent kidnapping at first, based on the ransom note and the information from the Ramseys. In
fact, the FBI still was consulting with the police, as
was the Boulder County district attorney's office.

Eller withheld details of the ransom note, except to
say it had demanded a specific amount of money and
was "a typical kidnapping ransom note that you
might find in any movie scenario." There had been no
additional contact from kidnappers, however.

He also offered a weak defense for the officers' failure to search the home thoroughly before the body
was found. They had, he explained, every reason to
believe that they were dealing with a kidnapping. "We
had no reason to believe the child would be in the
house at the time," he said. He added that applications
for search warrants were being prepared so the police
would have unrestricted opportunity to search the
house. Pressed by reporters, Eller insisted it was too
soon for the police to speculate if there had been a
bona fide kidnapping attempt.

The police still had not interviewed the Ramseys in
detail. "The parents are going through a tremendous
grieving process, we expect, and we're going to have
to work our interviews and those kinds of things
around it," Eller said.

He reflected on what had happened less than forty-
eight hours earlier to the victim in the photograph. "It
truly is a tragedy. This is a beautiful young girl, as you
can see—very vibrant and, from all reports we have at
this time, very precocious and a wonderful child."

Over the weekend, some of the details that would
spellbind Boulder and the world began to accumulate

in the media reports. Readers learned for the first time that the inexplicable figure of $118,000 had been chosen as the ransom demand.

In addition to repeated statements that police had no suspects and that the case remained a mystery, newspapers were beginning to assemble the first particulars about JonBenet, John, and Patsy Ramsey.

The accolades for JonBenet piled up quickly. Friends and neighbors called her a sweet, charming child—a joy to be around. Teachers at High Peaks Elementary described her as a wonderful child and an excellent, talented pupil. Costumed as a Christmas package, she had danced and sung "Jingle Bell Rock" at the school's holiday show. Counselors would be called in to help the other children deal with their fears and grief over their special classmate's death.

Her prowess in the juvenile beauty pageants was almost legendary, and it gave the public some insight into the little-known world of these "little misses." Eleanor Von Duyke, of Show Biz USA Pageant Productions, told the *Denver Post,* "With that long blond hair and big eyes, she just had that great Southern look that pageants really liked. She was just one of those natural-looking, beautiful girls that are so talented—the perfect pageant girl. Mothers are very competitive, and several told me that when JonBenet competed in pageants, they would take their daughters out of competition because they knew that if the judges saw a child that looked like she did, their girls would not win."

JonBenet appeared to come by that talent naturally. After winning Miss West Virginia of 1977, Patsy Ramsey had remained active in her home state's pageant as a sponsor, judge, and annual contributor to its

scholarship fund. Now she traveled the country with
JonBenet to attend her pageants. Patsy was well
known in Boulder's social and philanthropic circles as
a member of Opera Colorado and the Junior League.
But her life had been under a cloud even before Jon-
Benet was killed: she had been battling ovarian cancer.

John Ramsey had become a mover and shaker, a
highly regarded business executive, in the mere five
years he had been in Boulder. He had built a successful computer-sales firm, Access Graphics, in Atlanta
before that, and had merged it with others to form the
new corporation headquartered in Boulder. The company then had been bought by Lockheed Martin. As
president and chief executive officer, John had moved
to Boulder in 1991. In 1995 he had won the Boulder
County Business Report's Espirit Executive of the Year
Award. Access Graphics was one of Boulder's biggest
employers, with about 380 workers. John Ramsey was
said to be well liked by his employees.

But life had not been painless for John. In 1992 a
daughter from his first marriage had been killed in a
car crash. The death of Elizabeth Ramsey, twenty-two,
left him with two other children from that marriage—
John Andrew and Melinda.

When the Ramseys moved to Boulder, they had
paid about $500,000 for the house on 15th Street. Since
then, the newspapers reported, the couple had spent
$700,000 renovating the rambling three-story house
that boasted fifteen rooms, four bedrooms, six-and-a-
half baths, and a catering kitchen in nearly 7,000
square feet. The Ramsey home had been among those
featured on the Boulder house tour, a point of pride
for Patsy.

In keeping with their charitable and neighborly

WHO KILLED JONBENET RAMSEY?   39

reputation, the Ramseys had hosted a Christmas party for about a hundred friends at the house on Monday night, two days before Christmas. Santa Claus had arrived, bearing gifts for the neighborhood children.

JonBenet had given a gift to Santa—a box of "stardust."

Patsy Ramsey should have been celebrating her fortieth birthday on Sunday, December 29. Instead, the only event that afternoon was a special, invitation-only memorial service for JonBenet at St. John's Episcopal Church. About two hundred friends and neighbors attended, along with several police detectives there for what was officially called "investigative purposes." Neighbor Joe Barnhill said there wasn't a dry eye in the house as those assembled shared the grief of JonBenet's loss. They recited the Twenty-third Psalm. They sang hymns and listened to a soloist's rendition of the Lord's Prayer. A devastated Patsy Ramsey was so shaken that she had to sit throughout the entire service. On a cloth pendant around his neck, John wore a medallion JonBenet had won—a Christmas gift from the daughter he had come there to mourn.

Among those who spoke to the congregation was Bill McReynolds, the family friend who had dressed as Santa Claus for JonBenet just six days earlier—the man who had received her gift of stardust.

One of the detectives in attendance, Steve Thomas, later told the *Denver Post*, "It was an emotional service, which you'd expect for a six-year-old child who had been murdered."

The police released JonBenet's body to her family that day. After the memorial service, about a dozen family members accompanied the body onto a corporate jet for a flight back to Atlanta—and a funeral and burial in the town where JonBenet had been born.

As the next week began, the police had little new to say about the investigation. Leslie Aaholm, the city's director of communications who often served as spokeswoman for the police, said the Ramseys still had not submitted official statements. "They've been grief-stricken, and not in any condition to be interviewed," she explained. She said the Ramseys were in seclusion under protective custody of the police—but not under house arrest.

She added that officers still were processing the house for evidence and clues. The police had obtained hair, blood, and handwriting samples from JonBenet's brothers, Burke and John Andrew.

The architect who helped renovate the Ramseys' house had been contacted by the police less than a day after the body was found. Tom Hand had provided detectives with floor plans, and he offered the *Rocky Mountain News* his appraisal of the chances that someone had broken into the place—not likely in a house he thought would be "pretty difficult" to breach. "Patsy's pretty security conscious. She wouldn't . . . leave anything unlocked," he said.

Sergeant Larry Mason was leading the investigation and had thirty officers assigned to what he called a "damn tough" case. He said police had no suspect, but among the crucial developments expected in the immediate future was more information from the autopsy.

Meanwhile, doubts about what appeared to have happened in that house and what really happened were growing. Ted Rosack, the former agent in charge of the FBI in Denver, told the *Post* that the case was "too strange." He added, "This one doesn't compute." What about this ransom demand for $118,000? "It's too cheap," he shot back. "In the 1960s, we were getting notes asking for $250,000, which was a lot of money then. That's nothing today."

On Monday, mourners paid their respects to the Ramsey family during visitation for JonBenet at the Mayes-Ward Dobbins Funeral Home in the Atlanta suburb of Marietta.

Perhaps the most startling—and to some, troubling—development in the early days of the case was reported on Tuesday, December 31. John Ramsey, the mourning father, had hired a lawyer. Bryan Morgan—a prominent criminal-defense attorney—confirmed that he had agreed to represent John. The *Rocky Mountain News* reported that Morgan lived in Boulder, had served as assistant city attorney there for two years in the 1960s, and had developed a working relationship with the city's police department.

The *News* asked Morgan why John Ramsey needed a lawyer. "The district attorney has said no one is ruled out" as a suspect, Morgan explained succinctly. What had he told his new client about talking to the police? "I have zero to say about what I have or have not told my client." Only later would it be learned that he had told the police that they were absolutely not to speak directly to the Ramseys. All contact had to go through Morgan now.

The *News* noted that Morgan—who was once nominated but not chosen for the Colorado supreme court—had won an acquittal for a woman accused of murdering her doctor husband in 1978. Morgan convinced the jurors that the husband had been shot by two intruders, one of them a lesbian who had molested his wife after he was killed.

The *Denver Post* took a broader view of John Ramsey's legal move. Bryan Morgan, fifty-nine, was a partner in the powerful Denver firm of Haddon, Morgan & Freeman, housed in a stylishly renovated mansion on Capitol Hill. He had been involved in a number of high-profile criminal and civil cases in his thirty years before the bar. In 1984 he had run unsuccessfully as a Democrat for the board of regents at the University of Colorado. Colleagues called him the perfect lawyer to guide the Ramseys through the puzzling, perhaps dangerous, legal labyrinth ahead of them. Morgan was known to be a compassionate man, a passionate advocate, and an expert adviser.

Notable in addition to all of Morgan's qualifications, the *Post* reported, was one of the details in the résumé of the firm's senior partner, Hal Haddon. He had managed former U.S. Senator Gary Hart's successful campaigns in 1974 and 1980, and had been a top adviser on the senator's presidential campaign in 1988. Some sources would say later that had Hart not been sunk by his dalliance with Donna Rice aboard the boat ironically christened *Monkey Business,* a President Hart probably would have appointed Haddon to the cabinet post of attorney general. Hart's remarkable slide into oblivion had not taken Haddon with him, however. Haddon still was considered to be at the top of the politically connected lawyers in the Democratically controlled state of Colorado. He counted among his political allies Governor Roy Romer, former Governor Richard Lamm, and, *Vanity Fair* would add, Boulder County District Attorney Alex Hunter—the man to whom any prosecution in the JonBenet Ramsey case would fall.

That kind of political influence is known in the business as "juice," and Haddon had plenty of it. And he had just been drawn into the nation's most sensational murder case, on his home turf.

Some time later it would be learned that the Ramseys' decision to hire counsel had come on the advice of a close friend, lawyer and former prosecutor, Mike Bynum. He had told them immediately that they needed someone qualified to guide them through what was coming, and he recommended the Haddon firm. But exercising every citizen's right to counsel would cast a long and dark shadow over the Ramseys.

A few more legal and investigative details came out that day as well. The police said there had been no signs of forced entry into the house, a provocative detail that would be cited endlessly during debates about this case. Reports also confirmed that day that John had been the one who found his daughter's body in the yet undisclosed hiding place in the house where there had been no forced entry.

City spokeswoman Leslie Aaholm said the police still had not interviewed the Ramseys, not even before they flew out of Colorado for their daughter's funeral in Georgia. "It wasn't an appropriate time to question them," she said. But she confirmed that John Ramsey had provided the police with what she called "nontestimonial evidence"—samples of his blood, hair, and handwriting, the same cooperation already granted by his two sons. Those samples would be analyzed at the crime lab run by the Colorado Bureau of Investigation.

The police also announced that John Andrew Ramsey

and his sister, Melinda, had been out of the state when their half sister died. The police had for the first time ruled out two people as suspects.

Meanwhile, Lockheed named John Ramsey's supervisor, Gary Mann, as acting president at Access Graphics to fill in for Ramsey while he was away from the company to take care of his tragic personal business.

The same day that word of John Ramsey's decision to retain legal counsel was hitting the streets in Colorado, the Peachtree Presbyterian Church in Atlanta was filling with more than two hundred mourners who came to say a final good-bye to JonBenet. At ten o'clock on the last day of 1996, in a church still ablaze with Christmas garlands and poinsettias, a church where her parents had been married and she had been baptized, JonBenet was remembered in a service that would be recalled as heartbreakingly emotional.

In a polished maple coffin, JonBenet wore one of her pageant dresses and one of the glittering rhinestone tiaras that identified her as the winner of so many "little miss" titles. She held a stuffed animal in her arms.

Shirley Brady, a former nanny for the Ramseys when they lived in Atlanta, would later recount for the *Denver Post* her moments with a devastated John Ramsey as he knelt at the coffin, stroking his daughter's hair, talking to her, and weeping as he lamented to Brady that they had killed his baby, his little girl.

In death, Brady said, JonBenet looked like a china doll as she lay in the coffin.

Brady gave the Ramseys' son Burke a gold angel pin for his lapel. At just nine, he seemed overwhelmed by it all, she said.

"Anybody who thinks that this family could have committed this atrocious thing is insane," she insisted.

As the service began, the Rev. W. Frank Harrington—who had performed the Ramsey wedding and JonBenet's baptism—described the feeling that the future has been lost when a child dies. "The mind cannot accept and the heart refuses to grasp the death of one so young, who is suddenly taken from us by cruelty and malice by some unworthy person."

Dressed in a white robe, the minister assured the mourners that they were not alone in their grief. "I can tell you that the heart of God is broken by the tragic death of JonBenet Ramsey," he said. "Through our tears, if we look closely, we will see the tears of God."

He brought tears from everyone when he announced, "We're going to sing now the childhood song, 'Jesus Loves Me, This I Know.' We're going to sing now, and we can cry as we sing." They all did just that.

He turned to a different musical source to recall the close relationship between JonBenet and her mother. Quoting a song from Broadway's *Gypsy*, Harrington said the mother and daughter often sang the lyrics arm in arm. "Wherever we go / Whatever we do / We're gonna go through it / Together."

In the front pew, John Ramsey kept his arm around his veiled wife's shoulder and stroked her back. As the soloist again sang the Lord's Prayer, a weeping Patsy raised her black-gloved arms toward Heaven. Patsy lingered at the closed coffin at the end of the service. She knelt there, pressed her face against the wood, and clung to it desperately.

Then the pallbearers carried JonBenet to the hearse for the drive to St. James Episcopal Cemetery in

Marietta. Outside the church and across the road from the cemetery, television cameramen gathered to record the somber chapter in what was becoming a story of great national interest. The service inside the church had been taped by cameramen from Peachtree Presbyterian's video production department.

At noon on New Year's Eve, JonBenet's coffin was lowered into the grave under a dogwood tree and next to the burial place of her half sister Elizabeth Ramsey. As the mourners filed away, Patsy Ramsey stayed behind again to touch the flowers. When the family's limousine finally drove away from JonBenet's grave, Patsy turned and cast one more long look back.

The world would learn the next day that Patsy Ramsey was sharing something besides her grief with her husband. Like John, Patsy was represented by an attorney. She had her own counsel, Patrick J. Burke, another partner in the Haddon firm. Burke was a former assistant attorney general in Colorado and federal public defender, and had won an acquittal for the man who had been charged with gunning down Denver talk-radio personality Alan Berg.

Observers would find plenty to chew on in this latest move. Was obtaining separate counsel for Patsy simply a wise course? Or did it signal some divergence of interests, some conflict between husband and wife? Was it prudent or excessive? Was it just smart or was it necessary?

Either way, it would not be the only news that day.

CHAPTER 6

"There is a killer on the loose."

Patsy Ramsey, on the verge of tears, did not look directly into the television camera as she spoke softly.

"I don't know who it is. I don't know if it's a he or a she. But if I were a resident of Boulder, I would tell my friends to keep . . ."

She began to cry, and her voice dropped to a hoarse whisper as the husband moved to support her. "It's okay," he said gently.

She struggled to keep going through her tears.

". . . to keep your babies close to you. There's someone out there."

In a move that shocked the nation, John and Patsy Ramsey went to the Atlanta studios of CNN News on January 1, 1997, for an exclusive interview—just twenty-four hours after they had buried their daughter. For twenty-seven emotional and spellbinding minutes they offered their account of that awful morning, answered questions about the last seven days, proclaimed their innocence of any involvement in their daughter's death, and thanked their friends for supporting them in this terrible time. They announced they were posting a $50,000 reward for information leading to their daughter's killer, and that they were hiring private investigators to assist in the search for clues.

They began the interview with reporter Brian Koebel by disclosing that they both had provided blood, hair, and handwriting samples, as well as fingerprints, to the police. They hadn't been offended by that request. Patsy explained, "It was difficult, but, you know, they need to know. I mean, our handprints are all over our home, so they need to know if there are other ones."

Patsy followed with her stark warning of a killer on the loose, prodding Koebel to state that the FBI had said they didn't necessarily regard what had happened as a kidnapping.

John responded with his version of the old legal argument that if something looks like a duck, walks like a duck, and quacks like a duck—it's probably a duck. "I don't know. There is a note that said, 'Your daughter has been kidnapped. We have your daughter. We want money. You give us the money and she'll be safely returned.' "

Patsy finished her husband's thought. "That sounded like a kidnapping to me."

"Yes," John added in a serious tone as he addressed suspicions about a phony kidnapping, "that's what concerns me, because if we don't have the full resources of all the law enforcement community on this cause, I'm gonna be very upset."

He spoke like a man used to marshaling the maximum effort from those who took his orders.

Koebel moved quickly to the obvious issue. "Inevitably, speculation on talk shows will focus on you. It's got to be sickening."

John snapped at that bait. "Oh, it's nauseating beyond belief."

"You know," Patsy offered, "America has just been hurt so deeply with the tragic things that have happened. The young woman [Susan Smith] who drove her children into the water. And we don't want what happened with O. J. Simpson. I mean, America is suffering because they have lost faith in the American family. We are a Christian, God-fearing family. We love our children. We would do anything for our children."

"Do you truly think the perpetrator will be found?" Koebel asked.

"Yes, yes . . . has to be found," John said.

"Do you think it's a single individual?"

"Yes, in my heart I do."

"Do you take some comfort in believing that Jon-Benet is in a better place now?"

Patsy answered quickly, "Absolutely."

John echoed and elaborated. "Absolutely. That's the one thing that we want people who are dealing with us to know—that we believe that. We know that in our heart."

"She will never have to know the loss of a child," Patsy said as she began to recall the Ramseys' recent heartaches. "She will never have to know cancer or the death of a child."

John seemed wistful as he recalled the death of his older daughter Elizabeth. "We learned when we lost our first child that sooner or later everyone carries a very heavy burden in this life. JonBenet didn't carry any burdens."

The Ramseys explained that they decided to talk to the country on this holiday because they realized that

so many people had been praying for them and grieving with them, so many others had been touched by
JonBenet's death, and they wanted to thank them for
their concern. John said he had been touched when he
heard about a headline in a local newspaper that said,
"Georgia Says Goodbye." He began to choke up as he
explained, "I thought, 'Boy, this is hurting a lot of people,' and we thank them."

He said this interview also was a way to plead for
help from anyone who knew anything about Jon-
Benet's death.

Koebel again turned to one of the many questions
swirling around the case and the Ramseys. Why had
they hired attorneys? John said he had relied on guidance from friends, their minister, their doctor, and others, and a friend had suggested that it would be
foolish not to have a knowledgeable lawyer who
could guide them through this investigation.

Koebel pushed further, and drew an enlightening
answer. "Most laymen who don't understand would
say, 'Why? You're grieving parents. You want to find
somebody? Why an attorney?' "

John revealed his grand strategy. "Well, it's not just
an attorney. We are also assembling an investigative
team to assist. I want the best minds this country has
to offer to help us resolve this. This doesn't come from
anger. It comes from knowing that the only way my
family can move on now is to resolve who and why
this happened."

The Boulder police had been marvelous, he added,
caring and compassionate. "I know this has hurt them
in their hearts. They're parents as well, and I know
they're working very hard. But I want whatever re-

sources I can bring to bear; whatever it takes, we're gonna do."

Patsy's eyes begged. "Anyone . . . if anyone knows anything—please, please help us. For the safety of all the children, we have to find out who did this."

John added, "We can't go on until we know why. There is no answer as to why our daughter died."

Koebel asked about the ransom note, drawing Patsy's first public statement about what had happened that morning.

"I couldn't read the whole thing," she said through more tears. "I'd just gotten up. It was the day after Christmas, so we were going to go visiting, and it was pretty early in the morning. I had gotten dressed and was on my way to the kitchen to make some coffee. And we had a back staircase from the bedroom and I always come down that staircase. I'm usually the first one down. And the note was lying across—the three pages—across the run of one of the stair treads. And it was kind of dimly lit. It was just very early in the morning. And I started to read it, and it was addressed to John. It said, 'Mr. Ramsey,' and it said, 'We have your daughter.' And I, you know, it just—it just wasn't registering. I may have gotten through another sentence. 'We have your daughter,' and I don't know if I got any further than that. And I immediately ran back upstairs and pushed open her door, and she was not in her bed, and I screamed for John."

Was there anything in the note that struck John particularly? Koebel asked.

"Well, I read it very fast. I was out of my mind, and it said, 'Don't call the police.' You know, that type of thing. And I told Patsy to call the police immediately, and I think I ran through the house a bit."

Patsy nodded. "We went to check our son."

John elaborated: "We checked our son's room. Sometimes she sleeps in there and, uh, we were just—"

"We were just frantic," Patsy finished the thought. "And I immediately dialed the police, 911, and he was trying to calm me down. And I said our child had been kidnapped . . . and I was screaming, 'Send help! Send help!' And I think then I dialed some of our very closest friends. They didn't even ask. I just said, 'Come quickly.' And an officer was there. It seemed like an eternity, but I know it was just a few minutes."

Did the demand for ransom of $118,000 strike John as strange?

"Yeah." But their friends had the money assembled in an hour.

Koebel pressed again. "You have to wonder what happened. Was this a true attempt to get ransom?"

"I don't know," John said. "It makes no sense. I don't know if it was an attack on me, on my company . . ."

Koebel asked the difficult question about finding JonBenet's body.

"Well, we waited until after the time that the call was supposed to have been made to us," John explained, "and one of the detectives asked me and my friend who was there to go through every inch of the house to see if there was anything that was unusual or abnormal or out of place. I think she was actually asking us to do that more to give us something to do to occupy my mind. And so we started in the basement and, uh, we were just looking, and we have one room in the basement that, uh, when I opened the door— there were no windows in that room—and I turned the light on and I . . ."

John Ramsey choked up again. "That was her. I

hoped that she was okay, but I could tell she probably wasn't. I screamed, carried her upstairs."

He confirmed the reports from Denver that day that her mouth was covered by duct tape.

The Ramseys said they would be returning to Boulder within days, even though that would be difficult for them and they had felt at first that they would not return. But the only reason they were going back was to help the police find out who did this.

Would they be offended by a police request for another interview or by accusatory questions?

"No, no," John said. "We're ready now to get this resolved. It's got to be resolved for us to get on with our lives, to continue with the grieving process."

How was Burke doing?

"He's, on the surface, doing fine," John said. "We've talked about it a bit, when he wants to talk."

Koebel drew out more details about the note: printed with a felt-tip pen, with proper borders and indented paragraphs. Did its location on the back stairs used by the Ramseys lead them to believe the killer was someone familiar with their patterns?

"Well, that's certainly our suspicion, for several reasons," John said. "One, that it's a fairly large house, and to know where JonBenet's bedroom was . . . And the room that we found her in is kind of a remote part of the basement."

Patsy agreed. "A casual guest would not know where that room is. It's, you know, kind of out of the way."

But she said she would be crushed if the killer was someone close to them. "I'm hoping it's someone that we don't know, but they have some vendetta against the corporation or the parent company, and this was a way to . . . You know, if it turns out to be someone that we had known and had trusted in our home or has visited, I just don't know if I can take it."

Under all of the strain, how were the Ramseys doing as a couple?

John nodded. "We're closer than we've ever been."

Patsy's religious convictions surged forward. "I think God has a mission for us. We don't know what that will be, but if there is any good that can come from this, He will lead us, and we are waiting for Him to tell us what it is that we're to do. And if He can just ask this grieving nation to pray with us, pray for our child, love your children, love your family, and value every precious moment of every day with your children."

Had the police interviewed the Ramseys in detail on December 26?

Patsy nodded. "I had questions all the day of her death. For hours they asked us questions and questions, trying to get a chronology." But she said the police were compassionate and tried to help. "They immediately had two lovely ladies there who were, you know, trying to help us emotionally. And, you know, Boulder is not like . . . This is not something that happens in Boulder. Boulder is a small, peaceful town, unlike Atlanta or New York or L.A. where this, God forbid, is a much more frequent occurrence, this does not happen in Boulder."

Koebel asked again if they would be willing to sit down with the Boulder police.

"Absolutely," John said. "We want them to know everything possible."

"Everything," Patsy agreed. "Whatever they want. Whatever anyone wants. We will cooperate."

Koebel asked how the Ramseys wanted JonBenet remembered, and how they would remember her.

John smiled again. "Well, like all parents, we would say she's a perfect child. But the thing to remember about her was that if I would frown, she would look at me and say, 'Dad, I don't like that face.' And I would smile, and she'd say, 'That's better.' That's just the way she was."

Patsy offered her final thoughts. "She loved her daddy. She loved her daddy. She was Daddy's girl. She's such a happy, spiritual child. She would ask me, she said, 'Mommy, what's the difference in a day and a daydream, and how do you know if a day is real?' And I said, 'Well, you just know because you can smell the flowers and see the clouds.' And she's very spiritual. She had a deep sense of understanding the world around her for a very young child. I think that was because she had a wonderful Sunday school experience and a wonderful Christian education. She went to Christian preschool, and those teachers were just so wonderful, and she absorbed all of that much more deeply than I think I realized. And I am so grateful to them for the teaching that they provided for her."

And with that, the Ramseys' address to a confused nation ended.

At six-thirty that evening, four hours after the interview was aired, five detectives from Boulder boarded a flight from Denver to Atlanta to begin their investigation of the Ramseys' lives there. Sergeant Larry Mason would not comment when asked what they hoped to accomplish in Georgia, or if the trip had been planned after police saw the interview on CNN.

CHAPTER 7

His Caribbean holiday over, Dr. Cyril Wecht was back at work in Pittsburgh on Monday, January 6, when he took a call from Ken Harrell, a reporter at the *Globe*—one of the leading supermarket tabloids that are at once universally condemned and immensely well read. The *Globe* had not contacted Wecht before, and he was a little surprised when they asked him to review a case they were covering "on the West Coast." They needed it done in a big hurry, but Harrell didn't mention the name of the case and Wecht didn't ask. Being called in as a consultant was such a common experience that his curiosity was not yet fully engaged. He explained that he was unable to make a trip west right then, so he provided Harrell with the names of some of his colleagues out there who might be able to accommodate the *Globe*. Harrell offered his thanks and hung up.

But the reporter called back in a couple of hours. The *Globe* wanted Wecht and no one else. Reluctantly, Wecht acquiesced, on his terms; he would look over the material if they brought it to him. He suggested that Harrell call FedEx. But Harrell had something more dramatic in mind; he would have it hand-delivered to Wecht the next day. Harrell offered a consulting fee, but Wecht turned it down. When dealing with the media, he preferred to keep his professional opinions, conclusions, and integrity unfettered by fees. Later, the *Globe* would even send a check; Wecht returned it. There was nothing wrong with accepting pay for his professional services, but Wecht preferred to do it his way.

The next day, a woman working for the *Globe* in Cleveland flew to Pittsburgh and came directly to Wecht's office. She presented him with a number of photographs.

Wecht was stunned to realize that they were of the body of JonBenet Ramsey. The little girl whose photo had so confused him days earlier now had come to him in death, as had so many victims of violence in the past. But these photos did not resemble the one he had seen in the newspaper—the one showing a pint-sized showgirl dressed and painted to look like an alluring little vamp. No, these pictures the *Globe* had somehow obtained were entirely different.

One showed JonBenet's neck—but not her face. A white cord, apparently of some kind of woven fabric, formed a tight noose around the neck. The cord then was looped and knotted around a thin, rough, jagged-ended piece of wood, looking little more than a stick snapped off a tree. A tuft of blond hair was caught in the knot and under the cord—a pitiful image. Other photos showed the same kind of cord looped loosely around her right wrist, where a ring of gold lace adorned her middle finger—another adult affectation.

Cyril Wecht had seen similar photographs of violent death in the past, but not involving a six-year-old girl found dead in her home. Those well-known facts of the Ramsey case were important supplements to what could be seen in the photographs and could be inferred by an experienced forensic pathologist.

When Ken Harrell called for an analysis, Wecht told him that the photos immediately suggested that someone had been playing a dangerous game. The way the cords were tied around the neck and wrist suggested that JonBenet had been bound not with the intent to kill but to restrain. The cord around her neck showed several loops around the stick, indicating the stick had served as a handle to turn and to tighten the noose—as if it were a tourniquet. With the loop around the wrist, Wecht believed there may have been an effort to keep her from resisting her assailant.

All of that fit with something Wecht had seen from time to time in his autopsy work—the phenomenon of binding during sexual activity. Bondage appealed to some and was practiced in different ways, each an apparent sexual turn-on—physiologically and psychologically—to those being bound or those doing the binding.

But applying it to the neck had a distinct physiological effect that Wecht had also seen and investigated in the past—hypoxia, a decreasing supply of oxygen to the brain. This was not done with the intent to kill. No, the intent was to decrease oxygen for an entirely different, and very specific, purpose. Forensic pathologists saw this most often in men who applied ligatures around their own necks to decrease oxygen flow and thereby heighten the sexual experience during masturbation—a little-discussed practice known technically as auto-erotic asphyxiation.

Unfortunately, the men's search for the ultimate—if singular—sexual experience sometimes resulted in an overly enthusiastic pursuit. As they pushed the envelope to reach an even more spectacular orgasm, the nooses around their necks sometimes tightened too much, causing them to pass out and slump even harder against the ligature—in effect hanging or strangling themselves. The ropes or cords they used often were looped over bedposts, tops of doors, around doorknobs, or for nature lovers, even over tree limbs.

Such incidents occasionally were mistaken for suicides, but Wecht always thought that was an obvious error. To him, there were clear differences that should have been easily recognized by a capable forensic examiner. For one thing, Wecht had seen a number of cases that involved the use of women's lingerie by the men. A student at Carnegie Mellon University in Pittsburgh was found dead while dressed in a tasteful, expensive ensemble including panties and a bra, stockings, a skirt, and sweater. There were more bizarre fantasies acted out as well, such as a Westinghouse executive found dead after strangling himself accidentally while dressed in a complete scuba outfit, including the mask and wet suit. His wife found him in the bathroom, where he died while kneeling into the noose around his neck.

In JonBenet's case, Wecht concluded that someone had applied the noose to her neck to reduce the flow of oxygen to the brain in an extraordinary act—a vicarious form of auto-erotic asphyxiation. Someone had found sexual stimulation by forcing JonBenet to experience the terribly uncomfortable and even terrifying effect of this near strangulation; at least, it was supposed to be near strangulation. This had been what Wecht could only consider a sick, perverted sex game. Obviously, a six-year-old girl was too young to be seeking out such sexually aggressive activity or to find sexual arousal in it. Someone else—probably an adult—was forcing it upon her to feed his or her own sexual appetite. Wecht expected that this torture inflicted on JonBenet had been accompanied by some other kind of sexual activity—masturbation by the other person or the simultaneous sexual molestation of JonBenet.

Wecht could not help but believe this adult-level, extreme form of sexual activity was linked tragically to the first photograph he had ever seen of this little girl—when she looked like anything but a little girl. In that picture she was six going on twenty-three, he had thought. Had someone enjoyed dressing her as an adult, putting her into that sophisticated makeup and hairstyle, to feed some unnatural sexual desire for her? Had her participation in these troubling beauty pageants for kids played into her molester's hands? Had it even led her unknowingly toward her agonizing death?

The possibility that this variation of auto-erotic asphyxiation was involved in a death would shock many people, Wecht knew. But it was not unprecedented. In August 1990 a thirteen-year-old boy in the St. Louis area who had read about the practice experimented with it on his eight-year-old brother and a seven-year-old friend. The boys went to the woods and stripped—neatly folding and stacking their clothes—and the oldest tied their shoe laces around their necks to try this new game. Despite the harmless intent, both of the younger boys were fatally strangled. When their bodies were found, the community feared that a homicidal sexual predator had invaded their quiet neighborhood. But the oldest boy confessed—shocking everyone and generating a new level of discussion about this sexual phenomenon that many had never even heard of. He was prosecuted through the juvenile courts on charges of second-degree murder and sodomy.

The FBI estimates that as many as one thousand people die experimenting with auto-erotic asphyxiation every year. The mother of one of those victims from Scottsdale, Arizona, started a support group called Bereaved Parents, Inc., and travels the country hoping to educate young people to avoid what she called "The Silent Killer."

In JonBenet's case, the circumstances brought Wecht to another equally surprising conclusion. Since her abuser had not meant for JonBenet to die during this sexual game of torture, there had to be another explanation for her death. If the noose had not been tightened with death as the purpose, why had she died at all?

Wecht theorized that the rope had pinched the vagus nerve that descends from the brain down each side of the neck to control the functions of many of the body's organs. Among its purposes is the key role of regulating the heart and lungs. If the nerve's electrical messages are interrupted, cardiac and respiratory function may cease, resulting in what doctors call "electrical death." The heart and lungs could begin to slow down, develop erratic responses, and eventually stop—leaving no evidence to establish an obvious cause of death.

The tightening noose could have done exactly that to JonBenet. Her death would have been inexplicable to the one who had ignorantly applied the fatal pressure to her neck.

In fact, Wecht realized, JonBenet's death might not

have been the "murder" it was so universally being called. If Wecht's theory was correct, JonBenet's death had been accidental, even though it was caused by criminal conduct. It seemed more than likely that there had been absolutely no intent to kill her, or even do her great bodily harm. There had not been, as far as Wecht was aware, any beating that night. There had obviously been an assault, and there had been abuse. But Wecht, applying his medical and legal knowledge, could not find enough evidence to warrant a technical allegation of murder. In most courts these facts could be interpreted as the basis for a charge of voluntary manslaughter—acts dangerous enough to raise the possibility of harm or death, but still lacking any intent to kill. Despite the horror of this crime and this death, there might not have been a murder at all.

Ken Harrell recorded an interview for the *Globe* as Wecht offered his opinion that JonBenet had not been the victim of an intentional strangulation, but of a sex game gone awry. The *Globe* would print Wecht's conclusions in its January 21 edition, accompanied by some of the startling photographs that Wecht had studied.

The story of his analysis and the pictures of Jon-Benet's body would set off firestorms on several fronts, and plunge Cyril Wecht much deeper into this disturbing case.

CHAPTER 8

In the days after JonBenet's funeral and the Ramseys' interview on CNN, everyone was wondering how she'd been murdered and who was responsible. In the Ramseys' beautiful neighborhood along the front range of the Rockies, some residents wondered if they should fear for their children's safety. Was there some monster lurking out there, about to pounce on another innocent child? Or had this been a product of something sinister inside the Ramsey house? Reporters had begun knocking on doors in the neighborhood and beyond to ask such questions about the case dubbed by Mary George of the *Denver Post* as "the buzz of Boulder." She wrote, "Compassion and cynicism were running parallel through Boulder's collective psyche yesterday as residents struggled to make sense of the mystifying murder of a little girl."

Although some Boulder residents had recognized a paranoia, even an obsession, reporters found residents of the Ramsey neighborhood reassured by the police department's confidence that they had no reason to be afraid in their homes. The officer and patrol car assigned to the Ramseys' block reinforced that comfortably.

But one woman said her children had been disturbed

by the death of their playmate. They were asking the meaning of new words like *strangle* and *murder*, and had begun acting out violent crimes as they played. They were refusing to sleep alone, preferring the security of their parents' bed. The children also had found reassurance by assuming that some stranger had descended upon the neighborhood to commit the murder, but then moved on.

Rock-steady neighbor Joe Barnhill knew his community too well to be frightened, he told the press. "It couldn't have been anybody in this neighborhood. The people here are all good people."

A woman who lived across the alley from the Ramseys agreed. "I don't think we have to worry about someone on the loose. That's not the feeling I've gotten at all."

The Ramseys' interview on CNN had swayed Boulder resident Madonna Kao. As she and her husband, David, watched their young sons playing outside the student housing at the University of Colorado, Madonna told the *Post*, "At first I thought that it must be someone in the family. But when I saw the interview, I thought, 'Oh, no parent could do this.'" Her husband said they didn't feel threatened, but would be more likely to check on the children as they played outside.

The CNN interview had failed, however, to change the suspicions of a neighbor who had experienced the calm and quiet of the Ramseys' block at one a.m. December 26—perhaps within minutes of JonBenet's death. Carla Hanley lived two blocks away and had walked her dogs past the Ramsey house in the deep silence of that Christmas evening. Despite the murder she still walked her dogs past that place late every night without fear.

"We still think it's some sort of inside job," she said. "This was not a random act of violence. It's what most violence is in this country," she said, explaining her belief that it had been perpetrated by someone who knew the victim.

Two women walking down the Ramsey block on their lunch hour agreed that the Ramseys' televised performance had not been as effective as they might have hoped. It hadn't changed the opinions of Carrie Symons or her co-worker, Laney Wax, that someone who knew the family, possibly a family member, had committed the killing. "It's an awful thought," Symons acknowledged. "It's a judgment, and I don't know these people, though I have friends who do know them. But my theory of love is that you can love someone to death."

Mayor Leslie Durgin had been disturbed by Patsy Ramsey's warning, "There is a killer on the loose. . . . There's someone out there." Patsy was fomenting the fear that the residents of Boulder were not safe on their streets and in their homes, and the mayor could find no justification for that in the evidence she had seen so far. Patsy's whispered allegation demanded an official response. Durgin called her friend, Chief Tom Koby, to tell him how she planned to reply. She got his okay before turning to the media with a head-on challenge to the alarm sounded by Patsy.

"There *is* a killer," Durgin told reporters. "But I think the implication, which is completely erroneous, is that there is a murderer walking up and down the streets looking for young children. That's overlooking some pertinent facts. There was no forced entry into the home. The person who did it apparently knew the house. That does not imply to me a random act."

The mayor had no inside information from the investigation, no details not generally known to the public. That was the way she wanted it, she had explained to Koby. She didn't want to be in the position of protecting sensitive details and perhaps even having to lie or act dumb to keep secrets. She preferred to stay outside the loop. In fact, she decided her role would be to reverse the flow of information. Instead of letting the police tell her what was happening inside the case, she decided to be Koby's eyes and ears on the streets, telling him what their community was saying about the investigation and the officials in charge.

Patsy's comments brought a similar response from spokeswoman Leslie Aaholm. In conferences with Koby and other police officials, they had all decided that they would not engage in the practice of responding to media reports, not even rebutting the erroneous ones. Even at the earliest stage the case seemed likely to be built on circumstantial evidence, and discussing those details publicly could damage the investigation. The goal came to be keeping as much information private as possible—and that decision would generate as much controversy as it might have avoided.

But the policy didn't prevent her from responding to Patsy. At one of the daily news briefings, Aaholm announced, "Police don't feel there's some strange person in Boulder they need to be worried about." Clear, concise, and to the point.

But all of these back-and-forth comments confused a woman who worked as a nanny in the Ramsey neighborhood. She cut directly to the core of the issue haunting the whole country:

"The parents said, 'Watch out for your children.' Police in Boulder say there is nothing to worry about.

Somebody is lying. Either the parents are lying, or the city is lying."

Many reporters were assembling in Boulder and Atlanta to try to find the truth behind that contradiction. By Friday, January 4, fifty news organizations had inquired about the case and at least fifteen out-of-town reporters had taken up temporary residence in the beautiful Colorado town. The daily news briefing had to be moved from the police station to the City Council chambers to accommodate the crowds and at least a dozen TV cameras.

Mayor Durgin was shocked that this unresolved case had created so much interest, drawing requests from national television networks for interviews on their morning news shows—live at five a.m. She had been exposed to the national media spotlight once before, after a local reporter misquoted her as saying Boulder was soliciting low-income people as new residents. The wires picked that up, and soon reporters from all over the country were calling to get Durgin to expound on something she never said. But the response to the Ramsey case was far exceeding the earlier event, and Durgin found that baffling.

Under that kind of media onslaught, police detectives were forced to resort to various means of eluding the reporters and camera crews that wanted to shadow them. They began using decoy cars, stealthy maneuvers through back streets, and high-speed getaways—anything that worked—to protect their efforts from the unwanted scrutiny.

That same kind of intense and probing analysis was about to be visited on the city where this horrible event had happened. What was it about Boulder that seemed to invite reactions ranging from gentle teasing to sarcastic mockery?

Until JonBenet died, the most famous house in Boulder was an old Victorian on Pearl Street. The quaint house was used in the opening sequence of the seventies hit TV sitcom *Mork and Mindy*, the show that launched comedian Robin Williams to stardom and introduced many people to the name of Boulder. Some residents would look back on that period and mourn the loss of the town's fabled innocence.

Boulder had been a sleepy college town until then, snuggled up against the rocky, jutting peaks that form the Flatirons. It was by reputation a laid-back center for a comfortable approach to the counterculture of the sixties and seventies—kind of a hippie-friendly enclave with a wacky feel and a tolerance of alternative lifestyles and anti-war protests. A nice place, and not as strange as Berkeley, California. By the eighties and nineties, head shops that catered to the drug culture of the past had morphed into aromatherapy centers for those in the New Age. Volkswagens were replaced by Volvos or Jeep Cherokees. Leslie Aaholm noted the town's evolution with good humor, saying, "Yes, we have tofu factories and we don't allow smoking in bars and restaurants. But cigars and martinis are back." The boom in environmental concerns and a renewed focus on outdoor activities had introduced Boulder to many as a great spot for hiking, biking, and climbing in 34,000 acres of parklands that ring the town. With the mild climate, golf was possible year-round.

Some called it "the Athens of the Rockies." Others deflated that pretense with "Plant Boulder—twenty square miles surrounded by reality," or "the People's Republic of Boulder."

By the nineties it had become a center for the high-tech computer world, and was known as innovative and willing to try new things. The *New York Times* described it as "this mellow bubble of Buddhist studies and herbal tea manufacturing." The population edged near 100,000—a quarter were students at U of C and three-quarters were equipped with home computers linked to the Internet. With higher than average education levels and a median income of $44,500, housing prices shot up to an average cost for a single-family home of $290,000 in 1997, 50 percent higher than the national average. Urban sprawl had become an issue, with subdivisions springing up in the smaller communities outside Boulder and the highways in between hosting traffic jams usually associated with Denver, less than thirty miles to the southeast.

With that growth came some of the usual problems. A town where residents had given little thought to locking their doors began to worry more about security. But the crime rate remained low for major crimes. Everyone was sure that Boulder's karma would protect it from such grim realities.

This case had sent tremors through Access Graphics, John Ramsey's company, housed in a building along Boulder's fashionable and popular Pearl Street. Security had been tightened since JonBenet's death, partly to keep away the curious. Vice President Laurie Wagner told the *Post* that she had not heard anyone there suggest that the Ramseys were involved in their daughter's death. "Those doubts were not raised here," she said.

The CNN interview was heartbreaking for those in the company, she said. "There are many employees who have not seen John or Patsy since the tragedy, and for them, watching the broadcast brought the pain closer to the surface."

The police had interviewed workers there. "The police are investigating all aspects of the case, and that includes business. But we don't want to say anything about that."

She said she had spoken to John Ramsey, and he told her he would be back to work soon after the family returned from Atlanta in a few days.

The shock waves had hit Atlanta hard as well. In the aftermath of the emotional funeral, the Ramseys remained there, spending time with family and friends.

The Boulder detectives also were there, setting up shop in the police station in the northern suburb of Roswell as they began checking the family's background and interviewing the extended family and friends. They spent four hours talking to Patsy's parents, Don and Nedra Paugh in Roswell, and would interview some thirty people before they finished. But the police issued a statement saying they would not try to interview the Ramseys there, waiting instead until they had returned to Boulder. The police had been "completely taken by surprise" by the Ramseys' CNN interview, the statement confessed.

The electronic media circus had begun in earnest there, too. A Roswell police officer ran down the list of calls: CNN, Associated Press, NBC *Dateline,* MSNBC, Dan Rather for CBS, *Good Morning America* from ABC, CBS and NBC radio, *Newsweek* and *People* magazines, the *New York Times.* The newspapers and TV stations from Denver had even sent reporters to Roswell.

When the Ramseys spent Friday at her parents' home, about forty reporters and camera crews clogged the street in a stakeout. Spurred by the CNN piece, reporters besieged everyone close to the Ramseys with renewed requests for interviews. John's older son, John Andrew, turned them away at his mother's house in nearby Marietta. John's attorney, Bryan Morgan, fielded some two hundred calls for interviews. The media assault became so intense that the Paughs were forced to post on a sign on the white columns of their red brick home—TO THE PRESS: NO COMMENT. Even a courier bearing a personal request from NBC anchorman Tom Brokaw failed to raise an answer at the Paughs' door. When the Ramseys left the house later, Patsy covered her head with a coat. Reporters and photographers followed the white van carrying the couple, but lost it in traffic.

With the Richard Jewell fiasco fresh in Atlanta's collective memory, the Paughs' neighbors were in no mood to be generous to the media. After all, poor Mr. Jewell had been labeled a suspect in the bombing at the Summer Olympics; the media had accused and hounded him relentlessly, only to be humiliated when the FBI cleared him of suspicion. He would later win a hefty cash settlement from NBC for its overenthusiastic analysis of the supposed case against him. And now it seemed to be happening in Atlanta again. "Vultures," one of the Paughs' neighbors screamed at the pack of reporters. Another asked, "Haven't you learned anything from Richard Jewell?" Yet another offered, "You're sick! Why don't you get a life?"

But the story had arrived in Atlanta, and it could not be ignored. The *Atlanta Journal-Constitution* made an appropriate check with authorities and reported that the Ramseys had never been the subject of an allegation of child abuse while they lived there. Some of the

Ramseys' friends from Atlanta came to their defense more directly. Vesta Taylor, who had lived across the street from them in fashionable Dunwoody just north of Atlanta, was critical of the media coverage of people she was sure were innocent of any wrongdoing. "It's like they're being crucified after losing a daughter," she told the *Rocky Mountain News*. "But I'm sure it's all going to work out sooner or later."

Another former neighbor, Linda Saportas, was just as confident in her old friends. "I've known the Ramseys for years and years, and there's no way that anyone in that family is to blame for this. It's definitely somebody from outside."

Her husband, Joe, said the detectives from Boulder had asked if there had been any signs of child abuse or other troubles at the Ramsey house. He told them it was inconceivable that there had been anything violent inside that nice family. The Saportases remembered that some of Patsy Ramsey's jewelry had been stolen while they were renovating their home in Dunwoody. Joe Saportas concluded, "My feeling is that their daughter was seen by somebody while attending one of the beauty pageants, or by someone who had a key to the house. That sounds like a pedophile, and I don't know who that was. But it's definitely not John and Patsy."

Back at the center of the quake, where the pressure continued to build, police chief Tom Koby was flashing that abrupt manner that would befuddle and alienate the media. As he was questioned about activities in Boulder and Atlanta, he snapped that the investigation would develop at its own pace, and that the public had neither the need nor right to know what evidence the police were gathering. He said John Ramsey had the greatest "right to know," and Koby didn't care if his closed-mouthed approach angered the media.

"The things the public had a right to know, we've given them," he told the *Denver Post*. "A lot of things we're being asked to reveal might satisfy the public's appetite, but might have a detrimental effect on the investigation."

He refused to discuss the Ramseys' comments during the CNN interview, although he said it had caught him by surprise. The media learned that the police had requested a transcript. "Our interpretation of the interview is irrelevant," Koby said. "I don't want to speculate about grieving parents talking about their tragedy. John and Patsy are just expressing their concerns."

Koby had assigned nearly a third of his 125 officers to the Ramsey case, and was confident his department was conducting the investigation properly. "One thing about O. J. Simpson and the circus that developed is that people think that's the way it's done. We're trying to show how it should be done."

He offered a catchy quip to the *Rocky Mountain News* on Friday. "It's not O.J. and it's not L.A. here in Boulder. Our guy won't walk."

One keen observer of the cops' efforts "to show how it should be done" was considerably less than impressed.

Chuck Green, the take-no-prisoners columnist for the *Denver Post*, fired the first of many broadsides at Koby and his troops on Friday, January 3. Even if her killer was never found, Green wrote, the trial in her murder had started; the Boulder police were being tried in the court of public opinion, "and there is mounting evidence that a guilty verdict on charges of malfeasance might be justified."

The police had failed to secure the Ramsey house in the first minutes of the case. They "casually" had suggested John Ramsey search the house, leading him to locate the body and destroy precious clues. "The doorknob, the light switch, the duct tape, the position of the body, and the physical evidence such as hairs or fibers on her clothes all were disturbed in one desperate moment—while police idly mingled upstairs," Green charged in his rhetorical role of prosecutor.

All of that would be considered by the "jurors"—the public—in this trial. Green added with an air of wistfulness and doubt, "God willing, someday there will be a second trial, too."

Such criticism was becoming common as the second week of the case dawned. The head of the robbery-homicide division of the nearby Lakewood police department reflected on how frustrated the Boulder detectives must have been as John Ramsey carted his daughter's body up from the basement, and they realized how much evidence might have been lost because they hadn't made that vital discovery themselves. "This is going to be the case from hell," Sergeant Don Girson told the *Post*, "and I don't think it's going to get any easier."

One notable voice was raised loudly in defense of John Ramsey's actions. It came from a defense attorney, Larry Pozner of Denver, first vice president of the National Association of Criminal Defense Lawyers.

"For God's sake, this is his child! You don't ask a parent, 'Weren't you aware you were tampering with a crime scene?' They have a right to be human beings."

CHAPTER 9

Eight days after JonBenet's body was discovered, a series of startling revelations began to change the complexion of the case entirely. They marked the beginning of a course of news leaks from the oft-cited "sources close to the investigation" that would come to characterize the case and color the world's perception of everything that followed.

The first was a bombshell.

JonBenet had suffered a fractured skull. Beyond the grisly garrote that apparently had choked the life from her tiny body, there had been a blow to her head that had split the bone. A killer capable of inflicting a sadistic strangulation on this child now became someone who could also rain down a blow hard enough to crack her skull. What could be the source of that kind of anger and violence directed at such a child?

Before anyone could even begin to digest that gruesome news, there came another chilling development that changed the tone of the case again.

JonBenet had been sexually assaulted. There were no details provided, but the allegation was shocking enough by itself. First, a garrote asphyxiated her. Then a blow fractured her skull. And now a sexual assault.

The killer was moving rapidly toward the status of a true monster.

This new disclosure did not surprise Dr. Cyril Wecht. He had predicted it and, in fact, would have been surprised if she had not been molested. From the evidence he had seen, sexual molestation probably was the primary motive for what had happened that night. The rest of the horror she suffered was ancillary to the sexual activity.

He was surprised by the skull fracture, however. That seemed out of place in this attack. How had that become part of the scenario? Why would someone bent on sexual gratification introduce such violence? Wecht was eager to see more evidence that could provide an answer to this new quandary.

The next news bulletin moved away from the attack itself, but was almost as shocking. The police had learned that the three-page ransom note had been torn from an $8^{1}/_{2}$ x 11-inch legal pad in the Ramsey house. A detective's instincts and years of experience weren't needed to interpret that. To almost everyone this raised serious doubts about the theory of an intruder being responsible for this mayhem. Would a cold-blooded schemer bold enough to come to this house on Christmas night, determined to kidnap this rich couple's daughter for ransom, actually forget to bring along the ransom note? Or would a brutal child molester take the time after this foul deed to find a pad of paper in the darkened mansion and compose a three-page note setting up some fictional kidnapping? Would a kidnapper or a child molester consume the time needed to do all this, risking discovery every second?

This was all becoming preposterous, Wecht thought,

and another tidbit later would add another quirky twist. Not only had the authorities matched the three note pages to the legal pad at the Ramseys'—surely through microscopic comparison of the top edges of the torn sheets and the thin strip left in the pad—but the police also had found what was being called "a practice note" on the page just before the three that were torn out. It would be learned later that the words "Mr. and Mrs. Ramsey" appeared on this other sheet, and the police were convinced the writer had started a note, decided to limit the salutation to "Mr. Ramsey," and then started over on another page. "A false start," one source called it.

The *Rocky Mountain News* added another twist by comparing what was known about the note to the plot of a recent Mel Gibson movie entitled, appropriately enough, *Ransom*. Gibson delivered a powerful performance as a rich pilot and businessman—strikingly similar to John Ramsey—whose young son was kidnapped and held for ransom. The *News* learned that the note found at the Ramseys' warned John to prepare for a rigorous ordeal when he delivered the ransom. In the movie Gibson's character endured an exhausting course of events set up by the kidnappers. When Gibson saw an image of his captive son for the first time on a computer screen, the boy's mouth was taped—as was JonBenet's. The movie's ransom note said, "I have your son." Patsy told CNN that the note began, "We have your daughter."

There was more to be revealed. The Ramseys had returned to Boulder on Friday, but not to their home. Patsy's mother told a TV station in Atlanta, "Patsy will never return to that hellhole." And she added,

"We're mad as hell. Our friends are mad as hell. America is mad as hell about what happened."

Police sources told the *Denver Post* that the security system in the Ramseys' house had been off the night of the killing. How did that fit into the mystery?

Meanwhile, the Ramseys' attorneys confirmed that they had hired Patrick Korten, a communications consultant from Washington, D.C., to assist them in handling the media. Korten, who had once been a radio journalist and chief spokesman for the U.S. Department of Justice during the Reagan administration, said his firm, Rowan & Blewitt, specialized in "issues management" and "crisis communication" for a wide range of government, corporate, and private clients. Korten said he had worked with the Haddon law firm before, but he would not disclose details. The law firm had turned to him again, he explained, because it was not set up to handle the media deluge brought on by this case.

Korten's record put him firmly in the conservative Republican camp while following what the *Denver Post* called "the well-worn path through Washington's revolving door for more than two decades." He had worked as a reporter, government spokesman and flak, radio commentator, and now a public-relations consultant. In the Reagan administration Korten was spokesman for the Office of Personnel Management when it fired 11,000 air traffic controllers. At the Justice Department, he had been the chief spokesman for Attorney General Edwin Meese while his finances were under review by a special prosecutor. Korten called Oliver North "a man of great personal pride and honor . . . trying to serve his country faithfully" after North had been convicted of lying to Congress in the

Iran-Contra scandal. Korten was carrying the conservative banner on a radio talk show when he defended the controversial nomination of Supreme Court Justice Clarence Thomas in 1991. Korten also served as chief spokesman for the Pharmaceutical Research Manufacturers of America when it lobbied to streamline the Federal Drug Administration's process for approving new drugs.

Korten's firm had not taken a criminal case before. But he said his primary goal was to keep this one from becoming a circus. In one of many O. J. Simpson comparisons that would mark the Ramsey case, Korten told the *News*, "There are no Johnnie Cochrans on this team. We want to get the job done, and that's what we will do."

The private investigator hired by the Ramseys was identified as H. Ellis Armistead, a forty-six-year-old former police sergeant from Lakewood with an excellent reputation among cops, fellow P.I.'s, and lawyers. He was well known for his work with lawyers defending a man who ended up on death row for murdering four people at a Chuck E. Cheese pizza place in 1993.

Finally, the yellow crime-scene tape at the Ramsey house came down on Saturday, January 4, as the police ended the investigation after ten days there. The day before, police had carried in cardboard boxes—apparently to carry out evidence—while other investigators wearing rubber gloves had been seen removing doorknobs, placing them in evidence bags, and then installing new ones. The police also had searched the Ramseys' garaged vehicles—a 1995 Jaguar four-door and a 1996 Jeep Cherokee sport-utility vehicle. Reporters also observed several assistant prosecutors from District Attorney Alex Hunter's office—including some who specialized in sexual-assault cases—at the house. Hunter's chief trial deputy, Peter Hofstrom, was described by the *Denver Post* as talking excitedly with one of the police officers posted in front of the house.

Documents disclosed later would show that the police had seized a dizzying variety of items as evidence: a flashlight; two baseball bats; golf clubs and club covers; a hammer; a broken paint brush and wooden shards near a paint tray; white string from a sled; rope; numerous pens; a pink Barbie nightgown and fibers from the "wine cellar" where JonBenet's body was found; all the bedding from her bed; hair from the Ramseys' bed and from a brush in John's bathroom; men's and children's underwear; blue sweatpants; a black, red, and green Christmas sweater; sections of carpeting; a bathrobe; a toilet seat, toilet tissue, and water from a toilet bowl; a black velvet gift box; an item described only as labeled "victim's research paper and drawings"; an item labeled "My Science Project" from Burke's bedroom; cigarette butts; an angel from a Christmas tree.

And a letter to Santa Claus.

While the police were closing out their work in the house that Saturday, one Boulder resident arrived to perform an act oddly representative of the season. He placed three stuffed animals at the edge of the Ramseys' front lawn where the crime-scene tape marked the property line. The toys, he explained to a reporter, were gifts to honor JonBenet—one from each of his three daughters.

At the news briefing that day spokeswoman Leslie Aaholm offered an increasingly familiar refrain: the police were still trying to schedule formal interviews with the Ramseys.

When the search of the Ramsey home in Boulder ended on Saturday, it began anew at another house in another state. Two detectives flew to the resort town of Charlevoix, Michigan, to search the Ramseys' beautiful Victorian summer home on a bluff overlooking Round Lake—a house where JonBenet's sweet voice on the answering machine still greeted callers with, "We're having a great summer. Wish you were here." The Ramseys had planned to spend New Year's Eve there.

A Boulder detective's affidavit was enough to get a search warrant from a Michigan judge, and the search was conducted the next day. A local prosecutor convinced the judge to seal the affidavit by arguing that it "contains information known only to perpetrator or perpetrators of this crime, and if the information were to be released, it would severely compromise the integrity of this investigation."

The Ramsey case had now tracked the family's life to a third state. Neighbors in Charlevoix told reporters from the *Rocky Mountain News* that Patsy and the children had spent the last two summers in the $336,000 house they had bought in 1992, a house they had characteristically renovated inside and out, and turned into a stop on the town tour last summer. While his wife and children were summering there, John had flown to Charlevoix from Boulder as often as business permitted. The family had a powerboat at Round Lake and John's sailboat, predictably named *Miss America*, was docked at nearby Lake Charlevoix.

And there was one more piece of information that

seemed to make this resort town the perfect place for the Ramseys. In 1996 JonBenet had claimed the title of Little Miss Charlevoix.

On Sunday, January 5, John and Patsy made only their second public appearance in Boulder and the first since their return from Atlanta. This time, as with the first, they went to their church, St. John's Episcopal. They heard a special sermon from Bishop Jerry Winterrowd—a message on human dignity and judging others—that he said was in direct response to the Ramseys' travails and the impact of hurtful speculation on them and the entire congregation.

As John and Patsy left after the service, they paused in the doorway for a poignant moment, a private word, and an embrace with the Rev. Rol Hoverstock and the bishop—as the cameramen outside furiously snapped and taped away. And then, surprisingly to some, the family passed a side entrance and walked the long way around to attend the regular after-service coffee reception in the church hall. They were immediately protected by a phalanx of fellow Episcopalians who lined up shoulder to shoulder to run interference, to give their friends some shelter from the media, and to offer kind words of sympathy and support as the Ramseys passed. The slim Burke led the way, his sister's now familiar features vaguely discernible in his face but under dark brown hair. Patsy followed, obviously still pained and wearing a black dress and virtually black sunglasses, and supported every step by a friend. John was behind them with the clergy.

The convoy provided a priceless "photo op" for the starved media and paparazzi. The Ramseys' new media consultant, Patrick Korten, had in fact contacted television stations and CNN to alert them to the chance to get fresh footage of the reclusive Ramseys. "It was very important for them to come to church today," Korten explained, and he had tried to make sure the ever present media would not turn it into the circus he was hired to avoid. He would add later that the protective actions by other members had been an impromptu gesture, not part of his plan.

Cynics would suggest later that the event was the first of several orchestrated on the Ramseys' terms to cast them in the most sympathetic light to the public.

Later that day, police submitted a written list of questions to the Ramseys' attorneys—another unorthodox tactic for a homicide investigation. Although detectives from other departments questioned the move, Assistant District Attorney Bill Wise said it was simply a supplement and not a replacement for the formal, face-to-face interviews that police anticipated with the Ramseys at a later date. Any other course by the police, he told the *News*, "would not be treating them as they treat other suspects."

That remarkable statement was the first time anyone connected to the investigation had publicly referred to the Ramseys in the same sentence as the word "suspects." It certainly would not be the last.

Wise said the questions were fairly innocuous, general inquiries concerning FedEx or milk deliveries, the names of handymen with access to the house, the names of friends and neighbors. The D.A.'s office had advised the police not to submit written, direct questions about the crime; those would be withheld until formal interviews could be arranged.

* * *

One man with unimpeachable credentials finally said what so many others had been thinking. A scathing salvo at the conduct of John and Patsy Ramsey came from Marc Klass—the father of abducted and murdered Polly Klaas of Petaluma, California. Polly had been snatched right out of her bedroom on October 1, 1993, by her killer. So Marc Klaas could speak with authority on the question of how the innocent parents of a murdered daughter should act, even under the glare of the national spotlight.

And he did not approve of what he saw in Boulder.

"I think the parents have made some terrible decisions thus far by hiring lawyers and a publicist and refusing to talk to the police," he told WPVI TV, the ABC affiliate in Philadelphia on January 6. "And instead they go on CNN. They put themselves in a very defensive mode. I think it does not serve them well at all, to put themselves in that kind of position."

He had an entirely different approach. "I would have talked to the police immediately. In fact, I did an interview with the police within a day or two of the disappearance of my daughter. . . . You get on the polygraph and you do whatever you have to do to move suspicion away from yourself, so that law enforcement can focus all their resources on the other options that exist."

The pundits and commentators could expound and hypothesize. But Marc Klaas was the voice of sad experience, and he knew what he was talking about.

CHAPTER 10

If the ugly truth about the death of JonBenet Ramsey lay hidden under layers of mystery and intrigue, Dr. Cyril Wecht knew that many of those layers could be peeled away by the contents of one essential document.

The coroner's autopsy report.

As coroner of Allegheny County and in his role as forensic pathologist for several nearby counties in southwestern Pennsylvania, Wecht had prepared thousands of those reports himself. They have to be the unvarnished presentation of the medical and scientific facts revealed by the body and interpreted by the pathologist who conducts that surgical search for the final truth. In the passing of each life is a story that only the flesh-and-blood remains can tell. The pathologist has to reveal that story through the seemingly strange combination of medicine and detective work. Before the earthly remains are sent to their final resting place, they can provide the conclusive and definitive account of a life's final moments. Wecht's record as a forensic pathologist for thirty years had won him a reputation as one of the best medical detectives working in the field today. His experience and education, combined with his instincts and intuition, could unlock the doors that hid dark and dangerous secrets. He had done it many times before, and the challenge never ceased to set his pulse racing.

If he could get his hands on the report from Jon-Benet Ramsey's autopsy, what would it tell him about the way she died and why she died? Would it tell him who killed JonBenet Ramsey?

Getting the report would be the first challenge.

A judge in Boulder County sealed the document in early February, shortly after Coroner John Meyer, M.D., completed it. The judge agreed with Meyer and the county district attorney's office that revealing the postmortem findings could damage the investigation by listing the nature, locations, and numbers of wounds, and the other assorted details that only the killer would know. But lawyers for newspapers and television stations immediately challenged the decision, arguing that Colorado law required a coroner's autopsy report to be open to the public unless the authorities could establish "extraordinary circumstances" that justified sealing it. The media lawyers said protecting the status of the investigation and allowing them to use the information to test a suspect's knowledge of the crime were hardly "extraordinary circumstances." Those criteria could be applied to the autopsy report in every murder investigation or suspicious death. Nothing had been presented about the Ramsey investigation that justified putting it in a special category—at least when it came to the release of the autopsy report. Shouldn't public records be just that—public?

On February 14, the media won a partial victory as District Judge Carol Glowinsky ordered the release of seven pages of an edited—*redacted* is the legal term—

version of the report. Coroner Meyer said he could live with what the judge made available to be published; that much should do little damage to the investigation. The material withheld by the judge contained the details Meyer hoped to protect.

The judge decided that she could release only part of the report because the investigation, though seven weeks old, was still extremely active and in its "early stages." She ruled that the rest of the coroner's report would remain sealed for another ninety days or until an arrest was made, whichever came first.

What Cyril Wecht would find in the report would shock and sadden him as it provided indispensable, undeniable clues about what had happened that night.

But by the time the report was released, Wecht had already generated controversy with his earlier comments about JonBenet's death. His analysis of the photographs published by the *Globe* had drawn criticism from cops and prosecutors who said they had withheld all comment on the case to avoid compromising it, and everyone else should do likewise.

Nonsense, Wecht replied. His conclusion that JonBenet died during a sick sex game did not divulge any confidential, personal knowledge, or any secret investigative details. He certainly wasn't providing information the killer didn't know or details the killer had expected to elude the notice of the police. Wecht was not going to be an expert witness in the case later, so he had no ethical duty to remain silent. He simply was employing his years of vast experience and expertise to analyze evidence already known to the public. The natural reluctance of the police to say anything at all about any case was certainly no ethical or professional restraint on Wecht's right to offer informed speculation. He agreed that the police are justified in withholding some details while they conduct their investigations. But he also believed that shedding some light on any case was beneficial—to everyone involved directly and the public that had a right to know about the investigations into dangerous cases. Informing the public was not just feeding its curiosity or stoking the gossip mills. The citizens had a vested interest in knowing that their tax-supported law enforcement agencies were competently pursuing those who posed a danger—perhaps an evil, homicidal danger—to the people.

Wecht had been splashed a bit with the mud from the swirling controversy over the five photos published in the *Globe*'s January 21 edition. The reaction had been almost universal condemnation. All of the Boulder officials and most of the residents professed their outrage and disgust, as did so many people around the country. They called the *Globe*'s acquisition of the photos, presumably at a hefty price for the source, another terrible example of "checkbook" journalism. And publishing them was one of the worst examples of what was wrong with tabloid journalism—crass commercialism, brutal insensitivity, overhyped sensationalism, and a simple lack of basic human decency. The *Rocky Mountain News* almost gleefully reported that several tabloid publications had found no takers when they offered fat checks to Boulder residents to sell inside information about the Ramseys. Boulder was different from Hollywood, explained an editor at the *National Enquirer*; buying dirt on O. J. Simpson had been much easier.

When the *Globe*'s edition with the photos hit the stores, Coroner Meyer confirmed that the pictures

were authentic and then immediately contacted the
district attorney's office and the sheriff's department
to call for an investigation into how the *Globe* had obtained them from his files. As he had with his autopsy
report, he worried that leaking the photos to the
tabloid and, in turn, to everyone willing to part with
$1.39 would have a profoundly negative impact on the
investigation. Meyer said there was a very limited
number of people with legitimate access to those photos, and he wanted to know which one had violated
his office's confidentiality. He said the crime-scene and
autopsy photographs taken by his staff had been developed by a private company; perhaps the leak had
not come from his office. A few days later Meyer filed
a suit seeking a temporary restraining order to block
publication of any more photos by the *Globe*.

Boulder County Sheriff George Epp pronounced the
Globe's use of the photos "pretty sick," and assigned
three of his detectives to find the source of the leak. He
worried about the effect of the growing pretrial publicity on the ability to find a fair and impartial jury,
should criminal charges be filed later. He urged prosecutors to go to court to demand the return of the photos and seek a ban on publication of any more of them.
Epp said the *Globe* could theoretically be prosecuted
for obstructing justice or for theft, perhaps even at a
felony level if they paid more than $400 for the contra-
band snapshots. During his investigation Epp would
conduct lie-detector tests with several of the coroner's
staff members and others.

Pat Korten, the Ramseys' spokesman, called publication of the photos "ghoulish" and "beneath contempt." It revealed the editors to be jackals, not
journalists, he said. He worried about damage to the

investigation and complained about the infliction of
"unimaginable pain to the family." And he said they
would consider filing a suit against the tabloid for violating their privacy.

In the *Globe*'s offices in Boca Raton, Florida, editor
Tony Frost called the pictures "the essence of the case"
that had captivated the nation. They illustrated information already known to the public, and the decision
to publish them concerned issues of the First Amendment and censorship. He disagreed with allegations
that the photos were gruesome and ghoulish, explaining that *Globe* editors had carefully reviewed them to
determine which should be printed. He insisted that
no laws had been broken by the *Globe*, and said he
had no indication the photos had been stolen before
they were provided to his publication. He said he
would not compromise the reliable source that had
provided them to the magazine by disclosing that
identity. Still, he promised to cooperate with the authorities' investigation.

On the streets, the *Globe* found itself the target of
boycotts in Boulder and around the country. Outraged
citizens were contacting stores and newsstands to
plead that they refuse to sell the *Globe*. Many stores
pulled them from their shelves. In a few cases, however, stores defended the *Globe*'s right to publish and
said the brouhaha had led to higher than normal sales.
John Kareski, the owner of a newsstand in Denver,
even distributed free copies to protest what he called
the hypocritical effort to censor the *Globe*. In comments that echoed Wecht's opinion of the situation,
Kareski said the crime-scene photos were tame in
comparison to the pictures of JonBenet in her pageant

costumes; those were the really sick and obscene pictures to him.

Chuck Green at the *Denver Post*, ever a keen-eyed observer, wrote a withering column about the whole affair. He found it hardly worth the attention, insisting the published pictures were essentially "sterile" and suggesting they would "hardly offend a church choir." He said the incident had done little but give the Boulder police more ammunition in their war against the press. And he noted that more information about the "photo scandal" had been released in three days than had been provided about JonBenet's murder in three weeks. As for the "leak" of the photos to the tabloid, Green suggested that defense lawyers would find much larger holes in the conduct by the police in the first hours of the Ramsey investigation. Overall, he found the event a disappointing milestone in the history of shabby tabloid journalism.

In the end, the sheriff's investigation led to a private detective hired by the *Globe* to sniff out the photos and provide other information about the Ramsey case, then to the technician he coopted at the commercial lab that developed the coroner's film. District Attorney Alex Hunter filed charges against private eye Brett Sawyer, thirty-eight—a former deputy sheriff—and Lawrence Shawn Smith, thirty-six, who had worked at the Photo Craft lab for ten years. The *Globe* had paid Sawyer $5,500 for his assistance, and Smith got $200 for cranking out twenty prints for Sawyer.

In February, Sawyer pleaded guilty to a misdemeanor charge of obstructing government operations; Smith copped a plea to the same charge, plus a count of false reporting. A judge sentenced both men to three days in jail, four hours of community service, and an unusual act of atonement: they had to write letters of apology to the Ramseys. They also had to surrender their ill-gotten gains. Sawyer paid a $500 fine and was ordered to donate the rest of his fee from the *Globe*— five grand—to the district attorney's restitution fund. Smith, who was fired by the photo lab, also had to hand over his $200 in dirty money to the fund.

At the sentencing the judge delivered a stinging rebuke to Sawyer, telling him, "You made of that child an object—a thing—for people across the country to ogle and gape at."

Sawyer told reporters that the *Globe* had said it would not publish the photos he rounded up only four hours after getting the assignment. The tabloid was only supposed to show them to an expert for analysis, Sawyer said. He now regretted being involved in what he called "a huge error in judgment." He also said that, as the father of a six-year-old boy, he was sorry he had caused the Ramseys more pain.

The *Globe* returned the photos to Coroner Meyer, and he dropped his suit. But the tabloid retained the right to reprint the photos that already had been published. Meyer disagreed with the *Globe*'s claim to have handled them sensitively. "You can't use autopsy photos of a six-year-old girl sensitively, no matter what you do," he told the *News*. "It's a despicable thing to do."

CHAPTER 11

Cyril Wecht was looking at medical facts that seemed to confirm his fears. From the information contained in the edited version of the autopsy report on JonBenet Ramsey's death, Wecht could find sound reasons to support his theory, and nothing at all to contradict his belief that she had been sexually abused on the night she died. Beyond that, Wecht found what to him was clear evidence that her innocence had been taken sometime before the night her life was taken. The report told Wecht that JonBenet had been the victim of sexual abuse that may have begun before December 25, but he could not determine exactly how long she had endured that kind of perverted exploitation.

After Wecht received a copy of the report from the *Globe*, he studied every line scattered over the seven edited pages—the material from the original nine-page report that had survived the judge's censoring pencil. Although pages three and four were omitted completely, some riveting information remained on the others.

The bottom of the first page confirmed Meyer's announced conclusion about the cause of death— "asphyxia by strangulation"—but the report also added, ". . . associated with craniocerebral trauma." In addition to the strangulation, JonBenet's death was connected to the fractured skull that had been kept secret until reporters sniffed it out. The report's reference to trauma of the skull (*cranio*—) and brain (—*cerebral*) seemed now to confirm those reports.

But Wecht first turned his attention to what he believed was at the root of this tragic death. He found the answers to some of his fundamental questions in the very last paragraph of the last page, where just six lines of medical observation gave him enough information to deliver a substantial analysis.

Under the report on the "vaginal mucosa," referring to the internal membranes of the vagina, Meyer had written, "All of the sections contain vascular congestion and focal interstitial chronic inflammation. The smallest piece of tissue, from the 7:00 position of the vaginal wall/hymen, contains epithelial erosion with underlying capillary congestion. A small number of red blood cells is present on the eroded surface, as is birefringent foreign material. Acute inflammatory infiltrate is not seen."

Greek to the layman. Crystal clear to Cyril Wecht.

That paragraph meant JonBenet had suffered a penetration of her vagina that had left its internal wall inflamed. The most telling clue for Wecht was that the inflammation was "chronic." To a forensic pathologist, that unequivocal term meant the inflammation was at least forty-eight to seventy-two hours old. "Chronic" was not open to interpretation. The inflammation had not occurred shortly before her death. It was not fresh. It had not been inflicted in the minutes before she died, or even the hours before her death. If she died late on December 25, something had caused this inflammation on December 22 or 23, and perhaps even earlier. More recent inflammation would have been called "acute." This was "chronic"; this was older. By the same token, however, the inflammation had not been caused weeks or months before, because that would have healed before this postmortem examination.

No, "chronic inflammation" meant to Cyril Wecht that JonBenet Ramsey had been sexually molested a few days before her death.

He broke down the first sentence. Meyer's reference to "sections" meant the thin samples of damaged tissue taken from the vaginal wall and placed on a glass lab slide to allow examination under a microscope. When reviewed there, all of those sections showed "vascular congestion," which meant more than the normal amount of blood in the vessels. The engorgement of blood in the vessels was a natural response to the pressure or injury that caused the inflammation. "Focal interstitial chronic inflammation"? "Focal" meant in some spots; "interstitial" meant in the walls of the vagina.

The next sentence: "The smallest piece of tissue, from the 7:00 position of the vaginal wall/hymen, contains epithelial erosion with underlying capillary congestion." A tissue sample taken from the lower left area of vaginal wall at the hymen—the folds of membrane that partly cover the entrance to the vagina in a virgin—showed "erosion" of the layer of tissue, the "epithelial" lining. The chronic inflammation there had caused part of the lining to deteriorate and erode, or slough off. Under that area the capillaries had become congested by blood because of the inflammation.

This explained a vague reference by Meyer under "final diagnosis" on the first page of the report. It listed an "abrasion and vascular congestion of the vaginal mucosa." An abrasion is a scratch mark, but it was not explained—apparently another casualty of judicial editing. Wecht believed he had indeed found Meyer's explanation for the vascular congestion.

The location of the eroded tissue seemed especially important. If a child molester inserted a right-hand finger into a young girl's vagina and manipulated the finger—rubbing it against the vagina as a molester might—where would the finger touch the vaginal wall and cause inflammation? As the fingertip moved naturally to its left, wouldn't it strike at just about the seven o'clock position?

Next, "A small number of red blood cells is present on the eroded surface. . . ." Another essential observation and clue about what had happened. At the seven o'clock location Meyer had found red blood cells—proving the area had just suffered some trauma or injury sufficient to force some of the blood cells out of the vessels that carry them through the body. The cells were the manifestation of the injury. This, then, was the sexual contact that had occurred just before Jon-Benet died. This was "acute." It had been inflicted in the minutes before she died.

This medical evidence was also an important clue that supported Wecht's theory of repeated abuse. The red blood cells from the new inflammation were present at the same location as the chronic inflammation. The same damaged spot that proved prior contact of a sexually abusive nature had again been inflamed the night she died. At least over several days, someone had inserted an object—probably a finger—into JonBenet's vagina to sexually molest this tiny victim. If Wecht had had access to the microscopic slides of the tissue samples from that portion of the vaginal wall, he could have estimated the age of the injuries. The slides would show him which of the various kinds of white blood cells were present, and he could determine the age because different kinds arrive at different intervals after an injury. The white cells are the defensive soldiers the body dispatches to fight an infection or injury.

At the same location on the vaginal wall, Meyer also had found "... birefringent foreign material." That phrase referred to a substance that appeared under the microscope when exposed to polarized light and observed through a blue prism. Such material commonly contained silica, a component in lubricants such as talcum powder. Had a lubricated rubber glove been used by JonBenet's violator? Or had someone dusted her with talcum for natural purposes—to soothe an irritated genital area—or unnatural purposes—to provide lubrication for an illicit entry into this child's vagina? Whatever the purpose, some foreign matter had been introduced into her vagina.

The last sentence of this revealing paragraph: "Acute inflammatory infiltrate is not seen." Inflammatory infiltrate would be the white blood cells Wecht had wondered about before, the ones that would rush to the scene to defend the body. They were not found at this injured location on the vaginal wall because JonBenet had died before there was time for them to arrive. That would take an hour or so from the moment of the injury, and her body's vital reactions had ceased before then—along with her life.

She died too soon, in more ways than one.

There were more conclusions that Wecht could reach now that he had seen this much of the report— this brief but scientifically significant evidence. There was enough information in this document to draw more conclusions based on "a reasonable degree of medical certainty." That is the legal standard by which experts measure their work when testifying in trials. Wecht applied that standard when he provided diagnosis and analysis as a consultant and expert witness. He could apply it here.

More likely than not, Wecht could say, the abuse this little girl suffered had been inflicted during some kind of sexual game. He found no evidence that what Meyer discovered in the vaginal examination was the result of some natural condition—a bladder infection or the chronic bed wetting that would be suggested later. Wecht could not completely rule out masturbation by this six-year-old girl, but he found it highly unlikely, given the accompanying, fatal circumstances. How reasonable was it to suggest this little girl had masturbated in the moments before someone had killed her with a garrote and a blow to the head?

To Wecht, the material he had just read made it clear that she had been sexually abused by someone over a period of several days. The abuse certainly might have covered a much longer time, but the evidence here was limited to days. This evidence of abuse, tied literally and figuratively to the cords around her neck and wrist, was enough to draw the conclusion that a sick sex game had gone awry. The vaginal injuries documented in the autopsy report did not show the kind of extensive damage Wecht knew would be present if she had been raped—if a man's penis had violated her vagina. In fact, the medical evidence so far suggested that the vaginal penetration had been a carefully controlled, limited situation—not a savage sexual assault. There had been no tearing of the tissues. And Meyer had listed no bruises or injuries to the exterior genitalia. She probably had experienced penetration by some small, narrow object—most likely a finger. She had not been raped in the classic legal and medical sense of that word.

Wecht would not learn for many months that his colleague in Boulder—with the distinct advantage of having examined the body and the rest of the medical evidence—had arrived at some of the same conclusions: When several court documents were disclosed later, they would include an affidavit from Detective Linda Arndt swearing that Coroner Meyer had told her after the autopsy that JonBenet "had received an injury consistent with digital penetration of her vagina." Meyer had added "that it was his opinion that the victim had been subjected to sexual contact."

Just above the coroner's observations about JonBenet's vaginal injuries, Meyer had written a paragraph that next attracted Wecht's attention. Here Meyer addressed what he had found when he examined JonBenet's brain. Wecht had seen the reports that she had suffered a fractured skull, and Meyer had referred obliquely to that in his conclusion about the cause of death. The judge had obviously edited out the detailed analysis of the fracture from the pages showing substantial expanses of blank space. But three references on page one and this small paragraph of five lines on page nine offered Wecht details he could use.

From page one Wecht learned that the head injuries included a contusion to the scalp, subarachnoid and subdural hemorrhages, and small contusions on the tips of the temporal lobes of the brain. Two other items under "craniocerebral injuries" had been deleted by the judge.

The scalp contusion—a bruise—obviously was

associated with the skull fracture, surely caused by the hard blow that broke the bone beneath it. The subdural hemorrhage referred to blood from the injury to the brain that pooled under the dura membrane that lies between the skull and the brain. The subarachnoid hemorrhage was blood that collected under the arachnoid membrane, a spiderweb-like material under the dura. Those kinds of hemorrhages were almost always caused by trauma. They were not natural occurrences.

The third reference also fascinated the medical detective. He had seen such bruises to the temporal lobes of the brain—the portions that lie behind the temples on the sides of the head—and they often resulted from shaking someone and causing the brain to shift inside the skull, striking the bone on the sides. This report offered no reference to injuries on the outside of the head at those locations, so the internal bruises probably were not the result of blows.

Wecht wove this new bit of evidence into the rest of his developing analysis. While the attacker was applying the perverted use of the garrote that pinched the vagus nerve in her neck and eventually shut down her heart and lungs, the young prey had suddenly turned lifeless without explanation—perhaps literally in her abuser's arms. Wasn't it likely that the shocked and panicking molester had shaken JonBenet in a futile attempt to return her to consciousness? A few anxiety-driven shakes and a "Wake up! Wake up!" had failed to restore her to life, but had inflicted the bruises to the temporal lobes of the brain.

It all seemed to fit.

Coroner Meyer's examination of the neck also fascinated Wecht. The only reference to the cord around Jon-

Benet's neck that remained in this redacted report was on the first page, and it read simply "ligature strangulation." But on page eight Meyer described his careful—and, to Wecht, quite thorough—dissection of the neck. Meyer checked each layer for injuries that a pathologist knew were normally associated with strangulation by a ligature like that cord. Despite the noose wrapped around the neck, Meyer found no hemorrhaging in the so-called "strap" muscles on the sides of the neck. That was an important point to someone like Wecht, who really understood the physiology of strangulation. The lack of hemorrhages under the skin of the neck proved to him that there was no real intent to strangle JonBenet.

A lack of damage in the front of the neck was also noteworthy. Meyer noted no fractures of the U-shaped hyoid bone at the top of the throat or the delicate thyroid cartilages—the assembly commonly called the Adam's apple that make up the larynx. Below that Meyer still found no damage to the cricoid cartilages, which are the trachea. In many cases those structures are broken during strangulation, especially if manual choking is performed from the front. JonBenet's were intact. The tongue also failed to show any damage or injury, Meyer found.

To Wecht, all of that meant that this garroting by a rope tied to a stick handle was not designed to kill Jon-Benet, was not the work of some monster throttling the life from an essentially helpless child. There had been no desire to kill at all. The garrote had been just tight enough to perform its role in this sex game—to decrease the oxygen to JonBenet's brain and provide a perverse thrill for the molester through vicarious auto-erotic asphyxiation.

The other classic manifestations of asphyxiation

were there. Oxygen starvation caused pinpoint ruptures of tiny blood vessels, called petechial hemorrhages, on a number of organs and locations in the
body, especially the surfaces of the eyes, eyelids, face,
heart, and lungs. Meyer found the hemorrhages at all
of those places. He noted that he was uncertain about
petechial hemorrhages on the right eye and eyelids,
however, because of the livor mortis there. Livor mortis is the discoloration of the skin to a dark red shade
because of the collection of blood there after death.
Gravity causes the blood to settle in the body's lowest
areas, and that gives coroners, pathologists, and detectives useful clues about the position of the body after
death. JonBenet's face had been turned to the right,
causing the blood to settle on that side.

There were more injuries documented by the autopsy report as well. In a paragraph on page two
marked "external evidence of injury," Meyer described a "rust-colored" abrasion—a scratch—about
three-eighths of an inch long and one-quarter wide,
just below and behind the right ear. He also noted an
abrasion to her right cheek, and one on the back of her
right shoulder, which also bore a bruise. She also carried two scratches on her lower left back area and the
lower back of her left leg.

All of those marks, Wecht knew, could indicate that
JonBenet had squirmed while lying on her back or
standing against a wall as her molester inflicted the
sexual abuse. Another suggestion would come later
for some of those abrasions, but that was well down
the road and no one could have seen it coming.

A vague reference to a scratch on her cheek did at-
tract special interest, however. By inference he could

determine that she had not suffered serious injuries to her face from a beating or other brutal mistreatment. That fit well into Wecht's theory. The molester's goal had not been to injure or batter this child, but to use her cruelly to satisfy a perverse sexual drive.

Several organic observations were noteworthy but added little useful evidence. JonBenet's bladder was empty. Had she wet herself during the sexual assault, or voided her bladder when her body relaxed in death? Or, as some would insist, was she a chronic bed wetter? Had she wet her bed before she was taken on that fatal journey that night? Had the release of her child's bladder played some bizarre role in the events that night?

Her stomach contained a small amount of unidentified matter. The upper end of the small intestines held what Meyer thought to be fragments of pineapple. That was a small but interesting point for Wecht. If he had known what time JonBenet had eaten the pineapple, he could offer an approximate time of death because it would take about two hours for the stomach to digest the pineapple and move it to the small intestines. Here was another element of the mystery where he wished he had additional information; without more details, however, he could not interpret this one.

After the autopsy report was released February 14, JonBenet's pediatrician would reject any possibility that she had been a victim of sexual abuse. Dr. Francesco Beuf would firmly insist that he had never seen any physical or behavioral indications of that. "I can tell you, as far as her medical history is concerned, there was never any hint whatsoever of sexual abuse. I didn't see any hint of emotional abuse or physical abuse. She was a very much loved child, just as her brother," he told KUSA-TV.

He said he would have reported any suspicion of sexual abuse, as he was required to do by law and as he had done in appropriate cases. That was unnecessary here, he said, because he had always admired the close relationship between JonBenet and Patsy.

On *Primetime Live*, Beuf told Diane Sawyer that JonBenet had complained of pain while urinating during three of the twenty-seven visits to his office over the last three years; the rest were for colds, sinus problems, or other normal complaints. He believed the vaginal inflammation he diagnosed had been due to poor bathroom hygiene or common irritation from bubble bath. He also had listed bed wetting as an occasional problem, but said that was common in a high percentage of girls of that age.

Sawyer asked if Beuf would have detected a vaginal injury of the sort found during the autopsy if it had existed when he examined her. Probably, he said, but he wasn't certain because he had not given JonBenet a full internal gynecological examination; he had not used a speculum to view the area where Dr. Meyer found the injuries—the ones that Wecht believed were indications of penetration and sexual abuse.

Wecht understood why Beuf would not have conducted the complete exam needed to detect such internal injuries; using a speculum on a six-year-old girl would require full anesthesia, and there was rarely any need to be so thorough.

As Cyril Wecht thought about what he had read, he came to a grim conclusion. If a six-year-old girl had arrived at a hospital emergency room for treatment of those same vaginal injuries, the attending doctors and nurses would have been required by law to report their suspicions of child sexual abuse. The police in most places would have conducted an intense interrogation of the parents, followed perhaps by the arrest of the father or other adult male in the house. From the document now before Wecht, the medical examination had established probable cause—for a prosecution for sexual abuse.

The medical disclosures had not told Wecht who was responsible for the sexual abuse and the actions that killed JonBenet. The information didn't necessarily point to a man. Although the vast majority of sexual molesters are men, women also have been known to molest girls, even their daughters.

But Wecht was just as sure about another troubling legal point. What if more than one person was involved? What if two people were somehow linked in that night's reprehensible activities? How could the police and prosecutors determine which one was responsible for what—which one had inflicted the sexual abuse or which one had caused the death? How could criminal liability be assigned and pursued to justice? To Wecht, apportioning individual blame was not the issue. If one person caused the death, the other helped cover it up.

He wondered about those edited sections of the report, and eagerly anticipated their release some months down the road. Would they give him the rest of the story? Would they answer that single, maddening question:

Who killed JonBenet?

CHAPTER 12

Confronted by a cable television camera and a panel of five reporters, Chief Tom Koby addressed the intense curiosity exhibited by so many people across the nation about the JonBenet Ramsey case.

"Quite frankly, it is a sick curiosity in some ways."

The man at the head of the investigation into one of the most bizarre crimes in American history had just delivered his philosophy on the public's right to know about heinous criminal acts. Koby might have been revealing an understandable hostility toward the overdone, overly intrusive tabloid stories. Or he might have been showing his dislike and mistrust of the media in general. Either way, he seemed perilously close to suggesting that the people in Boulder and across the country who were following this saga with interest and sympathy and prayers and all of the rest of emotions churned up by the death of this amazing and beautiful child . . . well, they were all just sick.

On January 9, the dark, bearded Koby—dressed in a blazer, not a uniform—held a thirty-minute news conference that was televised on Boulder's local-access cable station. The camera lens captured an image that seemed to reflect much of the real Tom Koby—a forty-seven-year-old, modern, educated police officer with a tendency to project more of a corporate image than the old persona of a tough, street-wise cop. The *Denver Post* invoked the most popular fictional cops of the nineties to describe Koby as "more Bobby Simone than Andy Sipowicz."

Koby was born in Cleveland, grew up in Houston, and joined the police department there in 1969. While earning a bachelor's degree in business administration, he rose to captain in fourteen years, took command of the burglary and theft detectives division, and won the Manager of the Year award in 1985. By 1987 he was the deputy chief and became assistant chief four months after that. His chief and mentor was Lee P. Brown, who left that job to become chief in New York, federal drug czar after that, and then a sociology professor. Brown would later urge everyone to trust Koby's judgment and have patience. Brown pointed out that he had been police commissioner in Atlanta during the serial murders of young black men, and it had taken two years to arrest Wayne Williams in those cases.

Koby was an early proponent of what has been called community policing, known in Houston as Neighborhood Oriented Policing. The basic concept is to get cops out of their cars, onto the streets, and into the lives of the people they protect. That way, the theory goes, the police can understand what causes crime in each small area, reach out to the residents there, and try to stop problems before they start. In many cities the idea has been a hard sell among the officers actually required to implement it.

As Houston's crime rate shot up in the eighties, the chief who succeeded Brown was less excited about community policing than Koby. In 1991 Koby moved

on, becoming the chief in Boulder. He went from a
population of 1.6 million to one of less than 100,000,
and from a department with 4,000 employees to one
with just 213, and only 140 sworn officers. But his philosophy of community activism seemed to fit well
with the spirit of Boulder. The *Post* reported that some
of the changes implemented by Koby included abol-
ishing the city's police academy and sending officers
to other locations for training, and investigating shoot-
ings involving the police with more of an eye toward
learning what had gone right and what had gone
wrong than punishing the officer. Although he was
known as strongly supportive of the rank and file, he
still brought in an attitude as a disciplinarian; that created some paranoia among his troops.

He caused real controversy in 1993 when he refused
to allow the department to participate in a career-
oriented Explorer Scout project because of the Boy
Scouts' policy against admitting homosexuals. He also
drew criticism from the police union over training levels after a dispatcher failed to warn Officer Beth
Haynes that a man was armed, and the man killed her
before shooting himself.

Koby remained popular among the residents of
Boulder, who saw him as a modern leader suited to the
approach they favored from their police department.

When Koby appeared before the TV cameras and
five local reporters on January 9, he opened with a
prepared statement calling JonBenet "one of our inno-
cents." He hoped that this forum would help the community's grieving process and address some of its
concerns about the investigation. Without acknowl-
edging the source of the warning that a killer was

on the loose in Boulder—it wasn't necessary—Koby asked rhetorically if people should be living in fear that another child could be killed? No, he said, the police were sure this was "a one-time occurrence."

He promptly addressed what he called challenges to his department's integrity and competence, stressing that he had never worked with more competent or dedicated professionals than those on his team. "They are getting the job done," he asserted. And they would not lose their focus by responding to unfounded comments. "Prejudging and media hype have never solved a crime," he scolded.

The department's mission was to find justice for the victim. "Our allegiance is solely to JonBenet Ramsey," he vowed.

He acknowledged the painfully obvious fact that the "person or persons responsible for this act" had not been apprehended. But he reminded everyone that his department had solved thirteen of the fifteen murders committed between 1990 and 1995—an 85 percent success rate.

But when he and city spokeswoman Leslie Aaholm were asked questions that referred to JonBenet's death as a murder, both officials preferred a different word. Aaholm said, "I referred to it as an incident, not as a murder." Koby discussed his officers' early response by saying, "We were managing an incident."

When asked for more details, Koby responded by calling media interest intrusive and damaging to the investigation. But he said his earlier comment that the public had no right to know about the investigation had been reported out of context.

"This situation means a great deal to the Boulder community. This situation is a curiosity to the rest of the country and, quite frankly, it is a sick curiosity in some ways." He added, "I've never, in the twenty-eight years I've been in this business, ever seen such a media focus on an event, and it is in fact intrusive."

When asked if his department would have handled the case differently if JonBenet's parents weren't a rich corporate executive and a former beauty queen, Koby turned the question back on the media and its "assault" on the case. "Why has the media given so much attention to this case? If you and your colleagues would like to help us, back off a little bit and give us some room to do our jobs."

As a public official often working at the center of criminal investigations, Cyril Wecht could appreciate Koby's sentiments. Wecht thought the media pendulum had swung too far in reporting on some matters of crime and politics, often venturing too far into private circumstances that really concerned no one else. But he also knew that the public had legitimate concerns about crime, and a proper interest in learning what drives some people to the kind of horror that had just occurred in Koby's town. Why was it difficult for Koby to sympathize with the public's intense desire to learn more about what had happened to this little girl they had seen so many times—all dressed up and shimmying across the stage like a vamp, almost like Shirley Temple transformed into a little tart, when she should have been playing with dolls, riding her bike, joining a soccer team, or doing anything else that girls her age would normally want to do? Some were horrified by the images of feathers and sequins and high heels and makeup and tinted hair and swiveling hips and come-hither glances they had seen from these "tiny tot" beauty pageants, and they feared that

these events had somehow played a role in the horrible abuse and death JonBenet had suffered. People
genuinely wanted to know about this distressing influence on some of this society's children, and what it
really meant. How dangerous was it? They wanted to
know, most of all, what to do to make sure their precious children didn't fall victim to the same kind of
violence that had claimed JonBenet.

Didn't tax-supported authorities have a responsibility to offer a reasoned, appropriate response to their
citizenry's legitimate concerns? Imposing a total black-
out on such a case was unrealistic for a police chief. It
left the public in the dark, unable to decide whether the
police were doing their jobs and making progress on
such an important case. How could Koby be surprised
if his own stiff-backed approach had fed the flames?
Did the media go overboard sometimes? Absolutely.
Inveighing against the media's right to report the
news, to try to answer the questions that the people on
the street were asking, was courting trouble for any
public official involved in a high-profile situation.

After Wecht had offered his initial analysis of the Ramsey evidence, he had found himself consulted regularly
by reporters from newspapers, television networks and
local channels, radio, and even supermarket tabloids all
across the country. As was his nature, he never hesitated
to offer his educated opinion, provided he had a reasonable basis to support it. He had seen enough of the
evidence in this case to draw some well-founded conclusions, and he was not bashful about sharing them with
anyone who asked. He hoped to inform the public, and
perhaps even to promote a more active and courageous
approach to this case by those responsible for solving it
and pursuing justice in the courts.

His outspoken style and educated speculation resulted in dozens of appearances on a wide variety of television shows: network news programs such as *The Today Show* on NBC; cable news programs such as *Burden of Proof* on CNN; celebrity talk shows starring Geraldo Rivera, Johnnie Cochran, and Maury Povich; and tabloids shows like *Inside Edition*. He made more than a hundred appearances on local television shows from Pittsburgh to Denver, and gave an equal number of newspaper interviews.

But Tom Koby obviously disagreed with that approach. At the news conference that produced little news, Koby insisted that his department could not do its job under the glare of media lights.

Criticism of the police in this case, he said, suggested that people had failed to understand what was going on in the Ramsey house that morning. The officers had found themselves confronted with what legitimately appeared to be "an in-process kidnapping," and they geared up to respond to the situation that they had every reason to believe would proceed on that basis. They responded appropriately under those circumstances, he insisted.

"I've been in communication with police personnel around the country, and most legal experts will tell you we've done it just right," he boasted.

Wecht and many other consultants and experts would disagree strenuously with that sentiment. They would offer scores of criticisms about the department's response.

But Koby went even further. He called it "totally unfair" to insinuate that the Ramseys were involved in their daughter's death, or to criticize the Ramseys' decision to hire lawyers and "take precautions" during the investigation. He defended the Ramseys and his department: "There is nothing that's been done, either by us or the Ramsey family, that is out of order."

Did the police search the Ramsey house before the body was found? Well, Koby said, they performed "a preliminary search of the house and, remember, this is a very big house—it took us eight days to work through this house—and they were just trying to determine if there was anything obvious they needed to pay attention to."

Had officers checked the room where JonBenet's body was found? "It doesn't appear that we did. Keep in mind that this house is a large mansion."

Koby also offered his belief that there had been no corruption of evidence when John Ramsey carried his daughter's body up from the basement—more disagreement by the chief with expert opinions from other sources.

Koby said the police had talked to the Ramseys at their home that first day, of course, and were confident they would be able to conduct formal interviews with them soon.

"We were with the family for quite a period of time the first day, and there's a difference between talking with the parents and interviewing the parents. There is no way to interview parents at that point in time. It was impossible. So, were we communicating with John and Patsy? Yes. Were we interviewing John and Patsy? No, we weren't. That would have been totally unreasonable at that point in time."

Another contradiction of expert opinions.

Had the police given the Ramseys special treatment? Absolutely not, the chief said.

Did that mean that everyone in the Ramseys' position

would have been given their own copy of the ransom letter? If Koby knew it yet, he certainly didn't disclose that one of his officers had reportedly handed over a copy of the note to the Ramseys—the very people whose handwriting would be tested and compared to the penmanship in the note. Reports later would claim that the accommodating detective was Linda Arndt— something she would strenuously deny in her lawsuit against the city.

In a bar on popular Pearl Street, customers watching the televised news conference were disappointed. Nothing new to say. No breakthroughs by the cops. No penetrating questions by the reporters. What was the point?

Chuck Green would offer more eviscerating sarcasm in his next *Denver Post* column, shredding the officials for their insistence that the horrible death suffered by JonBenet was an "incident." Green recalled the comment from an editor when Green once referred to a murder as an incident. "It's more than that, much more than that, to the people involved," the editor had explained.

Now the veteran columnist had his own observations about police response to this "incident."

"They weren't investigating a crime scene. They were managing an incident. Welcome to Boulder," Green snapped.

Later, he would wonder about Koby's claim to be investigating the Ramsey case by the book. "Just what is the name of that book you followed, Chief?" Green would ask if it was "Kobygate."

Green proved to be an equal-opportunity critic. After the Ramseys' lawyers and "spin doctor" Korten complained several times about the slow pace of the investigation, Green suggested that the people who had advised the Ramseys not to talk to police should just "quit all their whining."

CHAPTER 13

Dr. Cyril Wecht was among the long list of experts who disagreed thoroughly with Chief Tom Koby's assessment of his department's handling of the JonBenet case. Wecht had participated in enough homicide investigations to know that Boulder police had ignored some basic procedures and violated some cardinal rules. The effects of those failures could be devastating to the investigation and its conclusion.

He was far from alone in that opinion. Another of the many experts with a lengthy list of criticisms was Gregg McCrary, a retired FBI agent with a national reputation for his work in an elite section inside the bureau. He was a so-called "profiler," one of the agents who had worked closely in the FBI behavioral sciences unit with John Douglas. Douglas had led the unit's efforts to blend insightful studies of criminal minds and careful analyses of crime scenes into a new method of investigating; what the unit had learned could be turned into guideposts leading authorities to society's predators. "Psychological profiling," it had come to be called. Douglas was recognized as the father of the emerging specialty that mixed criminology and psychology, fact and intuition. With the benefit of hours and hours of interviews with serial killers and master criminals, Douglas and the others tried to identify the behavioral patterns that would show up in the daily lives of those who operated so far outside the laws of man and God. Poor personal habits. Scruffy appearance. Low self-esteem. Menial jobs. Lives full of rejection. Alcohol and drug abuse. A recent turn toward religion. Obsessive thoughts. Dirty, banged-up cars. If any of those or dozens more characteristics the profilers could identify applied in a case, these experts could give the cops some distinct clues to watch for among their suspects.

Douglas had brought McCrary into the unit as it grew in stature. Douglas was rewarded with international attention that included working as an adviser on the blockbuster movie *Silence of the Lambs*. A tall, handsome, distinguished, and articulate man, Douglas had served as the inspiration for the movie's FBI agent Jack Crawford, played by actor Scott Glenn.

McCrary had retired in January 1995 after twenty-five years with the bureau. He now worked for the Threat Assessment Group, Inc., a company that identifies potential sources of violence in the workplace, as well as workers who might be inclined to act violently; the goal was to avoid such problems. McCrary still performed some profiling for police departments needing that special assistance.

He was drawn into the Ramsey case with a most intriguing offer the first week of January. In a call from Boulder, the Ramseys' attorneys had invited McCrary to join the defense team; they wanted him to construct a profile of the kind of person who could have killed JonBenet.

McCrary immediately knew what he had to do. He turned it down, for a couple of good reasons.

First, the descriptions of the scene suggested

strongly that the ransom note and the appearance of an abduction attempt had been staged by the killer. The note seemed fake, and there was little to suggest that there had ever been a genuine kidnapping attempt. All of the accounts had made him very suspicious about what the police had seen and heard in the Ramsey house. In his experience, intruders rarely go into houses and kidnap children. They don't leave phony-sounding ransom notes. But those elements of a crime often show up when someone in the family, or close to the family, commits a murder and tries to cover it up.

McCrary was convinced that the answer to the Ramsey case would be found in the family or very, very close to it. The facts as he knew them were consistent with what he called "a staged domestic homicide." These were common in murders among family members; someone close to the victim would try to make the scene look like something it wasn't to deflect suspicion away from the family. A husband who murdered his wife would want the police looking outside the home, perhaps toward a burglar. The problem with those schemes was that the killers rarely knew what a genuine crime scene looked like. They thought they did, using their misdirected perceptions from movies and books. All of that was make-believe, not what the police find in real crimes. A detective who had seen sexual homicides—especially an agent like McCrary, who had studied hundreds of them—would know they did not look like what was found at the Ramsey house.

That was not just McCrary's opinion. The facts proved that the murders of young children are overwhelmingly the work of someone in the family or close to the family. Studies by the Department of Justice have put the ratio at the about twelve to one, but it is even higher for younger children because their circle of acquaintances and activities is so much smaller, almost entirely focused on home and family. It's just common sense. Infants have no lives away from their families, and the sphere of possible killers grows slowly as children age. The younger the child, the more likely the killer is someone close.

If JonBenet had been killed while attending one of those troubling beauty pageants, McCrary would have been willing to consider the possibility that a homicidal pedophile was at work. Pedophiles are drawn to those pageants, McCrary had learned, and that could be a logical scenario for the murder of a popular contestant. There could have been an outside chance that a pedophile had stalked and killed her. But JonBenet had died inside her home on Christmas night—not a logical scenario for an intruder-pedophile.

McCrary had other good reasons to reject the employment offer from the Ramsey team. He simply did not want to take a chance on putting himself in the camp of the killer. After years of trying to put that kind of person in prison, he didn't want to find himself inadvertently at the defense table if someone in the family was charged later.

McCrary also assumed he would not have access to all of the information he would need to develop an accurate, credible profile. He would need all of the police reports and all of their investigative information to fully understand the crime, and he could only assume the police would not be willing to turn that over to the team representing people who hadn't even been charged. As a law enforcement officer, he certainly

never would have done that while a case remained
under active investigation. This sort of evidence didn't
fall within the normal exchange of information required in preparation for a trial, the process called discovery. There were no legal grounds for the authorities
to turn over reports and information to the Ramseys,
and in fact, there were excellent reasons why such
documents absolutely should not be surrendered to
them. McCrary thought it unlikely the cops and prosecutors would even consider it.

So his answer to the Ramseys was a prompt no.

He was shocked ten days later when he heard the
Ramseys had found an FBI profiler to take their
offer—John Douglas. Retired from the bureau and
working as a consultant and best-selling author,
Douglas had accepted the offer McCrary had spurned.
McCrary had tremendous respect for Douglas's abilities and performance. Although he was slightly disappointed that Douglas had joined the Ramsey team,
McCrary was interested to see what his former colleague could accomplish in this incredible case.

What had already been done by the cops had given
McCrary some deep concerns. He couldn't believe
Koby's insistence that experts said the department had
done everything right. The department actually had
done little right in those first, crucial hours. Serious
mistakes had been made early on, and they could have
permanent repercussions.

First, McCrary determined, the attitude of the police
at the Ramsey house hadn't even been appropriate for
officers responding to such a case. They had failed to
maintain the professional skepticism that is essential
to a detective. An investigator's job is not to believe or
disbelieve anybody, but to find the facts. When the

Ramseys told the police that their daughter had been kidnapped, the officers' attitude should have been, "I don't know if that has happened, but I'm going to find out." They should have taken all comments at face value, kept their minds open, and worked the case in every possible direction. As the investigation proceeded, directions lacking evidence would have shut down naturally one by one, until the police could focus on the most logical course. Instead, the police suspended their professional skepticism and immediately bought into the kidnapping story. Parallel lines of investigation could have been started, including a kidnapping, a murder within the family and a cover-up, a regrettable accident, perhaps even a runaway—all of the possibilities that could explain a little girl's absence from her home on the morning after Christmas. But even Koby would say later that the police had proceeded on the assumption that they were dealing with a kidnapping.

Second, even if there had been a kidnapping, the Ramsey house was still a crime scene. To McCrary, the police should have immediately cleared it out, secured it and the property around it, and turned the evidence analysts loose on every square inch of the place. The police never should have allowed the Ramseys' friends or clergyman to clomp around inside that house, contaminating every kind of trace evidence imaginable. McCrary had never heard of a kidnapping in which the police had allowed the family's friends and priest to stay in the house for hours, polluting the crime scene amid the initial investigation.

What about the report that John Ramsey left the house—alone, supposedly to get the mail—for about an hour before the body was found? McCrary was really stunned by that one. It showed a complete lack of control over the case by the police. Neither of the Ramseys should have been alone for a second that day, and certainly not outside the house.

Sending John and his friends to search the house without an officer to accompany them? Another mistake, almost too elementary to address. If there had been a good reason to have John Ramsey search his own house, obviously an officer should have been right there with him. A cop could have prevented John from making innocent mistakes that could damage the case, just as he might have done after he opened the door that led to his daughter's body.

What about the failure to conduct interviews with the Ramseys that first day? McCrary struck here on a point that Cyril Wecht also had found most troubling. Both experts challenged the police decisions not to interview the Ramseys immediately because they appeared to be the distraught parents of a kidnapped daughter, and not to interview them after the body was found because they were too grief-stricken. Wecht had seen too many investigations and McCrary had participated in too many to find Koby's explanation acceptable.

In kidnappings, detectives should as a general rule separate the husband and wife to ask them privately if there was something they would like to tell the police without their spouse's knowledge. Could a hidden extramarital affair by one of them somehow be behind this kidnapping? A jealous, spurned ex-lover perhaps? Was some other factor lurking in the shadows that could explain it? Gambling? Drugs? Debts? A failed business deal? A grudge or some other secret from the deep past? How could the police prepare to investigate a kidnapping without getting separate answers to such indelicate questions?

Once the body had been found, the grieving parents should still have faced intense questioning— separately. Wecht shook his head in disbelief as he described how the police had failed to follow the simplest, most basic approach that should have been applied. In a soft voice and a sympathetic tone, the supervising detective should have said, "Mr. and Mrs. Ramsey, we know this is awful for you. We're so sorry this has happened, and we're going to do everything we can to find out who did this. But we need to talk to you now if we are going to be able to solve this crime. This won't take long. So, Mr. Ramsey, we're going to ask you to go over here and talk to Detective Smith for a few minutes. And Mrs. Ramsey, we'd like you to go over there with Detective Jones for a moment. We'll get this over just as fast as we can, but we have to talk to you now."

The Ramseys could have refused to talk—even though that would have looked much more suspicious than their current reluctance to grant interviews. Or they could have "lawyered up," saying they wanted their attorneys present for any official interviews. But if the police had separated the Ramseys and got their accounts locked in right then, each spouse's statement could have been checked for inconsistencies with the other's—a damning problem for multiple suspects. And those interviews could have been examined for contradictions with later statements. More than a few cases had been cracked by suspects' inability to keep their stories straight over the long haul. Many had broken and confessed as the inexplicable inconsistencies piled up during intense interviews.

Even in a bank robbery, tellers and witnesses are interviewed separately—not specifically because they may have been involved criminally in the robbery, but to get their independent accounts, to learn exactly what they know about what happened, and to cover all possible bases.

The last kidnapping McCrary worked on for the FBI was a perfect example of a solid investigation. In April 1992, Exxon International president Sidney J. Reso was kidnapped as he was driving out of the long driveway from his home in New Jersey. The FBI sealed off the house and the substantial acreage around it, and began a multilevel investigation. The agents started at ground zero and even considered his wife a potential suspect until they developed enough evidence to rule her out. Then they moved to the next level of suspects. They would discover eventually that a former security consultant for Exxon and his wife had kidnapped Reso in hopes of financing a lavish lifestyle with $18 million in ransom. Reso had suffered a gunshot wound to the arm during the kidnapping, and then was handcuffed, bound, gagged, and left in a wooden box where he died a horrific death four days later. Amid intense interrogations the wife cracked and told the whole story. Her husband got life; she got twenty years.

When McCrary trained police officers and other agents, he taught them to conduct investigations of kidnappings and child-crime cases by moving through concentric circles of suspects, starting at the center. The first ring includes the people closest to the child— the immediate family of parents and siblings, and those with regular access to the child, such as aunts, uncles, and baby-sitters. The second ring comprises friends and neighbors. The police pursue the rings of suspects outward from there, each time moving further into society and away from the family. The furthest suspect from the center is the stranger, and the murder of a child by a stranger is the least likely scenario.

As a rule of diagnosis, McCrary liked to invoke a phrase that a friend had learned in medical school. "When you hear hoofbeats, think horses—not zebras." Other investigators had another expression: "Look at the in-laws before you look at the outlaws." The point of both was simple. Look for the closest, most obvious solution before considering those less likely.

In Boulder, it seemed the police had unfortunately started with the outer ring of suspects. Inexperienced investigators sometimes leaped all the way to the stranger first, McCrary had learned. A case may indeed take police there, and detectives always should remain alert for that one in twelve cases when that is the answer. But the review of those closest to the victim should be done first.

This case, McCrary was convinced, didn't fit the rare scenario of a murderous intruder at any level.

There was the inordinate amount of time an intruder would have spent inside the Ramsey home, threatened every second with discovery by the other residents. Criminals who invade other people's houses with evil intent get their business done and get out as fast as possible; they don't linger because they don't have enough control of the environment to feel safe. If JonBenet had unleashed a blood-curdling scream—as reported by the neighbor across the street—a kidnapper would have fled the house in a heartbeat; the risk of staying there was too great for even the calmest, smoothest criminal. Had the ransom note been written after JonBenet was killed? Had the incompetent kidnapper taken the time to find the pad of paper, compose the intricately plotted and written note, and carefully print it out in block letters? If murder was the intent, would the killer have stayed in the house to write out the bogus note after JonBenet was dead? The time it would have taken to do everything that happened in that house that night proved that the suspect was very comfortable there—not that he was worrying every second about being caught.

Wecht and McCrary agreed that the intruder theory was too implausible to warrant serious consideration. What it boiled down to was a series of completely improbable acts by a person who invaded the home of wealthy people on Christmas night. To accept the theory, one had to believe that the intruder had slipped into the house without leaving a trace of evidence—no hairs, no clothing or carpet fibers, no saliva or semen, no obvious footprints in the snow around likely points of entry. The intruder then found JonBenet in her second-floor bedroom, sexually molested her in a bizarre and convoluted manner, killed her, located the out-of-the-way room in the basement and hid her body there, found the legal pad, composed the complicated note, left it on the back stairs used by the family, and departed—without leaving footprints again.

Wecht's raucous sense of humor told him that the intruder theory sounded more like the bad ethnic joke of your choice. Pick your favorite target of ridicule and send him into the Ramsey house to pull off the kidnapping of a wealthy family's child. What really happened there that night could well be the punchline in a story about a bumbling criminal. Except that none of this was funny.

As the full details of the note were disclosed, Wecht and McCrary found even more reason to doubt the defense theory.

The ransom of $118,000 matched almost to the penny the amount of John Ramsey's bonus from Access Graphics for the year. That odd amount tied the writer of the note directly to the Ramseys and the company. Who else would know about that figure and find it significant enough to use it as the ransom amount of choice? It certainly wasn't a mere coincidence. In fact, such a low ransom demand from a multimillionaire kidnapping victim was suspicious on its face. McCrary knew that ransom demands are always round numbers, and much higher than this. Two hundred and fifty thousand perhaps, but even that would be low. A half million was more reasonable. Even a million or two million would have been logical.

The figure of $118,000 meant something special to somebody. McCrary's analysis was that choosing it had been born of panic; in a frantic search for a way to explain this little girl's death, the kidnapping plan had been hastily constructed. Without any idea of how to write a real ransom note, the writer had tried to be creative, but had reached too far and had grabbed a ransom figure that actually defeated the purpose. Instead of diverting suspicion from the Ramseys, it actually had focused attention on them. They or someone they knew very well had to have written the note, McCrary believed, and therefore had to have killed JonBenet.

The length of the note also was a problem. McCrary knew that ransom notes are short and to the point— not long, rambling epistles. A short note demanding big bucks. This one violated both rules. There had even been a first, aborted attempt to write the note; the police had found it still in the same legal pad at the house, containing only the salutation "Mr. and Mrs. Ramsey." The importance of that was, again, the time involved and careful consideration given to all of the details. The author had spent way much too much time composing this "letter"—it was too long to qualify as a note. Despite the time invested, serious mistakes had been made.

The letter was much too respectful and familiar with the Ramseys. It demonstrated no genuine anger toward them by this person who had hated them enough to sexually abuse and kill their daughter in their own home, and then demand money for their dead child.

"We respect your business but not the country that it serves." A ridiculous statement in a ransom note. The closest thing the writer could muster to an insult was the threat that "the two gentlemen watching over your daughter don't particularly like you." More faint stuff for a ransom note. If kidnappers take the time to address their feelings for the victim, they usually spew toxic venom and reveal their hate with intensely personal profanities.

The letter showed concern for John Ramsey, advising him to be rested because the ransom delivery would be exhausting. McCrary had to chuckle. Kidnappers don't give a damn about their victim's health and welfare. Warning that Ramsey would be scanned for electronic devices during the ransom delivery was ridiculous as well. It suggested a face-to-face confrontation between John and the kidnappers. That is the last thing a kidnapper wants. They almost always arrange what is called a "dead drop," a ransom delivery at some location where the money is left, the victim departs, and the kidnapper scoops up the loot unseen.

The whole tone of the Ramsey letter was too polite and familiar, especially toward the end when the writer continuously addressed John by his first name. "Use that good, southern common sense of yours." Another intriguingly familiar phrase. Who was writing this? Foreign terrorists? It certainly was not what kidnappers say, McCrary knew.

Clinton Van Zandt, another retired FBI profiler who watched the case carefully, said the tone of the letter suggested to him that it had been written by a woman or a genteel man. That seemed to point almost directly at the Ramseys, not hardened criminals or foreign terrorists. Van Zandt added the writer was educated, at least forty, had exerted authority over others, and was living a lie.

McCrary was sure the author was a very intelligent, manipulative person, but one completely devoid of criminal experience. A couple of simple words were misspelled—business became "bussiness" and possession became "posession"—in a clumsy attempt to suggest the author was uneducated or a member of "a small foreign faction" writing in English as a second language. But the precise, businesslike "attaché" was correct, even down to the accent mark over the *e*. That complete phrase—"bring an adequate size attaché to the bank"—exhibited the formal vocabulary and content of someone comfortable with writing or dictating for business purposes. That is not the normal background for kidnappers. And other words unlikely to be chosen by someone other than an educated writer of English were used, such as "hence" and "deviation." The misspellings even stopped after the first paragraph, suggesting the effort became too cumbersome to continue. The shaky penmanship so obvious at the beginning of the note also ceased and became more straightforward—as the strain of trying to disguise handwriting became too much to continue.

Even the choice of villains was revealing to McCrary. "We are a group of individuals that represent a small foreign faction." An interesting selection of bad guys, but no one really talks that way. Even the members of a small foreign faction would not call themselves members of a small foreign faction. And beyond that, this fictitious group reveals just who it is that the letter writer fears. When someone makes up a bad guy, McCrary had learned, they search their own fears for inspiration. Susan Smith said a young black man had stolen her two little sons—only to admit later she had driven them into a lake in her car because they were impeding her chances for romance. Tawana Brawley told people in New York that a group of white men, including a cop and a local prosecutor, had beaten and abused her; her story was later discredited. In the note at the home of a wealthy businessman in Boulder, the bad guys were vague, international terrorists. A most interesting choice.

All of those problems with the evidence in this case should have become apparent fairly quickly to any police department. In Boulder, where JonBenet's December killing was the first homicide in 1996, the bizarre collection of mismatched and outlandish evidence should have convinced the police to seek assistance from investigators more familiar with such situations.

Instead, McCrary had been told, the police spurned offers of help at the crime scene from the Denver police department's homicide squad, the Colorado State Police, and the Colorado Bureau of Investigation's crime laboratory. The CBI, according to McCrary, had been turned away twice—before and after the body was found. Getting the best crime-scene technicians available is always an immediate concern of anyone directing an investigation. The Ramsey detectives could have sealed off the house and waited a day to get the best. There would have been no rush once the crime scene was secure. Each room could have been thoroughly examined—even if there were fifteen rooms occupying almost 7,000 square feet.

Everything McCrary had heard indicated that this mystifying crime had been dropped on a department inexperienced in processing murder cases, and the people in charge had failed—for whatever reasons—to get the necessary assistance from other, more experienced sources. The result was an investigation that was seriously flawed. Some of the mistakes might be repaired by a renewed effort, but some of the evidence surely was lost forever.

CHAPTER 14

Who were John and Patsy Ramsey, that they had become the center of such a storm of controversy and suspicion and passion?

Intense reviews of their lives had developed some snapshot descriptions.

John Bennet Ramsey: A dignified, reserved, take-charge businessman who demonstrated a deep love for his family and their lives together. He struck some as a bit too cool or withdrawn, but others found that calm reserve to be part of his strength and even his charm.

Patricia "Patsy" Ramsey: A beautiful, loving woman who seemed to exemplify Southern grace without the pretense that could accompany someone with wealth and a background as a Miss America contestant. Many thought she found her greatest reward in her role as a dedicated mother who seemed to enjoy a special relationship with her children.

But just who were these people, that their storybook lives could take such a horrible turn into tragedy and suspicion?

A "wonderful, 'Leave-It-to-Beaver'" childhood. That was the description offered by John Ramsey's younger brother, Jeff, of their lives growing up as the sons of

Mary Jane Bennet Ramsey and James "Jay" Ramsey. Jeff Ramsey told the *Rocky Mountain News* that their parents were "very loving, calm people. You couldn't have asked for a better family life."

John was born in 1943 in Nebraska, but spent his teen years in Michigan, where his father, a highly decorated transport pilot in World War II, became director of the Michigan Aeronautics Commission. The elder Ramsey—whose stiff style at the commission reportedly earned him the nickname of "Czar" Ramsey—passed on his love of flying, boating, and golf to young John. In high school at Okemos, Michigan, John joined the cross-country team and the band, and was chairman of Christmas dance his senior year.

Newsweek quoted a friend as saying John was friendly, but didn't get excited about things. Quoting the caption under John's yearbook photo— "Some say he's quiet—others doubt it"—the magazine speculated that even then people didn't know what to make of his reserve.

Nancy Turner Lawton, a classmate who dated John for several years, remembered him for the *News* as "an upright person who had a desire to do things right." As an exceptionally responsible eighteen-year-old, John already had a savings account and a plan for his life. She often spent time with the Ramsey's at their summer cottage and described them as a reserved family of modest means.

John moved on to study electrical engineering at Michigan State University in Lansing in 1961, where he continued to make the right moves. He joined the Reserve Officer Training Corps and became president of the Theta Chi fraternity. Nancy Lawton also attended MSU, but she and John eventually decided to date others. She recalled for the *News* that she mentioned their break-up in front of some friends and one of them, Lucinda Lou "Cindy" Pasch, disclosed that John had just asked her out. The date must have gone well. John and Cindy announced their engagement in December 1965. They graduated the next June and got married a month after that.

John fulfilled his ROTC obligation with two years as a navy officer and flyer, serving at the Subic Bay base in the Philippines. In fact, investigators would believe later that the unexplained "S.B.T.C." printed under "Victory!" at the bottom of the alleged ransom note was a reference to Subic Bay, perhaps as the Subic Bay Training Center. But other reports said there was no mention of such a center in naval records.

After his tour at Subic Bay, John returned to MSU to earn his master's degree in marketing in 1971. He spent a year with AT&T's management-training program and in 1973 took a job in Atlanta with an electronics engineering company. One source said Ramsey got into computers early, and certainly not as the stereotypical computer geek. He became quite proficient, perhaps using the vision some acquaintances had recognized to see what was ahead for the computer industry.

Ramsey later told a trade publication that the company wanted him to move to California in 1976, but he decided against it. He called that a turning point in his life—although he could never have known how crucial it would be.

John and Cindy separated in 1977 and divorced the next year. She got custody of their three children— Elizabeth, eight; Melinda, six; and John Andrew, eighteen months—as well as the house and a 1977

Oldsmobile Cutlass station wagon. The *News* reported that John got "the 1969 Oldsmobile, the tape deck, and generous visitation."

Jim Marino began selling computer printers to John Ramsey for his company about 1977, while the Ramseys were divorcing. Marino was impressed that the ex-spouses had managed to remain friends and were rearing their children together even though they lived apart. Marino marveled at John's dedication—calling his children every morning and every evening, no matter where he was; it was like a religion to this loving father, Marino thought.

He was impressed with his new friend, seeing in him a forthright, honest, capable man who seemed to define the phrase "What you see is what you get." Although Ramsey would later find himself at the center of a shocking mystery, Marino could find no mystery in this man who seemed to do everything right and for the right reasons. Marino had never seen anyone as cool under pressure as Ramsey. He was a quiet gentleman who chose his words carefully. Marino never heard Ramsey raise his voice on the job or with his family. Marino was impressed with Ramsey's management style in the workplace. He said he never gave anyone anything except an opportunity. After that it was up to them to run with it. His leadership abilities struck Marino as someone in the dramatic mold of a General George Patton or an Andrew Carnegie or a Henry Ford.

Ramsey was shy, but in a way that Marino thought was good. He could find nothing artificial in Ramsey at work or at play. And the two men did play together. They toured the nightspots looking for women. In an observation that would seem important only years later, Marino found his friend's social and sexual interests "normal, with a capital N." Ramsey's quiet and reserve were not natural magnets for women, but they were drawn to his Porsche, expensive clothes, and gold credit cards. Ramsey was always discreet and a gentleman about his romantic relationships, and his generally respectful attitude toward women led him to reject Marino's occasional suggestion to take some clients to a topless bar. The most John would say about a woman was that she was "cute." Marino chuckled, "I doubt he would read a Victoria's Secrets catalogue."

While Jim Marino and John Ramsey were spending so much time together, John found the woman who would become his second wife. There were differing reports about how he met Patricia Ann "Patsy" Paugh. One said they met through mutual friends in Atlanta. Patsy's mother, Nedra Paugh, told a more romantic story to the *Boulder Daily Camera*. She said John had caught a glimpse of her stunning daughter entering an apartment complex, and had run up a flight of stairs to track her down, only to learn she had disappeared. He would find her later, of course. Marino said John was absolutely smitten with Patsy, whom Marino called John's "Jackie Kennedy." Marino did not know her well, but found her gregarious, open, and friendly—and an obvious social climber. She seemed to be from what Marino thought of as the "Donna Reed era," and being in the social registry was an important issue for her.

John and Patsy were married at the Peachtree Presbyterian Church near Atlanta on November 15, 1980. He was thirty-seven; she was twenty-three.

By then he had formed his own company. Microsouth distributed computer software out of his basement, and Patsy helped by answering the phone. He soon added another entity, Advanced Products Group, which sold computer hardware and other materials. He struggled, and even accepted a financial bailout from his father-in-law, Don Paugh, a retired engineer at Union Carbide. There was little evidence that John Ramsey was on the threshold of an impressive business breakthrough; he was driving an old pickup truck and spending off hours doing projects around the house.

Marino says it was during that period that he learned just what kind of man his friend really was. Marino was seriously injured in a motorcycle accident in 1978, and spent a year in a wheelchair and a walker. John Ramsey came to see him and then gave him a job. "He bailed me out when no one else would help me," Marino recalled affectionately. He took a different job in 1980, but the men stayed close.

John Ramsey made his move toward the corporate big leagues in 1988, when he merged Advanced Products Group with two other companies to form Access Graphics, a company that would distribute sophisticated computer equipment and services out of headquarters in Boulder. As vice president of sales for the new corporation, Ramsey spent most of the next year flying between Atlanta and Boulder. He told the *Boulder Daily Camera* in 1993 that the new corporation had not done well at first, and the executives worried that they had managed to turn three profitable companies into one unprofitable one. But that soon turned around, and sales began to rise sharply.

On the home front, John's second family was growing beautifully. His first child with Patsy was born January 27, 1987. The *Rocky Mountain News* quoted the Ramseys' former nanny, Shirley Brady, as saying that

John had chosen his son's name after a dream about a man in a long white robe, carrying a book in his hand. The child's name, this apparition told John should be Burke Hamilton Ramsey. And so it was.

Brady said she had turned to the Ramseys when she was desperate for work and had nowhere to live, and they hired her even though their first child was not due for several months. They remodeled their home in Atlanta to provide an apartment for her next to the nursery. "That's the kind of people they are," she said.

The Ramseys were blessed with a beautiful daughter on August 6, 1990. Patsy wanted to give the child a name with a French flair, and she created a unique union of her husband's first and middle names that would be pronounced as it would in Parisian high society. The striking result was JonBenet, a name that Pasty could not know then would be more memorable than she had ever dreamed, though certainly not in a way that any mother would hope for her daughter.

Jay Elowsky, the owner of the popular Pasta Jay's restaurants in the Boulder area, became friends with the Ramseys and told the *News* he was impressed with how patient they were with their children. Elowsky asked John how, as an older father, he could be so relaxed. He quoted John as responding, "I'm really digging fatherhood the second time around. I've got the time. I've learned. I'm really having a lot more fun with it."

As the Ramsey family was growing, so was the business. In 1991 aeronautical giant Lockheed Martin Corporation acquired Access Graphics and named John Ramsey as president. That would require him to relocate to Boulder, and the Ramseys reluctantly left Atlanta, the town and the friends that seemed such essential parts of them and their lives. They bought the charming mansion on 15th Street and began to adjust to an entirely different lifestyle in an entirely different world.

Dark clouds began gathering over the Ramseys early in 1992. On January 8, John learned his oldest child, Elizabeth—everyone called her Beth—had died in a car crash with her boyfriend, Matthew Derrington, outside Chicago. She was just twenty-two, a recent college graduate working as a Delta Airlines flight attendant in Atlanta. She and Derrington were visiting his family, and his BMW was hit by a bakery truck in a snowstorm, killing them both. Jim Marino said Beth's death devastated her father. The quiet, reserved man turned even more inward after that, focusing on his work to salve the pain in his heart.

Friends told the *Rocky Mountain News* that Patsy gave tremendous support to her husband, even locating a small Episcopal cemetery that she knew he would prefer over the larger one used by most people in Atlanta. The night before the funeral, Patsy called in their friends to gather around and support her grieving husband. After Beth was buried under a dogwood tree, Patsy had a small bench installed at the grave so visitors could sit and pray.

During the investigation into JonBenet's death, police would revisit the violent death of the first Ramsey daughter. Boulder detectives would check Beth's autopsy report, which said only that she died of massive internal injuries. And they would interview her sorority sisters, perhaps asking as they had other Ramsey associates in Georgia if they had ever heard any allegations of child abuse in that family. There was no indication that part of the investigation led anywhere.

A few months after Beth died, clouds arrived again

over the Ramseys. John's father died. His mother had died of cancer when John was in his late twenties, and his father had then married a woman named Irene Pasch; she was the mother of John Ramsey's first wife, Cindy. But now John had lost both of his parents.

There would be two more dark visitations to the Ramsey home in the years ahead, both of them carrying the specters of tragedy and death.

Who was the other half of this much probed couple?

Patricia Ann "Patsy" Paugh seemed the model daughter of middle-class parents in Parkersburg, West Virginia, a town of 34,000 on the Ohio River. The area had a distinctly Southern feel, and the Paughs seemed to foster that attitude of gentility and manners and grace in their three daughters. Patsy was born December 29, 1956, and blossomed in high school. Her friends recalled her as beautiful, but not the obvious beauty pageant type. They would happily describe her in warm and loving words for the *News* years later, remembering her more as a hardworking overachiever, not a prom queen.

Charlene Pearman, a year older than Patsy and a fellow student council member, described her as being the mover and shaker in the background, quietly getting things done. "She was so bright. She was just the kind of person who was a leader. If she had an idea, she wasn't afraid to try to get it implemented. It was just amazing. She had a lot of energy. She was more about doing important things. She was just so mature, and maybe saw life from a deeper point of view." Patsy was so unassuming about her accomplishments that Pearman remembered that she and many others were shocked on awards day to see Patsy collect two banquet tables full of trophies for speech, drama, and academics. She really excelled on the speech and debate teams, where she was described as a forensic coach's dream. Her specialty was oral interpretation—the dramatic presentation of a scene from a play or story without the support of props or costumes. She won the state championship as a junior and senior, and placed second in the national competition for her performance of a scene from the play *The Prime of Miss Jean Brodie*.

She was a sophomore when she opened a new and vitally important chapter in her life. A slender, green-eyed brunette with impressive intelligence and talents, she was chosen first runner-up in the Miss Teen-Age West Virginia pageant. She had caught "pageant fever." Four years later, as a sophomore at West Virginia University, Patsy took her shot at the big leagues of the pageant world, setting her sights on the Miss America title. *People* magazine reported that she had prepared the year before by attending the Miss America pageant and taking notes. She was runner-up in two preliminary competitions, but won a contestant-at-large title that got her into the state contest. She performed the same reading that had been successful in high school drama contests, and it must have helped. She was crowned Miss West Virginia for 1977.

Pearman, her friend from school, was surprised at Patsy's interest in the pageants because she had never emphasized beauty. "I really didn't think it was about wanting to put on a bathing suit and prance around," Pearman told the *News*. "I really thought it probably was more about what she was going to do with the scholarship money."

But Patsy went after her goal with zeal and dedication. Albert Cox, a state pageant official and friend of Patsy's, told the *News* that she was a terrific contestant.

"You have to be competitive. You have to have that spirit and drive to do it. But it's very difficult to be a phony. We're looking for somebody real up there." Cox said Patsy was everything a Miss West Virginia should be. Intelligent and ambitious. Charming and compassionate, with a deep spirituality. Sincere, down to earth—and driven.

Bob Anderson, who worked with her while she was the reigning state queen, described her as a dynamo. She especially enjoyed visits to hospitals and activities with children. "She loved being Miss West Virginia and was really into it. And the people loved her."

Patsy was quoted later as saying, "It's just like being Cinderella for a year. Wherever I went, people throughout the state treated me royally."

She prepared intensely for the Miss America pageant at Atlantic City. She wrote an original dramatic scene centered on a local controversy over school textbooks. Pitting a traditional journalist against an innovative young teacher, Patsy called the piece "Deadline." Some would see the irony in Patsy's literary protest against censorhsip then and her battering by the media later.

Patsy fell short of the real gold ring—the Miss America title—but came away from Atlantic City with one of the eight non-finalist talent awards and a $2,000 scholarship for her dramatic performance. Frank Deford, a contributing editor at *Newsweek* who also served as a judge at the Miss America pageant, reported that Patsy Paugh described herself as five feet six, 110 pounds, measuring 35–23–35—although he added, "That's what they all wrote." His notes on her performance said she spoke well but called her "a little automaton." Twenty years later, photographer Randy

Simons would tell *Newsweek* that JonBenet "could hold a pose forever."

Patsy loved the Miss America experience and returned to West Virginia with new fame. She recalled the excitement of the whole affair, explaining, "From the minute you arrive in Atlantic City, you're exposed to a barrage of reporters and photographers, watching your every move and every word." She even sponsored a fashion show to thank her supporters—a gesture those who knew her would call typical of her thoughtfulness and grace.

Patsy's pageant adventures would not be the last for the girls of the Paugh family. Nedra Paugh's influence over her daughters was evident, and some pointed to her as the impetus behind their tours on the beauty pageant circuit. Perhaps she saw it as their entree into society and their passport to financially secure futures. It became a family tradition, and Nedra became a fixture at the events. Dianne Lough, Miss West Virginia of 1970 and one of Patsy's friends, described Nedra for *People* magazine as "kind of a stage mother." Patsy's younger sister, Pam, followed her to the Miss West Virginia title in 1980—the first time that sisters had worn the crown. When Pam went on to the Miss America pageant, they ranked as only the second sister act in that competition.

Patsy still was not done with the pageants. She continued to be a sponsor and judge in West Virginia, and would introduce her own daughter to them at an age so young that many in America would be scandalized.

Immediately after the Miss America contest in 1977, Patsy returned to West Virginia University to complete her education. As a senior she ran the Student Services Committee, served as membership chairman for the Alpha Xi Delta sorority, made the dean's list, and graduated magna cum laude in 1979 with a degree in journalism with an advertising concentration.

She took an advertising job in Atlanta, charting a course that would lead to John Ramsey, Boulder, and disaster.

The marriage in 1980 of John and Patsy seemed a continuation of her Cinderella story. The newlyweds settled into a house outside Atlanta, and John marched on with his plan for success in the business world. Patsy worked in advertising until she began their family, but she also turned her efforts to the social scene of the Junior League, garden clubs, and charity groups. They redecorated the home John had bought while he was single, but then moved to a bigger, more fashionable colonial house with an unusually large yard in the exclusive Dunwoody area. Patsy really got into redecorating there, and John was always remodeling and expanding the place. A close neighbor, seventy-five-year-old Vesta Taylor, recalled for *People* that Patsy had the living room repainted five times in varying shades—all in the course of a week. Each time Patsy called Vesta over to see the newly painted room as the changing sunlight reflected the color. "Vesta, what do you think?" Patsy would ask. Vesta and her husband visited the Ramseys often and considered themselves another pair of grandparents for Burke and the infant JonBenet. Vesta marveled at how John and Patsy lived for those children.

During this time the Ramseys would make friends with a long list of people who would stand by them without wavering in the years ahead. Many of those friends would recall for the *Rocky Mountain News* examples of Patsy's constant caring hand outstretched to so many others. She spent a year turning a benefit Christmas card project for Eggleston Children's Hospital in Atlanta from a $80,000 fund-raiser to an $150,000 endeavor. Another friend said Patsy's efforts often were much more personal, such as making cupcakes for a sick child in the neighborhood.

The Ramsey home also included John's children from his first marriage. Nanny Shirley Brady said Elizabeth, Melinda, and John Andrew spent most weekends with the Ramseys, and Patsy made sure they were a welcome part of the family. John loved her even more for that, Brady said.

Patsy and Judith Phillips met at a business-related social event in 1982 when Patsy was doing some advertising work for the computer modem company where Judith's husband, Robert, worked in Norcross, a suburb north of Atlanta. Judith noticed immediately that Patsy was wearing a wig, an unusual choice for a woman in those days. Judith would see that many times later; some of the wigs were better than others, but Patsy never mentioned them. Judith assumed it was "part of the beauty pageant thing," but never really learned why Patsy wore them. They had nothing to do with a condition that would develop later.

Among Judith's first impressions were that Patsy was very friendly and John had a great smile. The Ramseys and Phillipses became social friends and saw each other occasionally. At that point John was still working hard to build his company. Judith remembered encountering him at a trade show when he had just a card table and folding chair, sitting there and trying to drum up business.

The Ramseys were a lot of fun. John was certainly the quieter of the two, but Patsy made up for it. Judith was surprised that Patsy, an alumnus of the beauty-pageant circuit, was so down to earth and lacked any pretense or "hoity-toity" airs. She enjoyed cracking dirty jokes and knocking off sarcastic, funny lines fairly regularly; she cracked Judith up all the time with her hilarious comments. John was more laid-back, the kind of guy who always said—no matter how dramatically his fortunes and surroundings improved—that he would be happy living in a log cabin. Judith thought there really was a part of him that would have been content with a simpler life than he and Patsy were building.

Patsy never struck Judith as the stereotype of a soft, coddled Southern belle. West Virginia may be part of the South, but it's not the deep South. To Judith, Patsy seemed like a Texas personality—strong-willed, not soft-spoken or quiet. She would be willing to give someone the shirt off her back, and people could take advantage of that. But Patsy also knew how to use her charm to get what she wanted.

"She was real out there, outgoing, flashy. She dressed to the hilt. She wanted to be the center of attention," Judith said.

In 1989 Judith and Robert realized their marriage and their life needed rejuvenation. They decided to move to Boulder, a town they had both visited several times and had come to love. Patsy was stunned to hear about the Phillipses' move. John already had merged his company into Access Graphics and was flying to Boulder regularly; Patsy had no idea Judith even knew the town existed. Judith's decision to move to Boulder was sheer coincidence—an unfortunate coincidence, she would believe later.

After Judith settled in Boulder, Patsy visited her from time to time when she flew in to handle big sales meetings for Access Graphics. She was in charge of any corporate reception or event that included food, music, and entertainment. Patsy would come to see Judith so their children—Judith's daughter was a month younger than Burke Ramsey—could see each other again.

Late in 1991 Patsy told Judith the Ramseys were moving to Boulder as well. John and Patsy took a condo while they shopped for a house. Judith told them about a beautiful place for sale on 15th Street, only blocks from Judith's house, which also served as the studio for her new photography business. Patsy favored a new house in adjacent Louisville, while John was partial to the mansion on 15th Street. Judith and Patsy went through the big house together, and Judith thought her support might have tipped the scales in its favor.

With her voice slipping into a lower and sadder tone, Judith Phillips said she never dreamed what would happen in that house.

She was not, however, the only one lobbying the Ramseys to buy that mansion. Joe Barnhill, who lived directly across 15th Street from the house, had met the Ramseys while they were looking at the place. Joe liked them immediately and thought they would make terrific neighbors.

In snowy November 1991, the Ramseys paid $500,000 for the house. In typical Ramsey fashion they set about renovating it. They made few changes to the original house and its elegant first floor, but they completely redesigned the huge addition on the rear to provide beautiful bedrooms for all of their children. The entire third floor of the addition became the master bedroom suite—redesigned specifically to give John and Patsy an unobscured view of the Flatirons. They even tore out the elevator that had been installed for the previous owner—a disabled woman. Judith thought the renovation had cost between $300,000 and $600,000, but would not quarrel with reports that put it at $700,000. "With Patsy, the sky was the limit in terms of her expenditures," Judith recalled.

When the construction work was finished, Patsy refurnished the entire house in her expensive, Southern taste that ran toward eighteenth-century styles and antiques. "She knew what she liked, and what she liked was expensive and historical. She had a real good flair for design," Judith said.

As Patsy developed a new social circle in Boulder, she and Judith saw less of each other. They remained friends, and Patsy was always there if Judith needed her; Patsy once lent Judith a dress for a charity event, and Judith borrowed one of their cars when hers needed repairs. But Judith was building her photography business and had little time or interest in socializing with Patsy's clique of society women. Patsy was actively involved at her children's schools, and often would ask Judith to take the photos—gratis—at one event or another. Patsy seemed to regard Judith's photography business as more of a hobby, and that left her friend "pissed." Judith tried making excuses a couple of times, and finally had to ask Patsy who was going to pay for these photographic services. Judith was earning a living with her camera, and she couldn't be donating her services at Patsy's beck and call. Predictably, that put a strain on the women's relationship.

But in February 1996 they had an occasion to spend

some fun time together. They were among the celebrities chosen to judge chocolate sculptures for a local charity event called the Chocolate Lovers Fling. Part of the assignment included eating the artwork. Patsy and Judith were joined by another celebrity judge, police chief Tom Koby. Judith sat across the table from Koby and found him quite charming and cute. She wondered if it was the intoxicating combination of champaign and chocolate, but she was impressed with Koby's "little boy face," his shyness, and his sharp sense of humor.

Judith never dreamed what the near future would bring to the relationships between those three celebrity judges.

Patsy Ramsey had gone home to serve as a judge for the Miss West Virginia pageant over the Fourth of July 1993 when she noticed an uncomfortable swelling in her abdomen. She and John flew to Atlanta, and Patsy underwent tests there. The diagnosis was two of the most feared words for a woman—ovarian cancer. And worse yet, the disease had reached stage four, the most serious and life-threatening. The Ramseys contacted an old friend in Atlanta, Dr. Gilbert Kloster, and he recommended the most aggressive approach. He referred them to the National Institutes of Health in Bethesda, Maryland.

She was scheduled for an immediate hysterectomy in Atlanta. The night before the surgery, Patsy was in tears when she called an old friend, Carole Simpson. Simpson spent the night with Patsy, and remembered for the *Rocky Mountains News*, "She said, 'I've got to live for my children.' That's all she said, over and over and over."

Patsy later described her battle for a newsletter called "Colorado Woman News." After the hysterectomy she remembered, "I went through menopause in five days. It was a total and unequivocal nightmare." The surgery removed all of the cancer that the doctors could find, but a CAT scan still showed a tumor and revealed that the cancer had spread to her lymph nodes. For the next few months she made grueling flights from Boulder to Bethesda every three weeks to undergo four days of chemotherapy with a potent, experimental cocktail of three anti-cancer drugs—cisplatin, cytoxin, and taxol. She would return home and await the inevitable drop of her white blood cells five days later, falling so low she would have to be admitted to Boulder Community Hospital so a specialist there could treat the toxicity of the chemotherapy. She credited the doctor in Boulder with saving her life on a monthly basis. She lost her hair, her weight fell dramatically, and she was left weakened and nauseated. When not in the hospital or flying east for chemotherapy, Patsy spent most of her days in her guest room; her beautiful master bedroom was too far from the bathroom to accommodate her emergency needs caused by the "chemo." The children or anyone else who visited Patsy in the guest room had to wear a mask to avoid spreading germs; the chemotherapy had ravaged her resistance.

Her mother stayed at the house to take care of the fatigued, debilitated Patsy and the kids while John was at work. Nedra Paugh told "Colorado Woman News," "When you find out your child has cancer, you cry all night. Then you pull yourself together and be strong for them."

Judith Phillips learned that friends were regularly

delivering meals to the family, but Nedra was keeping visitors away and even limiting Patsy's exposure to her children. Judith was furious when she heard that Patsy was making many of the flights to Bethesda alone, so sick that she was vomiting during the trip; Judith was disappointed in John for leaving his wife unassisted. Judith said Nedra began going with her daughter.

Patsy told "Colorado Woman News" that she began to devour religious and self-healing books, singling out one for special praise. *Healed of Cancer* by another survivor, Dodie Osteen, spoke intensely to Patsy, offering Bible passages and mantras to promote self-healing. Patsy said she combined the two into a special mantra that invoked Jesus' name. Aloud she chanted, "By His stripes, I am healed." She practiced positive thinking and visualized a beam of light from God bathing her body in healing power. In September, Patsy had the Rev. Rol Hoverstock perform a ceremony in which her family and friends "laid hands" on her as they prayed for God to deliver a medical miracle.

Two days later, another CAT scan could find no cancer. Patsy said she had considered herself healed since the service.

Patsy recounted her belief in angels when she described the CAT scan that would determine whether she was cancer free or required more chemotherapy. As she awaited the test, Patsy prayed to Beth—John's departed daughter, Elizabeth—who Patsy believed had become her guardian angel. When the technician arrived to begin the scan, she looked just like Beth and introduced herself as Bethany. Patsy had found her angel. The test showed no sign of cancer, and that was confirmed by surgery, another scan, and still another surgery. Patsy had never seen Bethany before and would never see her again. But in January 1994 Patsy was confirmed to be cancer free.

The interview for "Colorado Woman News" was conducted in the Ramseys' sitting room, which featured one of the eight beautifully decorated Christmas trees in their house for the 1994 holidays; the one in the sitting room was adorned in a variety of delicate angels. She told the newsletter that she was rebuilding her body and her life, strengthened by a renewed Christian faith and the miracle she had received. She said she rose every day at five o'clock to look out her window at the spectacular view of the Flatirons. "Every day is cause for celebration," she said.

Judith Phillips played a major role in the "Colorado Woman News" story by taking the touching photographs of Patsy and the children that accompanied the article. When Patsy, JonBenet, and Burke arrived at Judith's studio for the session, Patsy was wearing a wig again. Judith convinced her to take off the artificial cover-up, reveal the real Patsy, and display the short, dark growth of new hair growing back after the chemotherapy. "Funky," Judith described Patsy's new look. The photographs came out so well that Judith included one in her exhibit entitled "Something about Eve," made up of stunning black-and-white photos portraying motherhood.

Joe Barnhill quickly concluded that his first impression of the Ramseys had been absolutely correct. Joe was seventy-one and his wife, Betty, was sixty-nine when the Ramseys moved in. John and Patsy were wonderful people, and the Barnhills soon came to consider themselves surrogate grandparents to those terrific children, Burke and JonBenet. Patsy often would sit on the Barnhills' front porch and chat with them, as good neighbors do. John was quieter, not as bubbly as Patsy. Joe would never have known from John's conduct that he was a high-powered business executive. He never flaunted his wealth or position; he'd never have guessed the man had more than twenty bucks in his pocket. The men seemed to click, especially after they discovered they had something special in common—they both had been military pilots. Joe had flown propeller-driven dive bombers off an aircraft carrier in World War II; John was a "jet man" who had flown for the navy. They both loved flying, and it gave them plenty to talk about.

The Ramseys included the Barnhills in many of the wonderful social events held at the mansion, and often invited them over when John was just cooking burgers and bratwurst on the grill. The Barnhills met Nedra and Don Paugh, and came to like them very much. The Paughs even invited Joe and Betty to attend Don's birthday dinner at Pasta Jay's.

Joe was happy to return the affection to the Ramseys in any way he could. Every time a snowfall bestowed its postcard beauty on always picturesque Boulder, Joe cranked up his snowblower and cleaned not only his sidewalk but the pavement in front of the Ramseys' home. Joe, who loved decorating the outside of his house for Christmas, even painted a sleigh that the Ramseys featured in their front yard, complete with a Santa Claus figure at the reins.

It was a lovely life for the Ramseys and the Barnhills on 15th Street. But it was not destined to last.

CHAPTER 15

Jane Stobie was already the Hewlett-Packard products manager at Access Graphics when she met John Ramsey in the fall of 1990; he was still vice president of marketing and living in Atlanta. She liked him, thinking of him as a quiet, decent, well-dressed but still nondescript man. That first winter Ramsey's father-in-law joined the company. Don Paugh came to work for John Ramsey, and the portly, white-haired newcomer struck Jane Stobie as a grandfatherly fellow; she even gave him some golf balls, hoping to ingratiate herself with him. Stobie learned that Don Paugh, his wife, Nedra, and their daughter Pam had been working for John Ramsey in Atlanta, and that Don Paugh had actually helped create the company that had merged into Access Graphics.

Stobie noticed a change in John Ramsey after he became acting president in early 1991. She thought he seemed very cold, and going into his office gave her the "creeps." She never sensed they made a solid connection, and that was a difficult situation for people who needed to work together. He never even said much at business meetings, but she knew he made all of the important decisions back in his office later. He remained gracious but not very friendly. The only time he warmed to her was when she mentioned she was taking flying lessons. They began talking about that, one of John's genuine loves.

Stobie had limited contact with the new president's wife. She remembered their first meeting, shortly after JonBenet's birth. Patsy was wearing a pink top and a black skirt, and was accompanied by her mother as they visited the Boulder offices from Atlanta. Stobie later would learn more than she ever wanted to about Patsy's family.

Despite some mildly uncomfortable feelings about John Ramsey, Stobie watched as he led the company on a course of steady and impressive sales growth. From $50 million in 1990 Access Graphics rocketed past $1 billion in 1996—a year that ended on a note vastly overshadowing corporate performance.

Jeff Merrick and John Ramsey had become friends when they met in the management-development program for AT&T in 1971 and had to go to Chicago every four or five weeks for training. John impressed Jeff as a bright guy, though quiet; when AT&T let John go after a year, none of the others thought it was the right decision, but they attributed it to the company's concern that John was too quiet.

Jeff and John stayed in touch over the years, and Jeff even stayed with John and his first wife at their home in Atlanta one night on a business trip. The men didn't see each other again until 1982, when John had a different wife and lived in a different house. Patsy Ramsey was surprisingly young and quite nice—not a raving beauty, Jeff thought, but he could see how she could compete for Miss America. When Jeff was looking for a job in 1992, he called John in Boulder to see if he knew of any possibilities around the country. Almost as an afterthought, John mentioned that Access Graphics was looking for a director of distribution. Jeff had to remind his friend, "John, that's what I do."

Jeff went to work for John in March 1993, excited and enthusiastic about the new opportunity in Boulder. Jeff found himself working for Don Paugh—John's father-in-law brought in from Atlanta to be vice president of operations at Access Graphics. Jeff Merrick heard that Paugh had bailed John out years ago and now worked for him.

Jeff also was surprised that John was less friendly than he had expected. John never stopped by Jeff's office, some twenty feet from his own. Jeff would ask John to lunch occasionally, but the men sometimes sat silently for ten or fifteen minutes unless Jeff carried the conversation. When Jeff heard Patsy had cancer, he offered his help in any way John could use it. John thanked him unemotionally and never said another word about it.

At the 1994 company Christmas party Jeff met Fleet White and his wife when they attended as the Ramseys' guests. The two couples sat off in a corner by themselves, and others had to approach them, almost as if they were seeking a royal audience, just to say hello. Jeff thought it was strange that the Ramseys would bring personal guests to the office party, and it seemed uncomfortable for everyone.

At the party the next year, Patsy Ramsey surprised everyone by joining the band to sing the Patsy Cline classic, "Crazy." The performance seemed out of character and, Jeff couldn't help but feel, inappropriate. Patsy seemed to need the attention.

Jeff Merrick left Access Graphics amid continuing

friction with Don Paugh. Jeff had been transferred to the job of director of facilities and security. He went to John to thank him for the opportunity, reading it as possibly a promotion to prepare him to succeed Paugh later. Instead, Jeff learned he still would report to Paugh. But John stressed that he was happy with Jeff's work.

Six weeks later, Don Paugh delivered the bad news; Jeff's new job was being eliminated. When Jeff turned to John, his old friend claimed surprise at Don Paugh's decision, but said it was his to make; John washed his hands of the situation. Jeff asked Lockheed Martin to review his fate, but it backed John Ramsey. Jeff then hired a lawyer and negotiated a settlement with the company. When it was all over, Jeff Merrick's attorney told him the people at Access Graphics were not very nice.

That was becoming a popular conclusion. Jane Stobie and some others inside Access Graphics began calling it "the Evil Empire" about 1992 after a series of disturbing events that proved "something was not right, that these were not nice people." Jane had worked at other companies and had seen corporate politics, but she thought that what was happening at Access Graphics was worse.

Patsy was involved in a couple of those situations. First, she redecorated the Access Graphic offices at deluxe costs. High spending seemed to be a specialty, and Jane said everyone referred to Patsy's efforts as "Sherman shopping Atlanta." Then she arranged an extravagant company luncheon in Atlanta with a *Gone with the Wind* theme, complete with actors playing Scarlett and Rhett. Jane was shocked by how exorbitant it all was; an event that should have cost less than $10,000 rang up more than $30,000 in expenses.

Jane could not help but feel sorry for Patsy, however, after they had a chance to talk at a ball and dinner party in Denver. Patsy sat next to Jane and they chatted, while John made it clear he would have preferred they not converse at all. Patsy said she envied Jane for her career; that was something Patsy had given up when she married John. Jane saw a distinct sadness in Patsy Ramsey that night.

Jane found herself in the middle of another uncomfortable situation in January 1993—in a bizarre encounter with John Ramsey that she believed put her on the slippery downhill slope at Access Graphics. John had qualified for an expense-paid trip to Disneyworld for him and his spouse as a sales prize from Hewlett-Packard, the company whose products were sold by the division where Jane was products manager. John asked if tickets could be provided for Burke and JonBenet, and Jane explained that children were not covered by the Hewlett-Packard prize. John insisted that the tickets be arranged, and Jane insisted it was not possible. John was furious, and Jane was shocked that this multimillionaire would be so incensed over spending the money to take his kids to Disneyworld while he and his wife were going for free.

Not long after that, Jane was transferred to the computer sales division in Atlanta, where Nedra Paugh and her third daughter, Paulette Davis, worked. Although Nedra ran a tight ship and made a profit in Atlanta—while her husband worked in Boulder—Jane was informed that she was to go to Atlanta and begin the process of closing down the whole facility.

The Paughs were gracious and took Jane to dinner,

where they showed her Miss America brochures. But Jane soon began to see some of the signs that others had warned her about. The family seemed insular, like a closed society unto itself. Nedra appeared to exert extraordinary influence over her adult daughters. Patsy called Nedra several times a day, leading Jane to wonder whether Nedra was still influencing her daughter's life in Boulder.

Jane also found Nedra overly competitive and, behind a friendly and even charming appearance, potentially vicious. When Jane got engaged and showed Nedra her two-carat ring, Nedra sniffed, "That's a nice starter ring." Nedra's ring, she explained, was four carats. Nedra also recounted that she had seen another woman's ring when she attended a Miss America luncheon with Patsy and Pam; Nedra went out and bought a bigger one.

Jane eventually closed the operation in Atlanta in September 1993, sending the Paughs into a rage; they blamed Jane. Nedra got a job offer at the Boulder location, but she called the city "a hellhole" where the climate aggravated her arthritis.

Jane went back to the offices in Boulder to start a new products group, but she knew her days were numbered. In May 1994 she left to start her own company to do consulting and training.

Mike Glynn had gone to work for John Ramsey after they became acquainted through Jay Elowsky. Glynn, a former divinity student, was the recruiting director for the University of Colorado's football team, and Elowsky introduced him to Ramsey in 1991 as a source of donated computers for the program. The Glynns and the Ramseys became social friends, and

John offered Mike—who speaks several foreign languages—a job in the international division of Access Graphics. Glynn's account of their relationship for *Vanity Fair* included a description of the Ramseys as almost too perfect, almost a make-believe version of "Ozzie and Harriet came to Boulder." But Glynn also offered a rare portrait of John bursting into anger at work—"shouting and threatening, his eyes bulging like you cannot believe. It seemed like Jekyll and Hyde." Glynn later left for a better job, but called his old friend to express his condolences after JonBenet died.

Jane Stobie and Jeff Merrick and others who worked with John Ramsey sensed something ominous over the horizon, but they never could have predicted how it would descend on the Ramseys. Even after JonBenet's death, John's former friends and coworkers would never have expected the trail to lead to them. Jeff Merrick, Jane Stobie, Jim Marino, Mike Glynn, and others soon learned the Ramseys had put them on the list of suspects in JonBenet's killing. Detectives began showing up with pointed questions and even accusations for the people the Ramseys had reportedly called "disgruntled former employees."

Jeff Merrick gladly agreed to a request to go to the police station to talk to detectives a few days after the murder, only to be shocked when asked point-blank if he had killed JonBenet. He agreed to be fingerprinted and to provide handwriting samples, but turned down the request for blood and hair samples. Several weeks later another detective came to Jeff's house and asked him about a dinner with Mike Glynn, Jim Marino, his wife, and others from the company at Pasta Jay's restaurant about December 15. Yes, Jeff said, they all had gotten together when Glynn was in town that night. Apparently Don Paugh had witnessed that from another table and reported it to the police. Jeff was shocked that the detectives seemed to be taking the matter seriously, almost as if it had been a planning session among murder conspirators—at a popular restaurant where John Ramsey had an ownership interest with his friend Jay Elowsky.

Jeff was stunned by the absurdity of it, but did agree then to provide a hair sample. He and his wife even agreed to the detectives' request that they submit to a polygraph test. But later Jeff reconsidered and discussed it with his legal adviser, former Denver district attorney Norm Early. Early told them to reject the request and not to submit to blood tests, either. They had hair; they didn't need anything else. When the police called back about taking a lie-detector test, Jeff's answer was, "Sure, as soon as John Ramsey takes one."

At a third interview a couple of months later, the detectives asked, "Why does John Ramsey keep throwing your name out?" Jeff shrugged. "Maybe because I pulled on his halo a little bit. I challenged him when I left the company." The only positive word came when detectives told the Merricks they had been excluded from suspicion of writing the note.

Jane Stobie said she learned in a most curious way that she had been named a suspect by the Ramseys—a list she was told numbered 168. She was appearing on the Geraldo Rivera show when another guest—it might have been Marino—told her she was on the Ramseys' hit parade. Was she surprised? Yes and no; it was ludicrous, but nothing the Ramseys did surprised her anymore.

Glynn told *Vanity Fair* he was dumbfounded when a detective called him two weeks after the murder to say John Ramsey had immediately mentioned Glynn as someone who needed to be questioned. When word of that leaked out, Glynn spent three weeks under constant media surveillance, and a TV reporter even asked one of Glynn's neighbors if he was aware that the Ramsey family considered him a major suspect. After Glynn was visited twice by a private detective working for Ramsey, Glynn hired one of his own and learned that nearly everyone who had been interviewed by the police was later interviewed by a Ramsey private eye. Glynn said the police told him that the Ramsey team was trying "to obscure the truth."

Marino's place on the suspect list had hurt and saddened him at first. But he said John later denied that he had given the police Marino's name. Marino quoted John as saying, "The police are trying to piss you guys off and hope you'll say something." Marino could believe that; he said a detective told him that the police considered the Ramseys the prime suspects.

Despite some critical remarks about the Ramseys to *Vanity Fair*, Marino said later that he had come to believe in his heart that neither John nor Patsy could have had anything to do with their daughter's death. There had to be an outsider, an intruder; Marino believed it could have been a pedophile who targeted JonBenet, attended a Christmas open house at the Ramseys', eased open the lock on a window, and returned to abuse and kill her. As unlikely as some thought that scenario, Marino found the alternative unthinkable. "For anybody to whisper any sort of child abuse is absolutely ridiculous," he said.

He said he still talks to John Ramsey several times a

week. During an interview on December 2, 1997, Marino replayed a voice-mail message he said John had left the day before. A voice that sounded like Ramsey's said, "Hey, Jim, it's John. It's about five o'clock. Had one of those days." He went on to mention some problem about an airline flight.

Marino said he had consulted with John before appearing on some of the talk shows, like *Geraldo*, to defend the Ramseys. John used the term "sleazes" for the talk-show hosts and disdained journalism as an "entertainment industry." But John told Marino to go on the shows if he wanted to. He quoted John as saying he would speak out when it was time, and that would be when the culprit was caught.

Marino said he had been disappointed that few of the Ramseys' other friends had been as vocal in defending them as he has been. He said the Lord had even spoken to him about defending the Ramseys, recalling how the apostle Peter denied Jesus three times. Marino felt he would be doing the same thing if he allowed comments from people like Cyril Wecht to go unchallenged.

CHAPTER 16

Part of the tragedy that is the JonBenet Ramsey case is that those who grieve for this child may never really know who she was. The image frozen in the collective mind's eye is haunting—a strangely beautiful, pint-sized, sequined showgirl in feathers or a cowboy hat or a high-fashion costume, prancing and shaking her childish body across the stage and warbling a show tune. She wears too much makeup for a six-year-old, and her tinted hair is too teased and sprayed. Her smile dazzled the judges, but the sparkle came from baby teeth.

Some are horrified by what they see as an abuse of her innocence. Others think it harmless, little more than a special day of dress-up and pretend for a chance to learn poise, make friends, and carry away a crown, a trophy, and a "Little Miss" title.

But either way there was a little girl under all of that. "That baby was a little angel," former nanny Shirley Brady told the *Rocky Mountain News*. "She always woke up with a smile. You wouldn't know she was up because she hardly made any noise, but you would find her in her crib, laughing and cooing." Brady said Patsy's description of her new baby as beautiful didn't do her justice. "Oh, I couldn't believe it when I saw her. JonBenet looked like a big doll with those long eyelashes."

She was described repeatedly as being as sweet as she looked. John Ramsey's first mother-in-law, Irene Pasch, told the *Denver Post*, "She wasn't at all spoiled. I never saw her when she was cross." Pasch, who took a new role in the family when she later married John Ramsey's father, said she delighted in watching Jon-Benet come to the breakfast table, fold her little hands, and say her prayers out loud. "She was just a typical six-year-old, a very loving child."

The *Post* presented an array of images of JonBenet offered by those who knew her:

Sometimes quiet, sometimes a showgirl. This was JonBenet.

A love of sparkly things. Her homemade fruit roll-ups. Playing fetch with her dog, Jacques. This was JonBenet.

She was a funny, spunky kid who often spent kindergarten nap time trading secret hand signals and soft giggles with a little boy on the next mat.

She was a sweet, remarkably caring child who gave presents to Santa, who made sure her older brother, Burke, got his share of the warm attention that so often fell on her.

This was JonBenet.

She wanted to be an Olympic figure skater and liked cherries, making ceramics and watching videos of *The Sound of Music* and *Mary Poppins, USA Today* reported. One of her favorite TV shows was *I Love Lucy*, and her favorite color was purple.

The person she admired the most, she wrote on a

pageant entry form, was her dad. "He's the nicest guy in the whole world," she said.

Her older half brother, John Andrew Ramsey, told the *News* that JonBenet often tried to keep up with big brother Burke. "She was a tomboy with scrapes on her knees, just like any six-year-old," John Andrew said.

JonBenet's first and only report card for kindergarten at High Peaks Elementary School showed high marks for identifying words, counting to one hundred, and recognizing patterns. The *Denver Post* said the teacher praised her for being thoughtful, courteous, respectful, and diligent. "JonBenet is a pleasure to have in class," the teacher wrote. "She is a confident, positive student who works hard on all assignments. JonBenet's mature behavior makes her a positive role model for the other students."

The neighbor across 15th Street, Joe Barnhill, agreed completely. He found JonBenet "a superb little girl, so sweet. I felt like I had lost a granddaughter."

For her fourth birthday in August 1994, her parents gave her a white bichon frise puppy they named Jacques. He was cute as a bug's ear, Joe Barnhill said. When the Ramseys went to their summer home in Michigan in 1996, they asked the Barnhills to watch Jacques for them because they didn't want to take him on their new yacht there. When the Ramseys returned, they realized how attached the Barnhills had become to the dog, so they never asked for him back. A smiling JonBenet would come over sometimes and ask sweetly if she could take Jacques home to play with him for a while. "I'll bring him right back," she would promise. Barnhill would laugh later at the memory: "She would play with him for about twenty-five minutes, and that would be her fun," he recalled. The

Barnhills still have Jacques, even though the little girl across the street who first owned him is gone forever.

Joe Barnhill still treasures the last memory of the Ramseys as a happy, whole family. John had asked Barnhill to hide a Christmas present for JonBenet—a shiny silver bicycle. Late on Christmas Eve, Patsy called and said John would come over to pick it up. Barnhill met his neighbor on the front porch and rolled the bike out. In return John offered another example of his family's generosity and affection—two beautifully wrapped presents for Joe and his wife. "They were that kind of people," Barnhill remembered. "They didn't forget anyone. They were gracious that way."

Joe and Betty Barnhill attended the private memorial service for JonBenet in Boulder on December 29, and found their neighbors devastated. "They could barely talk. It was obvious Patsy was sedated. She couldn't talk coherently."

After the police finished their investigation at the Ramsey house in late January, Joe Barnhill took down the candy canes and other decorations that had festooned the Ramseys' yard in a happier time. He stored them under his porch, convinced they would never be used again. Barnhill couldn't even decorate his own house the next year, deciding to leave town for Christmas.

Many people found something special in JonBenet. The man who played Santa Claus at the Ramsey parties, Bill McReynolds, told the *News* that he was struck by her quiet smile, "pensive, almost retiring" ways, and an angelic glow about her. As he was about to leave the party in 1995, JonBenet handed him a little vial of gold glitter, like that which he sprinkled in his white beard when he played Santa. No child had ever given him a present before, and it touched his heart. At the party in 1996 JonBenet handed him another vial of glitter. He called it "star dust," and said he took it with him for luck when he went for heart surgery. Her death was harder for him than that operation. "She made a profound change in me," he said. At her funeral he walked up to Patsy, handed her one of those vials of glitter, and walked away. She called after him, "Santa, will you come to the party next year?" He said he couldn't do that; it would hurt too much to put the Santa suit on ever again. When he dies, he wants his wife to cremate his body, mix it with the star dust Jon-Benet gave him, scatter it behind their cabin in the Rockies, "and have it blow away in the wind."

As did almost everyone who knew JonBenet, Joe Barnhill said her success in the world of beauty pageants seemed to have no real effect on her personality. She never showed any sign that she thought her titles made her better than the other children. In fact, Barnhill said JonBenet had won several titles before he and his wife even learned she was entering the competitions. As with the Ramseys' wealth and status, they never flaunted JonBenet's success.

Patsy's friends said she and JonBenet saw the pageants that began about 1995 as a way to grow even closer and spend time together, a way to make up for the time lost while Patsy was recuperating from cancer. The pageants had been good for Patsy, and she believed they could be good for her daughter—a way to learn poise and self-confidence, a way to display her love of performing. Her friends were just as sure that there was not a single element of "stage mother" in

Patsy, no vicarious reliving of a fading glory for an aging beauty.

Pamela Griffin, who designed most of JonBenet's pageant costumes, told the *Denver Post* that Patsy was obviously passing along her grace to her child; it came out during the pageants. "If JonBenet did not win a pageant, she was always the first one in line to congratulate the winner, always the gracious loser. If she won—and when she won, she won big; she'd be standing there with five or six trophies and a dozen crowns—she'd immediately go give them to some of the little girls who didn't win."

Griffin's daughter, Kristine, nineteen, was close to JonBenet as her modeling coach and occasional babysitter. In an episode of the *Geraldo* show, Kristine disputed allegations that JonBenet's pageant performances sexualized her in any way. The routine in which JonBenet whisked away the skirt to her costume with a flourish wasn't meant to be seductive; it was designed to meet judging criteria by showing she could work with a prop. What some people interpreted as JonBenet provocatively wiggling her backside, Kristine saw as graceful moving to the music.

Kristine has been haunted by a dream in which JonBenet comes to her and says of the killer, "I don't know who he is, but I saw his shoes," Pam Griffin told the *News*.

Reflecting on JonBenet's pageant success later, Griffin would say wistfully, "We were grooming her for big things. Now it's just not going to happen."

Candy Cohen Reid, Miss West Virginia on 1981 and the mother of three boys, said she had been envious in the summer of 1996 when Patsy described how much she and JonBenet were enjoying the pageants. "They loved it because it gave them something they shared," Reid told the *News*.

Albert Cox, of the Miss West Virginia competition, was sure JonBenet must have liked the pageants and the time with her mother. "I'm sure Patsy and her family took it very seriously. But I couldn't see Patsy as a stage mom. Patsy's the kind of person—she wouldn't push it on her if she didn't enjoy it."

Babette magazine, dedicated to the Little Miss competitions, featured a photograph of JonBenet under the headline ROYALTY REIGNS. The story boasted, "JonBenet has had a great pageant year!" Among her titles, the magazine said, were Royale Miss America, National Tiny Miss Beauty, Colorado State All-Star Kids Cover Girl, and Little Miss Charlevoix—won while at the summer home in Michigan.

The Ramseys' Christmas newsletter for 1996 also recounted JonBenet's pageant successes and her plans to enter the National Hawaiian Tropic pageant in Denver on January 5. But the letter put all of that into perspective by noting JonBenet's academic success in kindergarten at High Peaks Elementary School, where she was now doing first-grade math. "Her teacher says she is so outgoing that she will never have trouble delivering an oral book report," Patsy wrote.

Brother Burke was not forgotten or ignored. His mother also described how he was excelling in fourth-grade math and spelling.

On Christmas afternoon the Ramseys' nanny from Atlanta called her old friends in Boulder. Brady said she could hear the kids laughing in the background, and Patsy told her John was cleaning the snow off the sidewalk so JonBenet could ride her new bicycle. Patsy also said the doctors had pronounced her free of cancer again. Brady quoted Patsy as saying, "I told you the good Lord won't let me die. I want to live so I can raise my children."

The Ramseys' holiday schedule was so full that Patsy hadn't been able to mail out their cards and newsletters until December 24. They arrived on December 26, shortly before the news of JonBenet's death.

Very few negative reports circulated about Jon-Benet. Some attention was given to allegations that she was a chronic bed wetter. Sources quoted the Ramseys' housekeeper in Boulder as telling police that Patsy changed and washed the sheets from JonBenet's plastic-covered mattress every day. Another report said JonBenet still wore Pull-Ups—the underwear-diaper combination for children still in potty training.

One source, however, offered an account of some critical comments about JonBenet's behavior, and those comments were attributed to her grandmother Nedra Paugh. Jane Stobie, who worked with Nedra in Atlanta, said Nedra surprised her with some frank descriptions of a difficult-to-control three-year-old with a habit of kicking people in the shins. Nedra laughed as she called her granddaughter "incorrigible." Patsy had trouble controlling the children, and John was of no help, Nedra told Jane.

But Nedra was thrilled about JonBenet's future on the pageant circuit; she was pretty enough to go all the way to Miss America.

CHAPTER 17

JonBenet's fate and the tapes of her stage performances not only propelled the story into the media stratosphere at heights approaching the O. J. Simpson case, but they combined to shine a harsh spotlight on these "little miss" pageants. Many Americans were unaware children so young were being paraded across a stage in sequins and stockings and high heels, and rewarded with trophies and crowns. Even some of those who love the spectacle of the Miss America pageants were alarmed by what they saw in the JonBenet tapes, and what they learned about beauty pageants for kids too young to ride bicycles without training wheels. From the CBS News anchor desk Dan Rather wondered if the JonBenet tape he had just seen was "kiddie porn." In March 1997 the publicity forced the cancellation of an event JonBenet had never even entered—the Miss Colorado Sweetheart Pageant.

As Geraldo Rivera brought his TV show to Boulder, he offered a succinct description of what many in the country were feeling. "This accelerated process—this pre-adolescent sexuality—there are a lot of very distressing, disturbing hints of abuse, even if the parents are absolutely innocent," he said. "She was tarted up and paraded in this neo-Lolita fashion that horrified us."

Cyril Wecht had already evaluated the pageants as a contributing factor in what had happened to JonBenet. His criticism of them, voiced on various television shows, had been met with thunderous applause. People were offended that these little girls were being dressed in scanty outfits, coated in makeup and hair spray, and then paraded around in such improperly provocative ways. The pageant defenders could call it anything they wanted, but Wecht and a growing number of people found it offensive and inappropriate. It was simply a disturbing transformation of JonBenet from a six-year-old child to a beauty queen who appeared to be twenty-five—as well as sexually knowledgeable and available. This context had created a unhealthily provocative appearance for her, and Wecht believed that had set her up for what had happened—whether her killer came from inside or outside of that house.

He did not oppose competition among children—as long as it was healthy. He had been an accomplished violinist as a child, as well as an athlete all the way through school, and he had competed in all of those activities. His children had played Little League and been involved in other competitive efforts. He supported genuine talent shows where children could display their abilities. But he found no real talent offered in these pageants. What, he asked, was proven by a contest based on whose parents could afford the most extravagant costume and which little girl could shake her childish fanny in the most alluring and sexually precocious way?

The pageants were not just a collateral issue in the

JonBenet case. To Wecht they were an integral part of her death script.

One of the leading critics of the pageants was someone with unquestionable qualifications—someone the Boulder police and prosecutors would turn to in February as an expert consultant. Marilyn Van Derbur Atler, Miss America of 1958, had shocked the world when she disclosed that she had been the victim of incest by her father—abuse that nearly devastated her life and propelled her into an almost fatal emotional crisis when she was forty. As she watched the mesmerizing images of JonBenet at the pageants, she was horrified. She knew that the average age for an incest victim's first assault was six years old.

She had always opposed the pageants for little girls—turning down every request to serve as a judge. But she had no idea how far they had gone until she saw the JonBenet tapes. She assumed the little girls wore cute little dresses. She never dreamed how these girls were being presented now. But she understood too much about what was really happening inside these little girls who supposedly were learning poise and grace and self-confidence. She knew they really were learning that they would be rewarded if they were pretty enough, if their bodies were perfect enough, if they found a way to please the eyes and desires of other people.

That was the message these tiny-tot pageants were sending to these girls. They were sending kindergartners to diets, fifth-graders to eating disorders, eight-year-olds to retainers fitted with teeth so their smiles would be perfect for competition, and teenagers to plastic surgeons for breast implants. They were sending them into hours and hours of costume fittings and dance rehearsals and voice lessons. When they could be outside playing games, they were inside learning to walk and dance provocatively. When they could be sporting pigtails and ponytails, they were getting their hair tinted and teased. Scrubby-clean little faces were layered in makeup and lipstick. Ask any college girl how many in her dormitory had eating disorders, Van Derbur Atler said, and the horrors of teaching girls to focus so intently on their figures would become real.

"What the JonBenet cycle of beauty pageants does, in my opinion, is set them up for major cosmetic surgery, eating disorders, an obsession about how they look, why they're loved, who likes them—those kinds of things. And it's the wrong message, in huge block print."

Surely, she thought, the damage done to girls by a society that places so much value on appearance should be obvious in the 1990s. After all, even the Barbie doll was finally wising up. The manufacturer that many said had contributed to outrageous physical expectations for young girls was retooling Barbie's image; she was getting a bigger waist and smaller breasts. Van Derbur Atler was immensely frustrated to hear that JonBenet had competed against twelve girls in one of the pageants in April 1996, but the year after her death there were fifty young entrants in that event.

Why, she asked, do so many of these young pageant contestants say they like it because it makes their mommies happy when they win? Some of the pageants even provide prizes—including cruises—for the parents of winners. What did that say about some of those entering the contests and their motives? As one mother who finally saw the light and pulled her daughter out of the pageant world told Van Derbur Atler, "These pageants are addictive."

Van Derbur Atler believed these competitions should be banned for anyone under high school age. "There is nothing about these pageants that is positive," she insisted.

She remains a strong supporter of the Miss America pageant for women of college age because it is the largest scholarship foundation for them in America today. It is not perfect; her vocal, dedicated efforts to end the swimsuit competitions have been frustrated by sponsors who recognize what attracts many of the viewers. Still, Van Derbur Atler did not see Miss America as a "beauty pageant," despite the spectacle of women in swimsuits parading down the runway. The rest of it remains a positive influence on the contestants, and she had a wonderful experience as the reigning Miss America.

But she still wishes she had the power to "will away" the tiny-tot pageants.

That would not be a simple matter. The *Denver Post* reported that at least 250,000 children take the stage each year in what has exploded over the last fifteen years to become a billion-dollar industry. A national registry lists some 3,000 individual pageant "systems." The *Post* called it "a tight-knit subculture of families [that] compete in malls and hotel ballrooms for cash awards, partial scholarships, TVs, and toys." Some contestants are infants just a month old. Girls can win in $50 dresses, but the miniature designer gowns of silk or satin can carry price tags of $3,000. Entry fees run from $25 to $500, and photo shoots for a polished competitor can cost $500. Then there are the

JonBenet in one of her extravagant
pageant costumes. (*Zuma*)

Patsy Ramsey
with JonBenet
and Burke.
(*Courtesy of
the* Globe)

Patsy Ramsey
in a recent
pose at a
photographer's
studio.
(*Courtesy of
the* Globe)

Toddler JonBenet uses a straw hat to accentuate her sweet face. (*Zuma*)

Without pageant makeup and costumes, JonBenet poses in jeans to let her childish innocence shine through. (*Zuma*)

Posing in the studio for these shots, JonBenet shows the smile and poise that made her a natural model. (*All photos by Zuma*)

Beaming for the judges, JonBenet displays the style and looks that made her a natural winner on the beauty pageant circuit. (*All photos by Zuma*)

LEFT: Reports have said no footprints were found in the snow around the heavy iron grate that covers the basement window that some consider a possible point of entry to the house. RIGHT: Arches on the second-floor terrace mark JonBenet's bedroom.
(*Photos by Charles Bosworth*)

Two police officers guard the Ramsey house in Boulder after JonBenet's body was found.
(*AP Wide World Photos*)

Boulder District Attorney Alex Hunter must decide the fate of the investigation into JonBenet's death. (*Courtesy of the* Globe)

Commander Mark Beckner announces in December 1997 that John and Patsy Ramsey remain under "an umbrella of suspicion" in their daughter's death. (*Photo by Charles Bosworth*)

Chief Tom Koby addresses reporters during a news conference in the JonBenet investigation. (*Courtesy of the* Globe)

Bill McReynolds played Santa Claus at Ramsey Christmas parties, where he said JonBenet's angelic personality touched him deeply. He and his wife, Janet (pictured with him), gave police hair and blood samples, and were ruled out as suspects. (*Zuma*)

Patsy Ramsey hugs her pastor as she and John leave their church on January 5, 1997. Behind them are their friends John and Barbara Femie. (*Zuma*)

John and Patsy moved to this $700,000 colonial mansion in Vinings, Georgia, outside Atlanta. (*Zuma*)

John, Patsy, and Burke leaving church in Boulder in February 1997. Behind them is family friend and restaurateur Jay Elowsky. (*Zuma*)

fees for dance and voice lessons, personal coaches, and makeup and hair consultants. Despite those costs, the *Post* said, the majority of the contestants come from working-class homes.

Some of those involved in pageants have worried about a specter that many others now speculate haunts these events. Do they unwittingly expose these dolled-up little girls to pedophiles? Are sexual predators trolling these waters, looking for victims?

Ted Cohen, president of an industry clearinghouse called the International Directory of Pageants, warned the *Post*, "They're an attractive package for somebody looking to violate a young person. The girls are certainly in a situation where they're in the limelight for [someone] looking for that type of person to abuse. It's a great temptation for people who are beyond control of themselves. And sometimes the parents are blinded by the stars and the trophies, and have a tendency to trust people more than they should."

He agreed that pageants should prohibit contestants before high school. "It can be psychologically not beneficial to the youngster," he said. "They put too much emphasis on physical beauty rather than the character we want them to develop."

The *Post* recounted stories of overzealous stage mothers whacking their reluctant daughters with shoes or dragging them into bathrooms for harsh pep talks that really amounted to blasts of withering criticism. Some mothers were so competitive, said one pageant operator, that they would not even enter their daughters if JonBenet was a contestant.

Many of the families involved in the pageants were first shocked by such criticisms and then outraged by them. Why should the events they saw as beneficial and just plain fun be seen as any different from Little League tournaments or figure-skating competitions? Some noted that the pageants could be stepping-stones to careers in modeling or even in Hollywood. They spoke of the enjoyment their daughters got from the pageants, from the friendships with other little girls, from the sharing and caring exhibited by many mothers and children.

"Unless you do this, you don't know," said Patsy's friend Pam Griffin. "Those of us who want to be involved in pageants shouldn't have to defend it," she told the *Post*.

The mother of Brittany Doolin, who at eleven took the 1997 Little Miss America title for Show Biz USA, said the pageants had been good for her. "She used to hide under the table when somebody would talk to her," Sherryl Doolin told the *Post*. Brittany described the pageants this way: "You get to have a lot of fun, and you're with your friends."

Mistina Regan said her daughter, twelve, had been in pageants since she was eighteen months old. Michelle Regan had shed her shyness and earned a spot on the honor roll at school. "This is not something she's doing for me or somebody else. She's doing it for herself," her mother said. "My daughter is a normal kid who goes outside and gets dirty and has fun with her friends. The only time she's a pageant kid is the day of the pageant. That's it."

Suzi Doland, who operated the Denver-area Royale Miss America system where JonBenet participated, said many pageants had different rules and different philosophies. Some didn't even allow makeup on children under five, while others limited costumes to dresses and most wouldn't allow swimsuits. Most of the pageants were run by people involved only for the kids' benefits.

Randy Simons, a photographer hired by the Ramseys to prepare a portfolio of shots for JonBenet, defended the glamorous images created for her and the other little girls for the pageants. "It's not sexy," he told the *Post*. "We're doing art, not painting makeup on this girl. Anybody who can look at that and think it's sexy—maybe they should reevaluate themselves. I think it's a very pretty, nice, angelic smile."

He said some of the close-ups were shot for photo contests where younger girls compete with eighteen-year-olds. "So we take them and put makeup on them. It's not done because I'm sick or her mother's sick," he said.

Simons later sold his portfolio of JonBenet photos to the Sygma Photo Agency for the relatively small amount of $7,500, spurning offers up to $100,000. He wept as he told the *Post*, "I wanted the pictures to get worldwide coverage so [JonBenet's killer] would have no place to hide."

After shooting thousands of girls for pageants since 1983, he recalled JonBenet as "special, unusually talented, unusually cooperative, very mature. She was one of the best little girls I've ever worked with. There's a certain kid you work with, you just know they're probably going to be a star."

He also said he was impressed by how attached Patsy and JonBenet were to each other. "These two were so close, so loving. There was an unusual bond. I said, 'You guys seem pretty close.' And Patsy said, 'This is not just my daughter. This is my best friend.' She meant it."

Patsy's sister Pam Paugh told *Vanity Fair* that her niece loved the pageants. "JonBenet would have done a pageant every day if Patsy had let her. But Patsy said, 'No, church comes first on Sunday, and the other days we'll do pageants or whatever,' " Pam said. Noting that Patsy and Pam were both former Miss West Virginias and Miss America contestants, Pam suggested it was entirely proper that they should help JonBenet prepare for the pageants and look as "exquisite" as possible. Pam was outraged by the coverage of JonBenet's participation in the pageants and some of the wild stories reported in the media, like the report of weekly French manicures. Pam said she and Patsy handled what they called the "pageant scrub," a fun time in the bathroom getting JonBenet bathed and ready for competition. They fixed her hair, and Pam applied "the little French manicure." Pam said she was a Chanel makeup artist, and helped apply only a little makeup; JonBenet didn't need much. Pam also explained that she designed most of the costumes, which were "very ladylike" and consistent prize winners. Pam also helped JonBenet with her lovely voice for the songs, but she had a dance instructor for her "Cowboy Sweetheart" number.

Despite Pam Paugh's comments, *Vanity Fair* reported that a former nanny recalled JonBenet saying, "I don't want to walk down the runway. It scares me." The woman said JonBenet liked to perform, but didn't like to compete.

Marilyn Van Derbur Atler stressed that she had no inside information about JonBenet, but the former Miss America could offer her informed opinion: it seemed likely to her that Patsy wanted her daughter

to become Miss America, the goal Patsy had fallen
short of reaching. "I don't think there is any question
that that is the path they were on," Van Derbur Atler
said, and that was for Patsy as much as it was for Jon-
Benet. Grooming her daughter as Miss America could
have been another part of Patsy's desire to project the
image of the perfect family. Van Derbur Atler knew all
about that, because she had lived that lie with her own
mother, who protected to her death the image of the
perfect family, despite the incest inflicted by her husband on their daughters.

Recognizing certain similarities between her family
and the Ramseys, Van Derbur Atler tried to project her
experiences into the allegations facing them. "Would
my mother have written a ransom note? In a heartbeat! Would my father have written a ransom note to
protect my mother? Never! But my mother would
have for my father, without any question. . . . Would
my father have killed me to keep me quiet? Oh, yes,
and then gone to lunch."

She said she was disheartened by naive comments
she often heard from people about incest and families
like the Ramseys. Surely, they would say, there could
not have been incest in such a beautiful family as the
Ramseys.

As she watched the JonBenet tapes, Van Derbur
Atler could not see behind JonBenet's eyes, but she
could see a little girl who was programmed. That is not
something that comes easily to a six-year-old. It takes
hours and hours of regimented rehearsal, Van Derbur
Atler knew. "In my opinion, she was used. She looks
like a little Las Vegas showgirl. She was taught to be seductive and coquettish. These are the exact opposite of
the lessons we should be teaching our children."

Later, when Patsy defended the pageants as just "a few Sunday afternoons," Van Derbur Atler would realize the "incredible denial" existing in the heart of JonBenet's mother. "This was not a couple of Sundays at all," she said. "This [had to be] a focus on their lives. One needs barely to look at all the outfits and all the routines. This was not a couple of Sundays at all, and for her to say that, to me, was just an indication of the world of denial she was living in."

In Patsy she saw a woman struggling to save her life—the life she had built around her home and her husband and her children, the image of the life she had built. If what happened that night was anything but the work of an intruder, everything Patsy had built could be destroyed in a flash.

As Van Derbur Atler looked at John Ramsey through eyes of experience, she saw a man "emotionally distanced."

As she watched the Ramseys' behavior after Jon-Benet's death, most notably their reluctance to meet with police, Van Derbur Atler could not help but draw her own conclusions: "They've incriminated themselves irreparably, in my view. If charges are never filed, they will be still be viewed, in my opinion, by most people as the two who were involved in her death, however it happened."

CHAPTER 18

There were many friends of the Ramseys whose hearts were broken once by JonBenet's death and then again as suspicion turned so intensely toward her parents. Many of those friends came forward in a special report compiled by the *Rocky Mountain News* months after JonBenet died.

Joe Barnhill said Patsy had called him to tell him it was all right to talk to the newspaper's reporters if they called. She knew he already had been besieged by the media, and she apologized for that. It was certainly true; Barnhill had been such a popular source that he finally posted a sign on his door reading, NO MORE MEDIA. But in this case the reporters from the *News* didn't call.

He would have been more than willing to tell them how convinced he was of the Ramseys' innocence. "As I have said all along, I don't believe the Ramseys killed their little daughter. They loved that little girl." If it turned out somehow that they were involved, it would break his heart. "It would be as hurtful to know they had done something as it was to lose that little girl," he lamented.

But the *News* did interview more than forty relatives, friends, and associates, many of whom had refused to speak out before. Despite all that had happened, they supported the Ramseys without qualm. They knew them too well, they said, to wonder about their guilt or innocence.

John Ramsey's daughter Melinda said the family had been plagued by the media. Her parents had been followed into a bank drive-through in Atlanta by a photographer who shoved his camera in her father's face and screamed, "Why did you kill your daughter?" as he snapped away. Melinda had been tracked down on her vacation by more obscenity-spewing photographers from supermarket tabloids.

"I know my dad better than anybody else," she said. "I've known him for twenty-five years. And I know he could not have done this at all. To me it is just so shocking that anyone could believe they've done this. It's just beyond belief." She added, "The most important thing is to find whoever did this, so this can't happen again. It may take years, but this person will be found."

John's younger brother, Jeff Ramsey, had wearied of it all. "I'm tired of waiting for the system to work, because it's not working. I'm tired of hearing all these innuendos. Somebody out there murdered a member of this family. It's not John or Patsy. So whoever did this is still out there."

Carole Simpson, the Ramseys' friend from Atlanta, said she had stopped and asked herself if they could have had anything to do with JonBenet's death. "I honestly can say it didn't make any sense to me that they had done it. You can't feign that kind of innocence. You can't make that up. I know the kind of people they are. I've seen them with their children."

A grief-stricken Patsy had called Simpson on December 27 to sob, "I can't believe someone did this to my baby! Someone came into my house and murdered my baby!" Simpson said Patsy kept repeating that over and over.

But the innocence so obvious to their friends hadn't protected them from public assault, Simpson lamented. "They have been hunted—haunted—everywhere. Unbelievably so. And when you lose your daughter, and you lose your house, and you lose your privacy, and you don't know who's out there who's done this, and you don't know what else may happen—it's overwhelming."

Mary Justice, another Atlanta friend, said, "There are people who are questioning them, but my response is always, 'Well, you don't know them.' People who don't know them are convicting them because they say there are just too many circumstances that are just too unanswerable, which is true, very true. But I know in my heart that I'll stick with them to the end. I know they've got a lot of friends who are doing that."

John Ramsey's first wife, Cindy Pasch Ramsey Johnson, said criticism of John for not showing emotion in public was unfair. "I think you have a private face and you have a public face. Everyone has two faces. What you see of John right now is his public face. You don't see his private face. You don't see the tears, and you don't see the grief. That doesn't mean they're not there."

Dr. Gil Kloster, the friend who helped guide Patsy through her cancer battle, said the Ramseys were existing in "a living hell" of losing their daughter to some unknown intruder and then being suspects in her death. People could suspect the Ramseys because they didn't know them. "The public is accustomed to being betrayed," he said. "Look at Susan Smith—this poor, grieving mother, so distraught. Susan Smith was pretty convincing. For a few days Susan Smith was a sympathetic person. If John and Patsy had anything to do with this, they would make Susan Smith look like a kindergartner."

The Ramseys' nanny knew the family too well to be suspicious. "It's funny how you can get so attached to people who are so good and loving," Shirley Brady told the *News*. "They were such good people. Never a harsh word. Kind expressions to one another.

"There is no chance of them being guilty."

CHAPTER 19

Judith Phillips was visiting her twin sister in Chicago over the holidays in 1996 when one of her neighbors called from Boulder to tell her JonBenet was dead, apparently the victim of a horrible murder. Judith was stunned; it was difficult to put the death of her friend's beautiful little girl into perspective. Judith was concerned about telling her own children what had befallen their friend. Her son's reaction was solemn silence. Her daughter's was intense fear; she slept in her mother's bed for the next month.

By the time Judith returned to Boulder, she had just missed the memorial service at the Ramseys' church, and the family had left for the funeral in Atlanta. When they returned the next week, Judith still couldn't contact them because they were in hiding with friends who fiercely guarded their location. Later, Judith wrote a letter to Patsy, and her husband wrote one to John; they had them delivered by a mutual friend who knew the Ramseys' location. Along with her condolences and offer of help at any time, Judith's letter asked Patsy what she wanted done with the photograph in Judith's motherhood exhibit. Under the circumstances, Judith certainly would have understood if Patsy wanted it removed for security reasons. Patsy did not respond.

After the *Globe* published the coroner's photographs, Judith called the Ramsey spokesman, Patrick Korten. She told him about the exhibit and explained that she had been approached by some media representatives willing to buy her other photographs of Patsy and the children. She asked the Ramseys to let her know within three days what she should do.

A week or two later, Judith received a curt letter from one of the Ramsey attorneys for the Haddon firm, William Gray, reporting that he had heard that Judith planned to exploit the family by marketing the photographs. She had no permission to market or even exhibit any of those pictures, he announced in perfect legal prose. He included a document for her to sign to acknowledge that, and to agree to neither sell nor display them.

Judith was outraged and hurt. The Ramseys had responded to her, a friend, as if she were a tabloid paparazzi who had snapped a couple of frames through their bedroom window. She filed the letter and form, and then tossed the photos and negatives in her safe. She pulled Patsy's photo from the exhibit, but decided not to dignity Gray's letter with a response.

In March Judith's husband finally called John to discuss the estate planning he had been doing for him. They had a nice chat; John told him where they were staying, invited the Phillipses by for a visit, and suggested they could even go to dinner together. Robert Phillips, aware of the continuing media siege, asked how the Ramseys could possibly eat out in public. "The media are really dumb and stupid," John responded, "and we can avoid them."

When Judith's daughter asked to visit Burke, Judith took her to the home where the Ramseys were in seclusion. Judith's knock was met by a pair of suspicious eyes in the window and a demand to know who they were. Judith explained, and they were admitted to see Patsy. The women had a long talk, and Judith was dying to ask a million questions. Instead, she just let Patsy talk. She broke down several times, but seemed to be crying without really shedding any tears. As she looked back on the events of Christmas night in her house, she kept wondering, "Why didn't I wake up?" Judith has always believed that the eyes are the windows to the soul. She kept looking into Patsy's eyes, only to find them remarkably blank. When someone mentioned how they had ditched the reporters shadowing them in Atlanta, Patsy said she didn't remember any of that, not even her daughter's funeral or the flights to and from Georgia.

Judith also was struck by what Patsy did not say. She did not talk about JonBenet. She did not discuss her grief. And she did not say anything about an intruder.

At one point Nedra came into the room, hugged Judith, and said, "God has a plan. His purpose for this tragedy will be revealed." Judith couldn't keep from rolling her eyes. The God she knew did not do these things to children for some unfathomable purpose.

Judith then got a chilly blast from the Ramseys' host because she had not made prior arrangements for the visit and might have been followed.

Before Judith left, Patsy asked her to pass on a message—actually a question—to Mayor Leslie Durgin. Judith knew the mayor, who also was a cancer survivor, and had introduced the women while Patsy was fighting her cancer. Patsy had called Leslie, and they had talked about their common experiences. Now Patsy wanted to ask the mayor why the police weren't protecting the Ramseys. What an odd question, Judith thought. She believed the police were protecting the Ramseys quite well; surely they were safe from harm. What did that question mean? What did they want, the national guard?

Judith passed the question to Mayor Durgin, whose response was a simple statement that she supported the police and prosecutors, and believed they were doing everything they could. Judith called Patsy's host to report the mayor's answer, but was stunned to be told that the Ramseys never wanted to speak to Judith again. The woman said the Ramseys did not believe Judith was their friend, and anything she needed to say to the Ramseys should be sent through their attorneys.

Judith was shocked. "What did I do?" she asked.

The woman's terse response was, "You know what I'm talking about."

Judith actually had not a clue. She just knew she was hurt and angry. She never made another attempt to contact them, and still wonders what she did to warrant their wrath.

She believed then that the Ramseys were innocent of any involvement in their daughter's death. But she was confused by their behavior, and all the secrecy and hiding out. The abrupt letter from their attorney had been disconcerting as well. If they were innocent, why were they going through all of this with the lawyers and public-relations experts? Why didn't they just make a statement to the media and be done with it? Why not face this head-on and end all the mystery?

Over the next weeks Judith thought more about how she would have responded if her child had been killed.

She discussed that at length with friends. They all said they would not be in hiding behind lawyers and turning away requests from the police for interviews. In fact, they all agreed that they would be literally camped out at the police station's front door, offering to help in any way they could and demanding unrelenting police action toward finding their child's killer. Instead, the Ramseys had offered such a bizarre response, such a troubling response, that she had to reconsider her beliefs about them. Were the Ramseys' actions really consistent with innocence? she wondered.

Not long after that, Judith decided to sell some of her black-and-white, emotionally affecting photos of Patsy, JonBenet, and Burke to the *National Enquirer*. It was time to end the friendship with the Ramseys that she believed they had abused and ultimately rejected.

This would not be Judith Phillips's last involvement in this case, and what she would see later with her trained, professional eyes would change her opinion again.

CHAPTER 20

Despite the lurid and hyped-up headlines screaming
from the racks in the supermarket check-out lanes, the
Globe and some of the other tabloids were pumping
out some bits of genuine news about the JonBenet
case, just as they had in the O. J. Simpson case before.
Readers were becoming accustomed to seeing Jon-
Benet's face on the same covers announcing Suzanne
Somers' new diet plan, Katie Couric's thrifty shopping
secrets, a bald Liz Taylor fighting brain seizures, and
the latest in John Kennedy Jr.'s marriage. The Ramsey
story was tailor-made for the tabloids, and they were
milking it for all it was worth. The *Globe* would receive
more mail about JonBenet's murder than any story in
its forty years. The *National Enquirer* would feature
JonBenet on the cover thirty-eight times over forty
weeks in 1997—more times than Princess Diana, O. J.
Simpson, or all of the Kennedys combined.

The real news about the Ramsey case inside those
tabloids had to be tracked, however, through hokey
stories analyzing John Ramsey's body language and
smile, dubious quotes from unnamed family friends
and official sources, salacious allegations and innuendos, dangerous speculation about who might be guilty
and why, and headlines unsupported by the stories

behind them. All the while the omnipresent covers featuring JonBenet's wonderful smile and amazing beauty contrasted with what many saw as some ugly coverage of her death.

A *National Examiner*'s cover "exclusive" trumpeted, "JonBenet Sexy Video Nails Killer," but all the story inside said was that pageant videos and other photos could reveal silent messages sent by JonBenet if she had been sexually abused all along. Holding her hands low suggested knowing what sex was all about, an expert explained. Fluttering eyes were due to stress 99 percent of the time, another expert said. Vacant eyes and stare also were indicative of sexual abuse, they suggested.

Stories in the publications openly speculated on how and why this person or that one might have killed the little girl. Any scenario was open to contemplation in print.

The tabloids also brought disdain on themselves by the constant photographic surveillance of the Ramseys and others in the case. Few people—even some avid readers—approved of the in-your-face photo ambushes and the constant shadowing of people just trying to get through the day. Patsy Ramsey would even call the *Larry King Live* show in September to compare allegations of paparazzi involvement in Princess Diana's death in a car crash in Paris to the tactics employed against the Ramseys. She blasted King's guest, *Globe* editor Tony Frost, for saying he wouldn't buy photos from Diana's crash—after he had bought illegally obtained crime-scene photos in the Ramsey case. "This is trash," Patsy protested.

But the tabloids did keep the light of public interest shining on the case, and the *Globe* had even posted a mammoth reward of $500,000 for information solving it. The reward offered by the Ramseys was $100,000.

The tabloids also excelled at offering succinct, bona fide analysis by qualified experts like Dr. Cyril Wecht, former FBI profilers Gregg McCrary and Robert Ressler, and many others. For some readers the *Globe*'s crime-scene photos and the later photographs of the inside of the Ramsey house provided valuable insights.

And there were legitimate scoops. In January 1997 the *Globe* published a photo of JonBenet in a pageant costume fit for a Las Vegas showgirl, and then pointed out a nasty abrasion on the inside of her right arm just above the elbow. Wecht examined the pictures and believed that the mark could have included a gouge from a fingernail. Did that mean JonBenet had been physically abused? Not necessarily; the injury could have been inflicted during play with her friends, or any of a dozen innocent ways. Was it something that child-abuse experts would have investigated? Quite possibly.

In late November, the *Globe* broke the story about what had been heard and seen the night of the killing by the Ramseys' neighbors—the details that open this book. The woman across the street disclosed to the *Globe* that she had told the police the next day about the scream that awakened her late on Christmas night. The man who lived next door to the Ramseys also had told an officer about the eerie lights moving around inside the kitchen area. Although no detectives had initially followed up on those leads, the officer who conducted the preliminary interviews said he had turned his reports over to investigators.

Cyril Wecht disapproved of some of the tabloid stories and tactics, but he had to admit that some valuable information had been dug out by those publications when it had remained hidden from the mainstream media. The scream reported by the neighbor, for instance, could be useful in establishing a time of death and in revealing other circumstances. If the scream had awakened a neighbor across the street, could anyone believe that the people in the Ramsey house had slept through it?

So, why hadn't the Ramseys sued the publications they dismissed as so despicable, those publishing such allegedly false allegations and speculations? Wecht's experience as a lawyer provided a simple answer. Aside from the difficulty of proving that a publication had knowingly or recklessly published false or defamatory information, the person filing such a libel suit had to submit to probing, questioning under oath—called a deposition. There is no right to remain silent in a civil suit—no pleading of the Fifth Amendment for protection. And if the case made it to trial, the plaintiff would have to endure cross-examination on the witness stand. The Ramseys were paying hundreds of thousands of dollars to lawyers for the sole purpose of keeping them out of court.

CHAPTER 21

"If they are responsible for the killing," former FBI profiler John Douglas said of John and Patsy Ramsey, "they are tremendous liars."

After interviewing the Ramseys for four to five hours, visiting their deserted mansion, talking to their attorneys and the police, John Douglas came away convinced that neither of the Ramseys could have had a hand in their daughter's killing. On January 27 Ramsey told NBC News that the Ramseys did not fit his profile of the killer.

Douglas admitted that his first suspicions had focused on the parents, as he said was proper in the death of a child. But when asked about the common suspicion that John Ramsey had killed his daughter, a sincere Douglas said, "I just don't believe in my heart that he did this." And he noted that a parent who killed his child usually didn't want to be the one who found the body, as John Ramsey had.

Douglas said he was experienced at interviewing manipulative criminals who claim innocence, and they hadn't been able to fool him. He had warned the Ramseys when they hired him that they might not like what he had to say about them. But now he was convinced they had not fooled him, either.

"The parents' grief seemed genuine," he concluded. He added, "From what I've seen and experienced, I'd say they were not involved."

He believed the police should look for the killer in the world around John Ramsey's business, perhaps a disgruntled former employee of Access Graphics and especially one who had been fired. The ransom demand that matched John's bonus was no fluke, Douglas said. He suggested that someone with a grudge against John may have watched "a lot of publicity that the child is a precious possession of the Ramseys," and then decided to kill JonBenet as the ultimate revenge.

Ironically, Douglas announced his conclusions just before the company revealed that a bomb threat from a raspy-voiced, profanity-spouting caller on Friday, January 26, had delayed John Ramsey's scheduled return to work. Access Graphics responded by adding guards and increasing other security measures. One of the problems, officials noted, was that reporters continued to try to interview workers or get into the building. The *National Enquirer* had gone so far as to offer workers $50,000 for information as they entered the offices, and a $5,000 payoff to someone who merely had an appointment in the building.

Douglas's announcement drew some flak in the Denver newspapers. They challenged his knowledge of the autopsy report from the coroner's office, reporting the next day that officials there denied discussing the still incomplete document with Douglas at all.

The *Rocky Mountain News* also took aim at Douglas's suggestion of a publicity-conscious killer who had specifically targeted JonBenet. The *News* checked publishing databases and could find no reference in any

Colorado newspaper or other general-interest publication that mentioned JonBenet before her death.

The *Denver Post* questioned Douglas's recent track record, noting that his profile of the Unabomber predicted he would have a girlfriend or wife who knew nothing of his activities, that he would drive a well-maintained older car, that he would live in the San Francisco Bay area, and would strike again after newspapers published his manifesto. Unabomber Ted Kaczinski failed to meet any of those criteria, the *Post* pointed out.

The newspaper also suggested that Douglas had "gone Hollywood" after his fame from *Silence of the Lambs* and his successful writing career. The *Post* quoted former FBI profiler Robert Ressler as saying, "Douglas is more into entertainment." Ressler had been to Boulder to study the case and participate in a television show. His analysis was remarkably similar to McCrary's—JonBenet had not been killed by a stranger, a kidnapper, or a career child molester. He insisted that the ransom note and kidnapping attempt were staged to cover up the identity and true motive of the killer, who he felt was someone in the "immediate circle" of people surrounding JonBenet—relatives, friends, neighbors, workers in the house. Ressler had studied thirty-six serial and sexual killers, and he said he had never seen anything similar to this case.

He would strengthen that analysis days later when the *Post* and *Rocky Mountain News* quoted sources as disclosing that JonBenet's killer apparently had wiped her body after she was sexually assaulted and killed. The *News* said the killer had used a cloth that left fibers on her skin, and that could account for the very small amount of fluid found on her body.

In the applications for search warrants filed by police, Detective Arndt quoted Coroner John Meyer as telling her that he had found "numerous traces of a dark fiber" when he examined JonBenet's vaginal and pubic areas. He also found dark fibers and dark hairs on her shirt. He had found strands of a green substance entangled in JonBenet's blond hair, but Arndt believed that to be from the green garland she saw wrapped along the spiral staircase where the ransom note was found. That would suggest that the killer had carried JonBenet down those stairs and brushed her hair along the brightly colored Christmas decorations—although it was impossible to know if she had been dead or alive then.

Ressler said wiping off the body showed great remorse by the killer and supported the belief that her death had not been intentional. A serial killer or sexual predator would not have taken the time and effort to wipe his victim's body, Ressler said. This killer, however, had been very concerned about being identified by forensic evidence left behind.

Meanwhile, the *Post* continued to hammer at John Douglas by noting the approaching publication of Douglas's fourth book, and a book signing planned for Boulder.

The story also revealed, in addition to a rejection from former FBI profiler Gregg McCrary, that the Ramseys had been turned away by the members of The Academy, an organization of eighteen former FBI and Secret Service agents who worked as consultants, investigators, and profilers around the world. A spokesman for the group told the *Post* that every one of the eighteen had rejected the Ramseys' offer to join their team.

McCrary knew Douglas well and was surprised that

he had issued such a strong statement in the Ramseys' defense and pointing toward a vengeful killer from John's corporate life. Douglas's conclusion certainly didn't agree with McCrary's analysis that the killer would be found inside the family. "I can't say the Ramseys did do it," McCrary said, "but I sure as hell can't say they didn't do it." He could not recall a single instance of a killer striking the child to get back at the parent. And this case spoke to him of psychopathic sexual behavior, not a revenge murder aimed at John. If that had been the motive, McCrary's experience told him, the killer would have placed the body somewhere it would have been seen readily, almost on display to shock and insult John, in addition to cause him pain. And a revenge killer would not have lingered in the house to write a bogus ransom note that would have confused the real issue. McCrary could find no way to reconcile the facts of Jon-Benet's death with Douglas's conclusions.

McCrary called Douglas and left him a message saying, "I hope you're right. You've really gone out on a limb. I hope you know something I don't know." The men met later when they lectured at a seminar in San Francisco, and McCrary told him the same thing. If Douglas turned out to be right, McCrary laughed, he would become "untouchable" from then on; no one would dare question his opinions. Otherwise, he may have inflicted a serious blow to his own credibility.

A week later, Douglas conceded on *Larry King Live* that his knowledge of the autopsy report was based on information from the Ramseys' attorneys, not from the coroner's office or other authorities. But Douglas said he still had been able to gather enough information to analyze the case and reach his conclusion clearing the Ramseys.

CHAPTER 22

When Boulder County district attorney Alex Hunter finally weighed into the JonBenet Ramsey case publicly with more than the occasional official comment, he did it with grand style and amid reports of growing strain between the authorities and the Ramseys.

On February 12, news reports quoted sources close to the investigation as saying the police had asked the Ramseys for more handwriting samples to help analyze the ransom note. Although getting several samples was not unusual in such a case, the new request arrived at the same time as reports of a widening rift between the cops and the Ramseys over the issue of formal interviews. The police had met a solid wall of resistance and special conditions erected by the Ramseys' defense team against requests that John and Patsy sit down separately with detectives for videotaped interviews. Reporters even began speculating about whether the conflict would lead the Ramseys to refuse to provide the additional handwriting exemplars and force Hunter to seek a so-called "41.1" order from the courts, a judge's ruling compelling the submission of handwriting samples.

The police were continuing that line of investigation with others as well. Bill McReynolds, who had played

Santa Claus for the Ramseys, had recently returned
with his wife from a month in Spain, only to be met
with police requests for samples of his handwriting,
blood, hair, and fingerprints. The sixty-seven-year-old
former journalism professor from the University of
Colorado said the police had interviewed him before
he left the country, but had just asked him on February 7 to provide the samples. McReynolds had given
them handwriting in block printing, just as the ransom
note had been written. But he couldn't remember the
exact words he was asked to reproduce.

Less than a month later, the police would return to
the McReynolds' mountain cabin to take the same kind
of samples from his wife, Janet, after some bizarre
coincidences had been discovered. On December 26,
1974—twenty-two years to the day before JonBenet's
death—the McReynolds' nine-year-old daughter had
been abducted with a friend in the nearby town of
Longmont. The McReynolds girl had watched the ab-
ductor sexually assault her friend before they were released; no one was ever arrested. Two years later, Janet
McReynolds wrote an award-winning play entitled
Hey Rube, a fictionalized account of the sexual assault,
torture, and murder of a sixteen-year-old girl in Indi-
ana in 1965. In another striking similarity to the events
in Colorado, the girl's body was found in a basement.
The McReynolds told the *Rocky Mountain News* that
they had not even realized the odd similarities. Janet
McReynolds said her play and her daughter's experience were irrelevant to JonBenet's death. What about
December 26, 1996? The McReynolds had gone to bed
at eight o'clock that night in their home in Rollinsville,
thirty miles up the mountains from Boulder. "Isn't life

strange?" observed the man who had played Santa for JonBenet.

While other news events were underway on February 12, a quiet but profound moment arrived at the Ramsey mansion on 15th Street. A moving van pulled up and workers began carting the Ramseys' possessions out of the house. John and Patsy had been unable to return after their daughter's death, and now it appeared that they never would. Those following the case remembered that Nedra Paugh had said that Patsy had vowed never to return to that house. Some reports later would suggest that Patsy had wanted the place burned to the ground.

The Ramseys' need for secret and temporary housing in Boulder also might have contributed indirectly to an incident involving their friend, restaurateur Jay Elowsky. While the Ramseys were staying at his home, Patsy called Boulder police on the morning of February 10 to complain that they were being stalked by the media; reporters and photographers were parking along the street near Elowsky's home and appeared to be surveilling the house through cameras and binoculars. Shortly after that call Elowsky was arrested on suspicion of felony menacing and carrying a concealed weapon. Police accused him of swinging an aluminum baseball bat at three people he suspected were reporters trying to locate the Ramseys. Police also found a loaded 9mm pistol in Elowsky's car. He told them he had seen some people near his backyard and followed them to a street in an industrial area near his home. He confronted them there, brandishing the bat, shouting at them, and ordering them to leave. Two of the men were local businessmen, but the third was a television reporter who said Elowsky had swung the bat at him. Elowsky later pleaded guilty of a misdemeanor charge of menacing, forfeited his gun, and drew a sentence of two weekends on a work crew at the county jail and a year's probation. Some media sources noted that the plea accepted by Hunter's office avoided a felony conviction that might have endangered Elowsky's liquor license at his restaurants.

Those events set the stage for D.A. Alex Hunter when he stepped before cameras broadcasting his news conference live across the country on February 13. He spoke at length about his desire to solve the killing "of this child who was really our child," about the difficulty of investigating a case based on circumstantial evidence, about the need for continuing secrecy despite media and public pressure, about his refusal to be rushed to judgment to satisfy meaningless deadlines, about his revulsion at some supermarket tabloids. He said he and Chief Tom Koby had ignored allegations that they were arrogant when they were actually being smart. They had ignored hurtful and inaccurate news reports. He added, "Our philosophy has been to concern ourselves only with the way the story ends, not with the way the chapters are being written." And he offered his own vow: "We know where we're headed. We know this case is going to be solved. We know it."

He then turned to the surprising news of the day and announced that he had assembled what he was calling the Expert Prosecution Task Force—what would be dubbed in the post–O. J. Simpson world as a "prosecution dream team." In what may have been the first effort of its kind anywhere, Hunter and Koby had sparked their team by arranging the assistance of

nationally known lawyer and DNA expert Barry
Scheck of New York and internationally recognized
crime-scene analyst Dr. Henry Lee, director of the
Connecticut State Police Laboratory.

Hunter also had gained the formal assistance of
four other district attorneys—Bob Grant of Adams
County, Bill Ritter of Denver, Dave Thomas of Jefferson
County, and Jim Peters of Arapahoe County. Hunter
said he had assigned his top assistants in his homicide
unit to the case as well: chief trial deputy Pete Hofstrom, chief deputy Peter Maguire, senior trial attorney
Mary Keenan, and senior trial deputy Lawrence
"Tripp" Demuth. Between them they brought seventy
years of prosecution experience to the table. And
Hunter had consulted with the capital-crimes unit of
the Colorado attorney general's office—the group that
handled death-penalty cases around the state. For the
first time the possibility that JonBenet's killer could
face execution had been raised officially.

Without mentioning the Ramsey defense team specifically, Hunter acknowledged that there had been a
sense of "almost a David-and-Goliath thing"—pitting
the high-powered lawyers and experts paid by the
Ramseys against the local authorities. Well, Hunter
was saying now, things have changed.

"We feel we can match the resources of anyone in
bringing to bear on this case—in our search for the
truth to do justice—the very best that is available," he
proclaimed.

The formation of the team amounted to a stunning
coup for Hunter and Koby, especially by snagging
Scheck and Lee. They had become well known as devastating presences on the "dream team" assembled by

O. J. Simpson. As one of the defense attorneys, Scheck had blasted the way physical evidence had been collected by the Los Angeles police and analyzed by the crime lab; his expertise in DNA analysis was masterful, and he played a major role in questioning its application against Simpson. Lee's powerful presentation as an expert witness also had been beneficial as he testified to the possibility of a second killer by analyzing blood-spatter evidence and shoeprints.

Only later would it be learned that the Ramseys had already called Scheck and Lee, only to be spurned by both. Hunter had called Scheck about joining the team, and the lawyer had consented. Scheck then sent Hunter to Lee for additional expertise, and Lee also agreed to serve as a consultant.

Hunter was not finished yet. Before he stepped away from the podium, he turned to the television lens and spoke directly to JonBenet Ramsey's killer—"to the person or persons that took this baby from us. . . . The list of suspects narrows. Soon there will be no one on the list but you. When that time comes—and as I have said to you, that time will come—Chief Koby and I and our people and the Expert Prosecution Task Force and the other resources that we bring together are going to bear down on you.

"You have stripped us of any mercy that we might have had in the beginning of this investigation. We will see that justice is served in this case, and that you pay for what you did. And have no doubt that that will happen.

"You need to know that everyone in America is watching. The death of this child has broken all of our hearts, except—apparently—yours. It has left a permanent scar on our conscience. There must be accountability. There is going to be accountability in this case, I promise you. That's my job, to make prosecution happen. And I say to all of you that there will not be any failure in that regard. We will ensure that justice is served for this community, for this nation, and most important, for JonBenet."

After the news conference the Ramseys issued a statement through Pat Korten: "We are encouraged by the decision of Boulder law enforcement officials to put significant additional resources into their investigation. We strongly support their intensified effort to find and bring to justice the person who brutally murdered JonBenet. In fact, we offered to pay for the more expensive DNA testing early in the investigation."

In a conversation later with talk-show host Peter Boyles on KHOW-AM Radio and *Denver Post* columnist Chuck Green, Korten said the Ramseys' investigative team had passed several promising leads on suspects to the police, but they didn't seem to take them seriously or to pursue them in good faith.

The Ramseys, Green quoted Korten as saying, believed they were "most probably the primary suspects" for the police, and there was a growing resentment about that. They also objected to the coverage of JonBenet's life and the concentration on the pageants, which were just a small part of it. She should be remembered as "a happy child with a normal childhood," Korten said, and the constant images of JonBenet's stage performances disturbed her parents.

Korten also revealed a moment that had been chilling for the Ramseys. When they had submitted handwriting samples to the police, they had been required to write out the text of the ransom note that had alerted them to what would follow and propelled them into this unending nightmare.

He disclosed that Patsy's emotional stability was a real concern to those around her. The family was moving regularly among their friends' houses, buoyed only by the private time they could share with son Burke. Korten said the Ramsey's were weathering the unimaginable storm by clinging to each other. "I wish my marriage was as close as theirs," he said.

In another note, Korten said Ramsey lawyer Bryan Morgan "went ballistic" over John Douglas's public comments about his work for the Ramseys.

Across the country, in a hotel suite in Pittsburgh, Dr. Cyril Wecht had watched Alex Hunter's news conference as a television crew from *Inside Edition* watched Wecht. He had agreed to serve as commentator for the program as Hunter delivered his first news conference—except to Wecht, Hunter had not produced any real news. He had scored by drafting Wecht's friends and colleagues, Barry Scheck and Henry Lee, for the task force. That was a smart, potentially beneficial move. But there had been no substance offered about the case itself. After seven weeks of investigation, all Hunter and Koby had said was that they had no idea how long the case would be dragged out.

After Hunter's emotional comments, Koby had spoken briefly and revealed that the testing of the DNA evidence collected at the Ramsey house had been completed by the lab for the Colorado Bureau of Investigation, and then sent for final testing to Cellmark Diagnostics in Germantown, Maryland, the largest independent lab for forensic DNA tests and the same one used in the Simpson case. Those tests, Koby said, could take another six weeks or more. "This case is going to take a while," Koby warned. Well, no kidding, Wecht had replied, and no news.

Wecht did wonder, however, about part of Hunter's impassioned closing remarks. "You have stripped us of any mercy that we might have had in the beginning of this investigation," the D.A. had said. Would any prosecutor feel mercy for an intruder who violated the sanctity of a family's home on Christmas night and hideously murdered a child? Wecht wondered. Would a prosecutor feel mercy for a pedophile, a sexual predator, who stalked a pretty young victim, and then stole into her home to torture and ravage and kill her? Would there be mercy for a kidnapper who sexually assaulted and then killed his intended ransom ticket?

Wecht could believe, however, that Hunter might have shown mercy for someone close to the child— even her parents—if some horrible, unintended event had taken her life. Even if loathsome, perverted desires had ultimately led to her death—accidentally— might not a prosecutor find some mercy in his heart if the person responsible had come forward and confessed those sins at the beginning? Would that mercy evaporate if instead the killer had done everything possible to misdirect and frustrate the efforts to deliver justice for this dead child?

Had Alex Hunter just revealed his own conclusion about who killed JonBenet Ramsey?

CHAPTER 23

The district attorney of Boulder County had been vacationing in a remote corner of Hawaii—far from a telephone—on the day JonBenet Ramsey died. Sixty-year-old Alex Hunter learned the next day about what would become the case of his career, a career that had begun in 1963 as a newly graduated lawyer clerking for a Colorado supreme court justice and blossomed as a seven-term district attorney in Boulder.

Alexander Munro Hunter, the son of parents he described as alcoholics, grew up in a suburb of New York City and came to the University of Colorado to get his law degree. After the supreme court assignment Hunter went to work as an assistant district attorney in Boulder. Six years later, in 1972, he ran as a Democrat for the D.A.'s post and won in a county that was changing from solidly Republican to the new center for the liberal counterculture spawned by the Vietnam War. His first victory was narrow, but the *Rocky Mountain News* reported he had never been seriously challenged in the six elections that followed, including 1996.

His record in office is replete with innovation and experimentation in a field where there generally is little room for either. He banned lie-detector tests for rape victims, and sponsored sensitivity training for cops and prosecutors working with them. He was the first D.A. in Colorado to hire a woman to investigate sex crimes. He favored publishing the names of drunken drivers in the newspapers. He fired seven staffers for attending a party where cocaine was snorted. Hunter set up a victims' compensation fund, implemented the reading of "victim impact statements" at sentencings, published a pamphlet on child molestation for distribution in the schools, and set up programs to combat drug use and teenage pregnancy. He sponsored hundreds of community meetings to discuss the issues with residents and for a while ran a call-in radio show dubbed *Dial the D.A.* And he actually responded to the citizens. When residents of Longmont complained about a police officer shooting a man who had been armed with a knife, Hunter put the voluminous investigative files in the public library and invited comments.

Such activities had made him a frequent target for sniping by opponents, and his philosophy on plea bargains earned him the label of "Monty Hall" from *Let's Make a Deal* fame. He once tried to ban all plea bargains, jammed the court docket horribly, and declared the effort a failure. He had never once sought the death penalty in twenty-five years, and explained that by saying he didn't oppose it, he just hadn't encountered the proper case.

Along the way he became a powerful force in Colorado politics, serving as the chairman of the local Democratic party. He was credited with recruiting party members and helping raise funds; a party leader called Hunter "one of our key people." He was considered close to Democratic governor Roy Romer and other influential political figures.

Hunter's personal life had been as active as his professional life. He filed for bankruptcy reorganization in the seventies after some bad real estate deals. He had been married four times; he told the *Denver Post* he was a marital "slow learner." He fathered five children, ranging from seven to thirty-seven.

He also told the *Post* that he saw the Ramsey case as more than just another murder. To him it was a chance to redeem the American court system after the debacle of the O. J. Simpson trial. Hunter said it took him a while to recognize the elevation of JonBenet's case to that level. But as the media calls grew daily, he began to realize what was ahead. It had even crept into his last moments with his mother, who died in early 1997. Among her last questions to him were inquiries about progress on the JonBenet case.

He told the *Post* his promise to catch the killer would be kept. "This is heavy-duty, high-stress stuff, but it's what I bargained for."

The day after District Attorney Alex Hunter made headlines with his new dream team, his top assistant made some brutally frank comments about the quality of the investigation by the police and the less than dreamy relationship between them and the prosecutors.

"There have been some allegations that the Boulder Police Department has had some problems with their investigation," Bill Wise said in a meeting with the county commissioners. "It's not as bad as [the media] are reporting, but there have been some problems, and we just need a good, experienced, probably retired police officer . . . maybe even an FBI agent."

Wise said the police had rebuffed an effort by Peter Hofstrom, the D.A.'s chief trial deputy, to get involved at the crime scene. "The Boulder Police Department says, 'Get out of our business.' They don't like lawyers sticking their noses into their investigations and trying to run crime scenes and so forth, so we've told Pete to back off a little bit."

Didn't the police recognize the value of advice from an expert like Hofstrom? a commissioner asked.

"Well, I'm not going to criticize the Boulder Police Department, but I'd sure like to. But I really don't want to get into that," Wise said.

If not for the close relationship between Hunter and Koby, Wise explained, "We wouldn't be in the case right now and the case would suffer for it. I can tick off in my head half a dozen—without even thinking about it—instances where they are being legally advised to do something, and with a lot of pressure they do it. But if they hadn't had that legal advice, there could really be dire consequences to some of the forensic evidence and so forth."

Wise also offered a startlingly candid comment while asking the commissioners to approve an additional $20,000 above the estimated cost of $150,000 for the Ramsey case. The commissioners asked if someone who was eventually convicted could be forced to reimburse the county for some of the expenses. Wise responded, "If he has the money, and one of the suspects has money."

Later, Wise would not elaborate on what obviously could be interpreted as a reference to the Ramseys as suspects. Wise would only call his statement "an off-the-cuff comment. It really was not directed at anybody."

The next day, Wise issued an apology for his remarks about the police. "I respect and have confidence in the Boulder Police Department and in their handling

of this investigation. My remarks to the commissioners were out of line, and I apologize for them."

Hunter offered an addendum, addressing Wise's
reference to a suspect who had money. While the list
of suspects was narrowing, as Hunter had said the
day before, it was too soon to identify anyone as a suspect. Wise had not intended to do so during the commissioners' meeting, and Hunter hoped that Wise's
comment would not be taken out of context.

A week later, Hunter's chief appellate deputy filed a
motion asking a judge to keep secret the search warrants issued for the Ramsey house. "The owners of the
property subject to these searches have not been eliminated from suspicion," Bill Nagel wrote in the first official document to call the Ramseys suspects.

CHAPTER 24

As the Colorado winter gave way to spring, no thaw could be found in the tension between the Ramseys and the police over the long-sought, suspiciously delayed formal interviews. There had been a glimmer of hope in January, but even that fell through when the police refused demands by John and Patsy to be interviewed together for just an hour, with her doctor present, and with detectives chosen by the Ramseys.

But there were other significant developments in the case.

John had been ruled out as the writer of the ransom note. But the handwriting experts for the Colorado Bureau of Investigation were unable to give Patsy the same clean bill of health, even after she had submitted five separate samples of her handwriting and the police had used a search warrant to grab several more unrehearsed examples from papers at her summer home in Michigan. Some of her writing specimens were useless because she was on medication or had been too controlled and deliberate when she wrote them, officials said. They even had the right-handed Patsy provide the fourth sample by writing with her right and then her left hand.

A source quoted the CBI report to *Vanity Fair* as

stating, "There are indications that the author of the ransom note is Patricia Ramsey, but the evidence falls short to support that definitive conclusion." The source reported that the CBI had examined samples from seventy-four people, but only Patsy's penmanship had set off alarm bells.

The experts hired by the Ramseys apparently disagreed, insisting that neither of the Ramseys could have written the note. While there may have been some similarities between Patsy's handwriting and the note, Pat Korten said, there were many dramatic differences that required eliminating her from suspicion. He said the police had declined an offer to meet with the defense experts to, one could say, compare notes.

But another source with a unique connection to the case had performed a special handwriting analysis—in an odd cooperative effort with authorities—and had come up with a much more definite opinion.

Judith Phillips, Patsy's banished friend and photographer, had been asked by the police to photograph a poster they had found in a remote corner of the Ramseys' basement near the furnace. Judith knew immediately what she was seeing through her viewfinder. With holly leaves painted around the hand-drawn legend, WELCOME TO THE GREAT NORTHWEST, Judith recognized Patsy's style of artwork. Patsy had wanted to become a serious painter but had never devoted the time. Judith had seen some aprons, however, that Patsy had painted for women volunteering at the elementary school. Judith recognized Patsy's style of outlining the image she had just painted, as she had with the holly leaves on the poster. Kind of a "country French" style, Judith thought.

At the police department's request, Judith produced an enlarged photograph of the poster for them to submit to their handwriting experts. But Judith then joined with a friend, investigative journalist Frank Coffman, to perform their own examination. Judith had no education as a document examiner or handwriting expert, but she had a sensitive eye that could recognize shapes and forms and all of the other special elements that went into professional photography. Judith and Coffman identified forty-seven similarities between the letters Patsy had written on the poster and the letters that appeared in the ransom note. Judith found it impossible to miss the way the letter *t* was rounded off at the bottom or the way the letter *l* was formed; both exhibits before her contained identical components.

Judith and Coffman prepared an exhibit of their own, juxtaposing the poster and a reproduction of the note side by side, and documenting each similarity they had observed. They delivered that to the police, but never received a response.

Faced with such striking and numerous similarities, Judith Phillips concluded that Patsy Ramsey had written the ransom note. "It was her penmanship, even though it might have been left-handed."

There would be another startling revelation related to the source of the ransom note. The *Rocky Mountain News* would report that John Ramsey had been the one who handed over the legal pad to police when they asked for paper to take handwriting samples from the Ramseys on December 26. A detective who leafed through the pad discovered the page on which was written, "Mr. and Mrs. Ramsey"—the apparent "false start" to the ransom note.

* * *

Although the police had not released much information about the case officially, they had made some formal decisions—and they involved some Ramsey family members and former friends.

Four days after the Ramseys turned to their own Web site on the Internet to post a plea for the cops to clear John Andrew and Melinda of suspicion, the police obliged them. In a departure from their say-nothing policy, the police issued an official statement saying the older Ramsey children had been eliminated as suspects; they had been in Georgia with their mother when JonBenet died.

Chief Koby provided an even more rare concession by personally clearing Fleet and Priscilla White of suspicion. Koby said he was making an exception to his policy of silence because the Whites had been cast as culprits by some publications. Koby called them "key witnesses who have cooperated fully with us from day one of this investigation." Fleet White, after all, had been able to provide important details: he had been with John Ramsey when he discovered Jon-Benet's body in the room that White claimed to have seen empty sometime earlier.

The Whites' break from the Ramsey camp had become legend in Boulder. The *Globe* claimed in August that in the hours after JonBenet's funeral, White had angrily confronted John Ramsey over his refusal to cooperate with the police; the men almost came to blows, according to the tabloid's account.

Vanity Fair expanded on that in October. That report said the showdown between the men had happened at Nedra Paugh's house when White demanded to know why the Ramseys had hired attorneys and were refusing to cooperate with the police. A furious Nedra

Paugh was quoted as describing White as "a wild man and a lunatic."

Not long after that encounter, both magazines said, John Ramsey told his lawyers and the district attorney that he considered Fleet White a prime suspect. Ramsey consort Pam Griffin would offer her opinion that White knew something about JonBenet's death that he had not revealed. "This man has a dark side," Griffin told *Vanity Fair*.

But the police disagreed. The Whites had been cooperative, key witnesses—not suspects. And they would be heard from again later.

The day after Koby cleared the Whites, Alex Hunter provided a different perspective on the Ramseys. "Obviously," he told the Associated Press, "the focus is on these people. You can call them what you want to. . . . I have more people call me and say, 'Why are they doing this? Why are they behaving that way?' That would be something that would be very interesting to discuss later."

Hunter tempered that surprising admission, however, by stressing to the *Denver Post* that "this is an open-minded investigation."

By then Hunter had beefed up his task force by calling a veteran homicide cop out of retirement. Lou Smit had spent twenty-four years investigating more than two hundred murders—and solving ninety percent of them—as a detective for Colorado Springs, as well serving as the sheriff and district attorney of El Paso County. He had been credited with solving the murder of Karen Grammer, the sister of television star Kelsey Grammer of *Frazier*.

Called "the fox" by admirers and known to carry

photos of victims in his pocket while he searched for their killers, Smit said he had ended nine months of retirement because "I want to be part of representing that little girl and catching the person who took her life." He was known for his ability to crack tough unsolved cases, and for approaching his work with a literally religious fervor, almost as if he were appointed by God as an avenging angel.

His first order of business was to sift through some thirteen thousand pages of police reports in a new location—a "war room" set up by prosecutors and police in secure office space in the county's Justice Center to serve as combined headquarters for the investigation. Not even janitors would be allowed into the three-room complex where windows were treated to turn away sensitive microphones, computers were "hacker-proofed," and documents were shredded to foil tabloid reporters searching the trash for tips. The reports to be read by Lou Smit were contained in fifteen binders, each with a photo of JonBenet's face laminated to the cover.

There had been other developments to occupy the interest of Ramsey case buffs as well.

Cyril Wecht had been consulted again as the *Globe* tabloid raised more hackles in Boulder by getting its hands on another batch of secret photographs—this time of the inside of the Ramsey house. Eight photographs published in March started in JonBenet's pink bedroom and followed the path her killer might have taken, down the spiral staircase and into the basement room where her body had been found. The pictures showed where sections of beige carpeting had been removed near JonBenet's bed to look for trace evidence;

where doors and banisters had been dusted for fingerprints, and where, Wecht explained, the chemical
called Luminol had been applied to test for blood or
other fluids that couldn't be seen by the naked eye. The
Globe noted the bag of golf clubs by the door into what
it called "the dungeon of death"—the concrete room
where the body lay. The tabloid suggested a golf club
had been the weapon used to fracture the girl's skull.
The photo of the basement also showed a safe sunken
into the concrete floor where detectives had hoped to
find pornography, but instead found nothing.

Alex Hunter called publication of the photos "reprehensible," and the police suggested it could cause
some difficulty by providing even more detailed information to the public.

The Ramsey team demanded a police investigation
into how the photos had fallen into the *Globe*'s hands;
a special prosecutor was appointed in Denver, where
the lawyers' offices were located. This second *Globe*-
photo investigation led again to a photo lab, but not to
criminal charges. The lab that had developed photos
taken by the Ramseys' private investigators inside the
home had thrown out a test batch; someone found the
prints in the trash and sold them to the *Globe* for "a
modest four-figure sum." The photos were deemed
abandoned property and the investigation was closed.

The visual arts played a role in another flap related
to the case. An art student at the University of Colorado enraged the sensibilities of most residents by
creating a mural that covered two twenty-five-foot
sections of wall in the fine arts building. Over three
copies of a *Newsweek* cover featuring a glamour shot of
JonBenet, the artist had stenciled foot-high letters that

read, DADDY'S LITTLE HOOKER. He told reporters that he was protesting child beauty pageants. By the time the display had been torn down twice, he had been unfavorably portrayed in the media, received a death threat, and warned of copyright infringement, the young artist was reconsidering his effort and wishing the furor would just blow over.

Even the DNA tests created conflict between officials and the Ramseys. Alex Hunter went beyond the requirements of the law and offered to allow the Ramseys to have an expert present to monitor DNA testing at Cellmark Diagnostics in Maryland. The law only required admitting a defense expert after someone had actually been charged with the crime—something that seemed in the distant future in this case. But Hunter said he would allow the Ramseys to send in someone, anyway. That was interpreted widely by the media to confirm the Ramseys' position as suspects in their daughter's death. Other experts called it a smart move, taking away a defense point if the Ramseys ever were charged; they couldn't do the O.J. thing and complain about sloppy lab work and contamination if they had been there to watch it.

The Ramseys said they would consider the offer, and soon hired Moses Schanfield of Denver, a widely respected expert. But they also announced that their earlier requests to observe tests at the CBI lab had been rejected. The lab's director, Carl Whiteside, said state regulations only allowed representatives of defendants in a criminal case; there was no defendant in this case. In the end, the Ramseys decided against monitoring the Cellmark tests because they had been barred from the earlier CBI tests.

About that time the *Denver Post* reported that, contrary to earlier rumors, no semen had been found on JonBenet's body. That seemed to be a damaging blow to the investigation, since semen would have provided a direct DNA link to a likely assailant.

Court documents showed that the police had examined JonBenet's body under a black fluorescent light, which makes bodily fluids and certain other trace evidence more visible. They thought they had found semen on both of her thighs and for some time hoped the analysis of that sample would provide the proverbial "smoking gun." But as with so many events in this case, hope turned to disappointment.

Moses Schanfield told the *Rocky Mountain News* that he understood the sample about to undergo DNA testing to be a combination of fluids from two people, and that the major component was blood. He was still waiting to hear what the minor component was, but he offered this confirmation: "It's my understanding that there is no semen."

Patsy Ramsey found herself under a different kind of scrutiny when the *News* disclosed that police had investigated reports of what was called her bizarre conduct when she served as a juror in 1996. The six-member jury in Boulder Municipal Court had acquitted a man charged with third-degree assault for punching another man in the mouth during a pickup basketball game. The victim needed extensive dental work, according to testimony. But when the prosecutor and defense attorney met with the jurors after the acquittal, a source told the *News*, Patsy fired a broadside at the defense case. She complained in severe tones that she had not heard testimony from a dentist or any evidence about damages. The lawyers found her criticism odd and bizarre because it had not been the defense attorney's duty to present such evidence. The cops on the Ramsey case didn't consider the incident a major addition to the case, but found it useful because of its "behavioral significance."

Questions about Patsy's jury duty were among the last that spokesman Patrick Korten would field for the Ramseys. He soon left their employ. The family's attorneys now would handle media calls and public statements to reduce costs and simplify logistics. Korten said the job had been designed to last a month or two, but had become "more marathon than sprint," he explained.

As Korten left, John Ramsey went back to work. On April 9, 1996, he returned to Access Graphics offices in downtown Boulder to resume his work as company president. Vice President Laurie Wagner called the occasion "upbeat," saying the employees were delighted to have him back.

After months of negotiations, the Ramsey interviews with authorities finally were scheduled for April 23 at a neutral lawyer's office in Boulder. John and Patsy had agreed to meet separately for no-holds-barred sessions with D.A. Alex Hunter, Sheriff George Epp, his detective Steven Ainsworth, Special Investigator Lou Smit—anyone except the detectives leading the Boulder Police Department's efforts.

But at four o'clock the day before the agreed date, Chief Tom Koby cancelled the sessions on the advice of the FBI's Child Abduction and Serial Killer Unit. The bureau's experts had found the Ramseys' conditions unacceptable and damaging to the case, and urged the police to call off the meetings. Koby said the Ramseys' refusals to meet with the police continued to hinder the investigation of their daughter's death.

The response from the Ramsey team was immediate. In a letter to Hunter that crackled with animosity toward the police, Haddon and Patrick Burke, Patsy's lawyer, blasted the day's developments as "incomprehensible." The police were leading "a cowardly smear campaign against John and Patsy, fueled by leaks and smears attributable only to 'sources.' We will no longer endure these tactics in silence. It is beyond comprehension that law enforcement authorities prefer to leak information rather than interrogate the persons who they characterize as 'suspects' in this investigation. It is apparent that the leadership in the Boulder Police Department lacks the objectivity and judgment necessary to find the killer of JonBenet Ramsey."

The lawyers alleged that authorities had misled the Ramseys at a meeting on April 11 to discuss the interviews. Assistant D.A. Peter Hofstrom and Detective Tom Wickman had told the Ramseys they had been treated unfairly in the past, the investigation was on a new track, and their cooperation was needed to solve the case. In that atmosphere the separate two-hour interviews had been set for nine-thirty and one-thirty April 23.

Then the letter leveled a charge that many observers would find shocking. The lawyers said the police had attempted to hold JonBenet's body as ransom, as leverage to squeeze her parents into a hostile interview with detectives. "We had to threaten legal action to obtain her release for burial," the letter said.

The police rejected that version of what had

happened. They had, in fact, been reluctant to release the body, but only because they were unsure all of the forensic work had been completed. Within twenty-four hours of the family's formal request, the police had turned over the body.

When the dust cleared, the reasons the police cancelled the interviews were fairly obvious, even when wrapped in bureaucratic terms by the FBI: "The conditions were inconsistent with sound investigative practices and would not likely lead to a productive investigative review." What that really meant was that the two-hour lag between the interviews with John and Patsy would give them time to powwow with their lawyers and experts, discuss what was asked and what was answered at the first session, and be sure the second session jibed with the first.

The war of words escalated from there. Patsy even called KCNC Channel 4 in Denver to blast the cops and insist she and John had nothing to hide. "You'd think, if they believe we are guilty, they'd want to talk to us," she said. "I'm just sadly disappointed by what's happened. I pray we can still work this out, that the killer of JonBenet will be found. . . . I will sit with investigators around the clock if that's what they want." She said she and John still cried themselves to sleep every night.

Both sides exchanged news releases the next day as well. Hunter and Koby referred to "the unfortunate miscommunication," and hoped the interviews could still be arranged. The authorities' conditions were clear: separate, tape-recorded sessions, with Patsy's first; no time limits; conducted by Boulder detectives chosen with Hunter; at a neutral location.

The Ramsey lawyers responded, calling the police

version of events and conditions inaccurate, but not responding to the new conditions.

Amid the hostilities Coroner John Meyer weighed in with his version of the flap over releasing the body. Yes, he said, the police had asked him about holding it until they had interviewed the Ramseys. But no, there was no pressure from the police, no reason to hold it, and no attempt to do so.

Then one of the most surprising developments yet broke. Alex Hunter revealed that he had agreed to a request from Ramsey attorneys to get copies of initial police reports of the first day in exchange for the interviews that later were cancelled. That had been an "absolute condition," Hunter said, and the reports contained meager information that the prosecutors and detectives thought worth the exchange for the interviews.

Columnist Chuck Green put that in his special perspective. "The Ramseys for the reports, but the police didn't get the interviews. Such a deal."

Gregg McCrary also weighed in with his amazement at the flea-market bargain that could help a suspect avoid making any contradictory, incriminating statements to police. "It's crazy. It's bizarre," he told Green. "Plain common sense tells you that's not the proper way to conduct an investigation. . . . You just don't give suspects that kind of information. It makes whatever interview you get invalid."

In the midst of a hurricane powered by public blasts of anger, John and Patsy Ramsey met with the police and prosecutors for lengthy interviews.

On April 30, under conditions required by the authorities, the two were slipped into the County Justice

Center's underground garage about 8:00 A.M. and escorted to the district attorney's offices on the first floor. Patsy went in first for a six-and-a-half-hour interview with two police detectives and Chief Deputy D.A. Peter Hofstrom on one side, and her attorney, Patrick Burke, and their private eye on the other. John then submitted to more than two hours of questioning that ended about five-thirty.

Hal Haddon pronounced them "formally interrogated," adding that they "fully complied with the agreement and answered all questions posed to them."

After 126 days the Ramseys finally had met with the police.

But it wouldn't take anywhere near that much time to get them to talk again.

CHAPTER 25

"I did not kill my daughter, JonBenet," John Ramsey said quietly and firmly to his specially invited guests.

"Let me assure you that I did not kill JonBenet," Patsy said softly.

With their formal police interviews completed just the day before, the Ramseys held their first news conference on May 1. It was hardly a public event. It smacked more of *Mission Impossible*—vague messages to reporters to be in Boulder by 10:00 A.M., calls to their pagers and cell phones to give them the secret hotel location and the password "subtract," and finally small white identification badges for admission to a secure room at the Boulder Marriott.

The Ramseys met with seven hand-picked reporters from local newspapers, TV, and radio stations. As the Ramsey attorneys stood in the back of the room, the reporters were given conditions: no questions about the facts of JonBenet's killing; no questions about the police interviews the day before; no photos of the Ramseys arriving or departing the hotel, or of the attorneys; no discussions with the staff or the attorneys.

John kicked off the session by explaining that they had felt they needed to wait until they met with police before publicly addressing other concerns and offering other comments. One question that John recognized as causing "some bias of opinion" against them was their decision to hire lawyers so quickly. That was the result of advice from a close friend who was also a lawyer, advice that came while friends and family were consoling the Ramseys the day after JonBenet's body was discovered. Without naming Mike Bynum as the catalyst, John said the friend had asked permission to arrange counsel for them. "Fine. Do it," John had responded. Only later did the Ramseys learn that they would automatically be pushed into the suspect pool because of the experience of law enforcement with child-murder cases—"a tragic statement for our country," John thought. Amid feelings of helplessness, he then brought in his team of experts to "do what I can do to help solve this case. Had it been in my power, I would have called out the national guard, frankly."

Then he drove head-on to the question haunting everyone.

"To those of you who may want to ask, let me address very directly: I did not kill my daughter Jon-Benet. There also have been innuendos that she has been or was sexually molested. I can tell you those were the most hurtful innuendos to us as a family. They are totally false."

And then, in one of those awful moments that criminologists and psychologists and armchair experts everywhere would leap upon, the little girl's grieving father stumbled over the name that had been created especially to honor him.

"JonBuh ... JonBenet and I had a very close relationship. I will miss her dearly for the rest of my life."

He passed the torch to his wife, and she picked up where he had left off.

"I'm appalled that anyone would think that John or I would be involved in such a hideous, heinous crime. But let me assure you that I did not kill JonBenet. I did not have anything to do with it. I loved that child with the whole of my heart and soul."

She began to cry, and John reached over and took her hand.

Patsy turned quickly to the spiritual source of her strength. "We feel like God has a master plan for our lives, and in the fullness of time, our family will be united again and we will see JonBenet."

The Ramseys offered their gratitude to the hundreds of people who had expressed their concern and compassion in cards and letters from across the United States, Canada, and Europe. And then Patsy spoke directly to the assembled reporters.

She held up a copy of a quarter-page advertisement they had run the Sunday before in the *Boulder Daily Camera* renewing their reward of $100,000 for information solving their daughter's murder. With the ad's sweet kindergarten photograph of a smiling JonBenet—sans makeup or pageant regalia—held close to her face, Patsy said, "We need your help, from this moment on. . . .

"We feel like there are at least two people on the face of this earth that know who did this, and that is the killer and someone that that person may have confided in. And we need that one phone call. We need that one phone call to this number that will help the authorities come to a conclusion to this case. Please, please, if you know anything, I beg you to call us. Call us."

When they opened the session to questions, they came fast and furious. What about the criticism from other parents, including Marc Klaas, that no lawyer's advice could have kept them from talking to the police if their child had been murdered? John insisted that he and Patsy *had* talked to the police—for eight hours on December 26 and two more on the 27th. They subsequently gave the police every piece of information they requested; the suggestion that they had not spoken with the police was "totally false." They were insulted to be considered suspects in JonBenet's death, and they thought a formal interrogation was a waste of their time and the detectives' time. Ultimately, the day before, they had submitted to the interrogation.

What did the Ramseys want to say to their daughter's killer?

John said firmly, "We'll find you. We will find you. I have that as a sole mission for the rest of my life."

Shaking her finger toward the camera, Patsy added, "You may be eluding the authorities for a time, but God knows who you are and we will find you."

John also said, "An arrest is absolutely necessary in our lives for closure."

What about being considered suspects? John said they had been shocked at first and then outraged. But they soon learned that statistics about child-murder cases assured that they would be investigated as suspects, and they accepted it. They still were concerned that "any time spent looking at us is time that's wasted." That was why they had formed their own investigative team.

Patsy said they had been taking the grief and suspicion cast toward them "hour by hour, day by day, week by week. There's no rule book as to how to handle something like this.... It's just overwhelming.

We're grieving. It's hurtful. I can't tell you how bad it's been."

John recognized the nation's curiosity about them, and addressed what might be stoking it. "I think we also as a country, and perhaps some of you as a reporting entity, are cynics, and that's kind of sad. We are not perfect people. But we are not bad people. We are a normal family. We love our children dearly."

Did the Ramseys want the death penalty for Jon-Benet's killer? John said solemnly, "I would absolutely want the most severe penalty to be brought." Tears welled in Patsy's eyes, and she nodded silently.

Was John worried that the delay in the interviews with police had hampered the investigation? No, because he and Patsy had not provided any new information the day before that the police had not already known.

What about those pageant photographs that had helped feed the public's curiosity? Did the Ramseys wish now that JonBenet had never competed in those events?

Patsy leapt to the defense. "Those were beautiful pictures. I'm so happy that we have those pictures. They're all we have now."

John added, "That was just one very small part of JonBenet's life."

Patsy agreed: "A few Sunday afternoons."

Was there any improper activity going on in the Ramsey home?

"Absolutely not, absolutely not," Patsy insisted.

How was Burke doing? Very well, Patsy said. John added that his older son, John Andrew, had returned to classes at the University of Colorado.

A message for the viewers about the Ramseys and this sad event?

John said, "We think we are a normal American family that loves and values their children, much like most of the families in this country. And one thing we have learned—we learned it, frankly, with the death of our oldest daughter—we learned that life is precious." If JonBenet's death had convinced one parent to spend more time with their children, "then JonBenet's life had some meaning."

How did they feel about some of the "mind games" played by the police, such as the attempt to hold Jon-Benet's body until the Ramseys were interrogated?

Patsy showed a flash of anger: "I can tell you we were outraged by that. We didn't know about that until we returned from Atlanta. Atlanta was our home; we lived there for twenty-one years. We were absolutely nauseated by all of that, and appalled. That's when the worm turned."

John explained that they had felt they were coming back to Boulder to assist in the investigation, but that feeling was damaged by police tactics. Now, they hoped, the relationship between them and the police was moving to a new level, and the Ramseys were more assured that the police would be looking outside the family for a solution to the crime.

Did they believe the killer would be caught?

"I do. Yes, I do," John said. "We have been told by some of the experts that we have consulted with on a national level—as well as assured by the people that the Boulder D.A.'s office has brought in—this is a solvable crime. It will be solved."

The news conference ended on a strikingly emotional and unexpected moment when Patsy was asked what she would say to JonBenet right then. In a quiet voice Patsy offered a stunning response:

"I talk to JonBenet, and I tell her that I love her, and that I'll be seeing her real soon. It won't be long."

None of the reporters pursued that solemn thought from the tortured woman.

The analysis and speculation began as soon as the news conference ended.

Did the timing of this surprise event mean arrests were imminent? Were the Ramseys looking for sympathy, or trying to influence potential jurors that might be called to a trial someday? Or were they just trying to counteract the negative implications of their five months of silence? Were they trying their own case in the court of public opinion?

What did Patsy mean when she said she told Jon-Benet that they would be together soon?

One of the most stinging rebukes came from the host of one of Denver's most popular morning radio talk shows, Peter Boyles of KHOW-AM. "The Ramsey infommercial," he dubbed the event sarcastically. His acerbic comments about the case had won him national celebrity, and he popped up often on various TV news and talk shows, offering his critical opinions about the way the Ramseys, their lawyers, the police, and the prosecutors were conducting themselves. He would be heard from again later, and words would not fail him then, either.

CHAPTER 26

The Ramseys' news conference was just the beginning of a campaign to take their case public. Their next maneuver was a grabber.

In the May 11 edition of the *Boulder Daily Camera*, the Ramseys ran an advertisement asking for information about a dangerous mystery man—a young man the ad said had been approaching children on the streets of Boulder in late 1996.

Could this be the intruder who stole into the Ramsey home and brought such tragedy to their lives? That certainly was the impression created by the advertisement.

Rachelle Zimmer, now the family's spokeswoman, would say only, "We have a reason for including the new material in the ad."

Mayor Leslie Durgin was not pleased by the Ramsey endeavor suggesting that a man was stalking the children on the streets of her town. She told the *Rocky Mountain News*, "They obviously have a public-relations strategy they are following. If they think they know something, I wish they'd tell it to our police department." She later called it "nothing more than a public-relations ploy to divert attention away from them."

As the advertisement hit the streets that Sunday, the

most common reaction seemed to be a knowing chuckle, as if to conclude that the Ramseys had stooped to a fairly transparent, perhaps desperate effort to redirect suspicion. The public's response seemed to be that something more substantive would be needed.

But the media attention over the ad's suggestion of a mystery man forced the hand of someone else in the case. On Monday, May 12, Alex Hunter disclosed that an unnamed assistant in his office had authorized the Ramseys' inclusion of the controversial information in the ad. Hunter felt compelled to explain that it had not been solely the actions of the Ramseys, but also his office's commitment to follow all reasonable leads. He would not discuss how seriously his office or the police were pursing that lead.

The police, however, did. Spokeswoman Leslie Aaholm said she had no information that the detectives were working on the angle suggested by the ad. Sources told reporters that the cops appeared to be focusing on the Ramseys, while the prosecutors were pursuing the mystery man and other leads outside the family.

Chief Koby wouldn't discuss the ad. But when asked if residents should fear a predator stalking their children, he delivered one of his characteristically wordy responses: "No."

Hunter's office generated even more debate, however, in a motion filed May 22 by Deputy D.A. Bill Nagel as he tried to keep search warrants under court seal. Referring to the Ramseys, Nagel wrote, "Nothing has been discovered which would unequivocally eliminate them from suspicion, and they remain a focus of the investigation." Then he added, "However, there remains the real possibility that the murder was committed by an intruder, and that possibility continues to be a serious and ongoing focus of the investigation as well."

He said no smoking gun had been found among hundreds of pieces of evidence, hundreds of interviews, 700 photographs, 10,000 pages of investigative material, and 850 tips from the public.

Nagel's comment lending authority to the intruder theory sparked a lot of conversation, including speculation about growing differences between the directions being pursued by the prosecutors and the police.

The Ramseys were not ready to abandon their advertising and publicity campaign just because of a lackluster response to their first effort. Throughout the summer they would make several more dramatic attempts to spur public interest in looking for the intruder they said had killed their daughter.

Before that effort could continue, the Ramseys and the Boulder Police Department both had unrelated matters to resolve.

May was a terrible month for the police and the image of their laid-back, politically correct enclave. When some rowdy, drunken students at the University of Colorado lighted a bonfire and threw bottles at the responding police, the town's tie-dyed seams came apart. Chief Tom Koby led his troops back in, dressed in full riot gear, ostensibly to prevent any more violence. Instead, the rioting escalated and lasted for three tumultuous days as students ran amok and smashed windows. Later, Koby threw fuel on the fire by suggesting that his officers would have been justified in shooting some of the student offenders.

Koby also announced that fewer hands were needed on the Ramsey case and he was reassigning detectives Linda Arndt and Melissa Hickman to regular duty. Soon after that Arndt was reported to be on medical leave due to exhaustion—which she would later deny in a lawsuit she would file against the city. After her reassignment, former Denver prosecutor Craig Silverman told the *Rocky Mountain News* that Arndt should be noted for her compassion in the case.

With all of that coming on the heels of increasing tension in the department, the officers' union called for a no-confidence vote on the chief, and it carried 78 to 31. Koby was humiliated, and other city officials professed to be surprised and stunned. Everyone, including police union officials, denied that the vote had anything to do with the Ramsey case. Mayor Durgin insisted it had to do with Koby's efforts to change the philosophy of the department to community policing. Leslie Aaholm said the negotiation of police contracts also played a role, and there was frustration over the handling of the student riots. Regardless of the true factors, many saw Koby as seriously wounded in his role as department leader. Durgin and others said, however, that he retained wide and deserved community support. Durgin would later seem to lose some of her patience with the chief, however. Citing a growing anger and frustration among her town's residents at the police and the Ramseys, she would demand that Koby brief the city council on the progress of the investigation.

Before long there were more tremors in the People's Republic of Boulder. On June 3, the detective leading the investigation, Commander John Eller, confirmed that he was seeking a chief's job elsewhere after eighteen years in Boulder. A few hours later, City Manager Tim Honey—the man who had hired and vocally supported Koby—resigned amid continuing disputes with the City Council over several issues.

Eller returned to the spotlight four days later when Sergeant Larry Mason announced that he intended to sue Eller for accusing him of leaking details of the Ramsey investigation to the media. Eller had yanked Mason from the case eleven days into the investigation and placed him on administrative leave. Some sources claimed that Mason had found himself at loggerheads with others leading the investigation because he immediately had favored a more aggressive approach to the Ramseys. Later, the Internal Affairs unit cleared Mason of Eller's allegations, and he returned to patrol duty. But he said the stress had caused illnesses for him and his wife, and Eller should pay the damages. Mason later would accept $10,000 from the city in return for not suing.

The interim president of the chamber of commerce reacted to the series of developments in consummate Boulder form: "It's hard not to say, 'Wow, what kind of alignment of the planets is going on here?' "

The only good news for the cops came from Dr. Henry Lee, the expert criminalist serving on Hunter's task force. At a conference with Hunter and three detectives at the Denver airport to discuss the investigation, Lee was asked if the police had fumbled the case. "I don't . . . No, no, I don't think so," he said. The *Rocky Mountain News* reported that as "tempered support" from Lee for the police. He later would say that the evidence pointed in many directions, and it was too early to tell if it aimed toward one, two, or five people. To make an arrest, he concluded, the police would "need some luck."

Others observed that good vibes had not been abundant around this case.

The rift between the police and prosecutors drew more attention June 7 when the *News* reported that the detectives had refused to brief the D.A.'s office on the results of DNA tests—reported to be inconclusive and of little value. Even Dr. Lee and DNA expert Barry Scheck—the big guns touted when Alex Hunter announced his task force—had not been told of the test results that the police had got back almost a month earlier. One source said the police and prosecutors might be in the same canoe, but they seemed to be rowing in different directions.

There was more concern about that the next week when police found evidence that their Ramsey-file computer in the investigative team's "war room" had been compromised. Nothing was deleted or destroyed, but there was evidence someone had used it about one o'clock on a Sunday morning. The Colorado Bureau of Investigation was brought in, and eventually decided that the computer had played with itself; an internal battery had short-circuited.

Despite that conclusion, *Vanity Fair* would later quote a source as saying that three experts had told police the computer had definitely been "hacked"— broken into. The magazine offered no suggestion of the perpetrator's identity.

But by the time CBI had completed its review, authorities were investigating a report of another computer caper. A social worker for Boulder County had interviewed ten-year-old Burke Ramsey in January, and the social services department now feared that

someone had tampered with the computer that held
that file in late June. Later, Commander Eller would
say it appeared that someone curious about the contents of the file had tried to get into it, but there was no
way to tell if they were successful and no criminal
charges would be filed.

In July, the Ramseys completed an important piece
of personal business. While they spent the summer in
Charlevoix and John commuted between Colorado
and Michigan, they bought a $700,000 brick colonial
house in the upscale Atlanta suburb of Vinings—quite
near JonBenet's grave. The Ramseys, it seemed, would
leave Boulder behind forever. They hired $30-an-hour
guards to provide round-the-clock security for their
new home. Their mansion at 755 15th Street remained
on the market for a reported $1 million plus—later re-
ports would estimate the market value at about
$800,000—but it had not drawn a single inquiry. Ran-
dall Bell—a real estate agent in Los Angeles known as
Dr. Disaster for his ability to sell tainted properties like
Nicole Brown Simpson's condo and the estate where
Charles Manson's followers murdered Sharon Tate—
suggested a bulldozer was the best strategy for the
Ramsey house. He said selling it would be harder than
finding a buyer for the mansion in Rancho Santa Fe,
California, where thirty-nine members of the Heaven's
Gate cult committed suicide in March. Bell called the
thought of selling a house where a child was murdered
nauseating—like trying to sell Jeffrey Dahmer's apartment in Milwaukee.

In late June and early July, the police got permission
from the Ramseys for detectives to return to the house
to take measurements to be used in production of an

architectural model—ostensibly for use at a trial some day. They also wanted to take additional photos from different angles and different lighting conditions, and to conduct a considerably more invasive search. The first effort in December and January had yielded a wide variety of items, from golf clubs to letters to Santa. But this new, four-day venture employed a plumber and a locksmith, and a lot of detectives crawling all over the place. They checked outside bushes and windows. They carried back inside a door that they had carried out before and still bore an evidence tag. There were even plans for some "role-playing" efforts in the house.

Although the police would not explain the presence of the plumber, Dr. Cyril Wecht knew what few members of the public understood. Evidence that could be important in a case such as this—hair, blood, bodily fluids, fibers—often remained in the drain pipes and traps of a house, even if someone tried to wash or flush it away. That was one of the points that had troubled Wecht about the O. J. Simpson case. If O.J. had butchered his wife and her friend by himself, he would have been covered in their blood. If he had cleaned up at home, much more than the small traces recovered there would have been found in shower or sink drains, perhaps even in the toilet. The lack of significant amounts of blood there led Wecht to speculate that another killer had been involved.

There was one more item to be disclosed as the police ended their search at 755 15th Street on July 3. The detectives had long ago brought in an expert from the nearby Arvada Police Department to check the Ramsey house and computers for child pornography; none was found. The detective even used his knowledge to

search pornography databases on the Internet for any
links to the Ramsey case.

The family's attorneys were outraged, calling the release of that information another slanderous effort to
smear the Ramseys that should cause Boulder's citizens to doubt their leaders.

With apologies to Shakespeare, the winter of Boulder's discontent seemed to have become its spring and
summer of silliness.

Although no one had been arrested for killing Jon-
Benet, charges and criminal prosecutions continued to
pile up on the edges of the case. On May 21, a man
who worked for a company that transported bodies
for coroners and funeral homes was arrested for the
theft of a morbid souvenir in the Ramsey case. James
Michael Thompson, thirty-three, of Denver, admitted
taking two pages from the morgue book at Boulder
Community Hospital—pages that logged the arrival
of JonBenet's body on December 26. He also was
charged with five counts of abuse of corpses for allegedly posing them in macabre positions, with noise-
makers in their mouths and holding signs reading
HAPPY HALLOWEEN or the witty YEE HAW. He called it
"shock art." He told the *News* that taking the morgue
pages on April 30 had been a spontaneous decision he
regretted, and one made while he was drunk.

He was held in jail overnight and gave samples of
his blood, hair, saliva, and handwriting—just in case
ripping out the pages was something more than a sick,
spontaneous lark.

But apparently Mr. Thompson did not learn a lesson
from that escapade. He later was accused of trying to
burn down the Ramsey house on June 18 by shoving

burning papers through the mail slot in the front door; damage to the carpet and door was minimal. Thompson was charged with attempted third-degree arson.

There was another unusual tidbit. *New York Post* columnist Cindy Adams reported that an artist in Boulder had asked the Ramseys to commission her production of a sixteen-page book of paper-doll cutouts of JonBenet and thirty reproductions of the outfits she wore at beauty pageants. The artist proposed the title of "Tribute to JonBonet," with the tragically famous child's name misspelled. A family attorney rejected commercial use of JonBenet's image; "It's too painful for the family," he said.

Just after that Ramsey attorney Hal Haddon confirmed that his investigators had told prosecutors of a bizarre theory linking the $118,000 ransom figure to a Bible verse in Psalm 118. The psalm is on the list of forty healing Bible verses in the book Patsy had clung to desperately during her illness, *Healed of Cancer*. In the King James version, verse 27 of Psalm 118 includes the phrase, "bind the sacrifice with cords."

Commander Eller was asked if the tip on Psalm 118 had advanced the investigation. "The question is insane," he told the *Post*.

To round out the activity in July—a missile from the East to the West. Darnay Hoffman, a lawyer in New York City who had become frustrated by the lack of progress in Boulder, announced his intentions to sue D.A. Alex Hunter. Hoffman, who described himself as a victims-rights advocate, cited a little-known Colorado law that allowed a judge to order a prosecutor to file charges if he had refused to do so. Hoffman would eventually file his suit in November, seeking appointment of a special prosecutor and attaching affidavits from two handwriting experts who linked Patsy Ramsey's penmanship to the ransom note. Hoffman called the note "almost nuclear" in its impact on the case, and said Hunter had shirked his duty by refusing to file criminal charges against Patsy. Hunter responded that he hadn't refused to file; the police hadn't even brought him a case yet. A judge in Boulder eventually would throw out Hoffman's suit in January 1998.

With the purchase of a new home completed by late July 1997, the Ramseys returned to the search for their daughter's killer. John released a prepared statement expressing his growing frustration because the police still were limiting their investigation to him and members of the family. His team had developed "solid leads" and were continuing its investigation. To assist that effort, Ramsey said, he would begin a more aggressive bid to inform the public and seek its help in solving the mystery of who killed JonBenet.

The opening gambit was the release of details from the profile drawn up by John Douglas. The killer, he believed, was someone who might have been in the Ramsey house before that night. The expert assumed the killer was a man, and the profile said he might have been suffering from stress in the weeks before the crime, which could have been triggered by an event such as a crisis on the job or in a personal relationship. He might have committed the crime to vent anger, perhaps at a female close to him, or even at John Ramsey. After the killing he might have read and watched the news reports intently, might have increased his consumption of alcohol or drugs, and might have turned to religion. He might be rigid, nervous, or preoccupied. He might have tried to appear very cooperative with the authorities if he was interviewed, and he might have quickly constructed an alibi for that night, repeating it several times to those around him as if to rehearse them on it.

Gregg McCrary had drafted profiles for the FBI many times—and had refused to provide one to the Ramseys. But what he read now from the Ramsey team could only be described as "silly and juvenile." It contained some vague elements of truth, but it betrayed a lack of real experience or sophistication, and came across as a pedestrian effort. Most of the points would apply to any murder.

Most grievous to McCrary was the fact that this rudimentary effort ignored most useful, telling evidence in the JonBenet case—the obvious staging of the crime scene and the writing of the bogus ransom note.

The day after releasing the profile, the Ramseys announced they would use that information in another newspaper advertisement—cast as an open letter from John and Patsy—as well as bright orange fliers to be distributed in the Ramseys' neighborhood in Boulder. "You may know him," the flier read. "You may be his alibi. He may have discussed JonBenet's murder with you in casual conversation and made a point of repeating where he was the night of the crime."

Even the D.A. could not let those efforts pass without comment. He echoed the mayor by saying the Ramseys obviously were trying to shift the focus away from themselves and to alter public opinion.

But defense attorney Hal Haddon insisted the ads—at $3,000 each—were proving productive and had drawn several useful tips.

The same procedures were used again the next week, this time focusing on individual letters from the ransom note. The ad reproduced examples of the capital letters *M*, *D*, and *W*, as well as some distinctive lower-case letters such as *k*, *w*, *u*, *r*, and *f*—all copied from the note. Anyone who recognized that writing style was asked to call the Ramsey tip line. Haddon said the team was seeking permission from the authorities to release the entire note to help the public analyze the writing.

Columnist Chuck Green ripped the whole idea, reducing it to game-show significance with the quip, "Give us an *M*, Vanna."

Peter Boyles of KHOW-AM carried his outrage to an unprecedented level, answering the Ramseys' full-page open letters in the newspaper with one of his own, addressed to John and Patsy. On Sunday, August 3, Boyles paid for a page in the *Boulder Daily Camera* to tell the Ramseys, "I am angered by your behavior in hiring investigators, experts and lawyers in what appears to be an effort to protect your interests rather than to find the killer." He called their criminal profile laughable, a description of the average American. And then he offered a ten-item list of the Ramseys' behavior that he said had elicited "suspicion and mistrust."

His letter slammed the Ramseys for hiring a public-relations firm, hiring separate teams of lawyers, refusing lie-detector tests, delaying police interviews with bizarre conditions, offering inconsistent theories on who killed JonBenet, ignoring foreign terrorists as suspects without explanation, charging on CNN that Boulder was unsafe, alleging now that a family acquaintance suffering from financial or marital stress was the killer, suggesting in fliers that the killer still was roaming Boulder streets, and picking selected reporters for interviews while refusing to talk to objective journalists such as Ted Koppel.

Boyles ended his letter with a howitzer: "Fred Goldman's behavior exemplifies the true crime-victim parent of a child who has been murdered. You, on the other hand, have led Colorado and the nation on a seven-month, low-speed, white Bronco chase."

The Ramseys were undeterred. Another ad on August 24 compared phrases from the ransom note to dialogue from recent movies, and concluded that the killer was obsessed with "techno-crime" films like *Dirty Harry, Ransom*, and *Speed*. In *Speed*, the kidnapper cautions, "Do not attempt to grow a brain." The note at the Ramsey house said, "Don't try to grow a brain, John." In *Dirty Harry*, the kidnapper warns, "If you talk to anyone—I don't care if it's a Pekinese pissing against a lamppost—the girl dies." The ransom note told John Ramsey, "If we catch you talking to a stray dog, she dies."

Alex Hunter still was unimpressed. "This will not advance the case at this time," he said flatly.

Sources would tell the *News* later that, in the wake of the ads, the Ramseys had hired private investigators to conduct surveillance on "a handful" of potential suspects. But by the time the string of ads ended, Hal Haddon was moved to offer the *Denver Post* a startling reassessment: "As far as public reaction to the ads, it's been a disaster. All the feedback from the public has been pretty negative. Everything we've said has been turned against us." And he recognized futility in trying to restore the Ramseys' public image. "Their reputation has been totally mutilated."

There was one development over the hot summer that seemed in the Ramseys' favor. A source close to the family told the *Rocky Mountain News* in August that a single pubic hair from JonBenet's bedding had not been matched to anyone in the family, although the final efforts to trace it were underway. The importance of that was obvious: any incriminating evidence—especially of that nature—that came from someone other than the Ramseys lent credibility to the intruder theory.

There also was a development on the police department's side of the equation: they got their own attorneys. The police, saying they were hoping fresh eyes would help fine-tune the case, obtained the assistance of three private-practice lawyers for what everyone now called the police "dream team." Commander John Eller said the lawyers would help the police prepare their case for presentation to D.A. Hunter. Hunter said the idea was unusual, but all right with him. "Almost everything about this case is unusual," he said with a flair for understatement.

The advisers were Robert Miller, a former U.S. attorney and Weld County district attorney; Daniel Hoffman, former law school dean from the University of Denver; and Richard Baer, a former homicide detective and prosecutor in New York before moving to Denver.

But even this development did not come without problems. The *Denver Post* disclosed that Miller had teamed with Hal Haddon in a suit that won $45 million in a verdict in July against a drug company. Eller said the police were aware of their adviser's relationship with the leader of the Ramsey team, and it was not a problem.

One informed observer of the legal machinations in

the Ramsey case, former Denver prosecutor Craig Silverman, told the *News* that the cops' decision to hire their own lawyers made it clear that Hunter's office had rejected the police theory about who killed JonBenet.

As July ended, John Douglas resurfaced on *The Today Show* to explain that what the Ramseys had published was not a full psychological profile. He had provided them only with a general outline suggesting that the police search for a killer who would have been subject to precipitating factors and events in his life, and who had some knowledge of the Ramseys and their home.

Douglas urged authorities to release the complete text of the ransom note, reminding everyone that Ted Kaczynski had been arrested after newspapers published his long-winded manifesto.

But Douglas admitted he was pessimistic about a solution to the JonBenet Ramsey mystery. Her death may fall into the category of 35 percent of all homicides in America, he said—unsolved.

Douglas, it seemed, could provide no answer for the question—who killed JonBenet?

CHAPTER 27

Dr. Cyril Wecht stared sadly at the document before him, a new portion of the autopsy report just opened to the public on July 14. Boulder County coroner John Meyer and the district attorney's office had fought the release all the way to the Colorado supreme court, but the justices refused to overturn a district judge's ruling that ordered more information released to the public because the investigation could no longer be called in its "early stages." Under the court order, the seal on the final portions would be lifted later. Wecht had never heard of an autopsy report released piecemeal as this one was—another first for this case.

But now Wecht could evaluate this new evidence, and he found more of the horror that was JonBenet Ramsey's death. Not only had she suffered a fractured skull, she had been subjected to a blow so severe that it split the bone on the right side of her head from front to back. That kind of crushing impact would have dropped a three hundred-pound NFL defensive tackle in his tracks. Wecht shuddered to imagine the effect it would have had on a four-foot, forty-five-pound, six-year-old girl.

On the newly disclosed page seven of Coroner Meyer's autopsy report, Wecht had begun a journey that would support and refine his analysis of how Jon-Benet came to her fate, and how she suffered along the way. And it would startle him all the more.

Under the title of "Skull and Brain," Meyer described what he had found when he examined the cranium that had been so badly fractured. The break in the bone—a shocking eight and a half inches long—began behind the right ear, then moved up and forward, toward the top of the skull and all the way to the front of the skull. It essentially covered the whole right side of the child's head. The fracture was "comminuted," Meyer noted, meaning portions of the bone were pulverized and displaced along the broken line.

Wecht's instincts as a medical detective were alerted as he read that the fracture also was marked by a different kind of damage behind the right ear. Meyer described a displaced piece of broken bone as a roughly rectangular shape, measuring three-quarters of an inch by a half inch. To Wecht, that established what was called a "pattern injury," meaning inferences could be drawn about the shape of the instrument—the weapon—that had delivered the blow. A fracture that was essentially a line with a rectangular fragment on one end suggested something with a shaft and a larger head—a heavy flashlight or a golf club, for example, both already suggested as the "blunt instrument" in this case.

Wecht noticed, too, that the blow had not broken the skin of the scalp; there was a bruise but no laceration, no cut. That suggested a rounded object with a smooth edge, or one that was flat and broad with no edge or sharpness—such as those already listed.

Wecht could understand now why this part of the report had been withheld before; it would be useful in determining if a particular object could have been the weapon that dealt the blow to JonBenet's head.

Meyer's examination moved to the scalp—the skin covering the skull—where he found a hemorrhage that covered an area seven by four inches; that was where the blood had collected in the unbroken skin from the damage inflicted by the blow. The hemorrhage was fresh and showed no "organization," which meant JonBenet had died before the blood cells could form a network to fight the injury. That was to be expected, a normal event under the circumstances, Wecht knew.

But he was shocked as he read on and learned what Dr. Meyer had discovered under the broken bone, inside the shattered skull. As the first court-edited version of the report had revealed vaguely in February, there was the predictable "subdural hemorrhage"— the collection of blood under the dura membrane between the skull and the brain. But the additional information included a detail that Wecht would not have predicted. The hemorrhage consisted of only seven or eight centimeters of blood—less than two teaspoons (a brimming teaspoon holds four or five c.c.'s of blood). This development, Wecht realized, was a major departure from what he had expected and had to be given serious consideration by anyone trying to reconstruct what had happened.

A blow to the head of this magnitude should have caused significantly more bleeding inside the skull. In Wecht's experience, the lack of a more substantial hemorrhage under the dura membrane could only mean one thing: there had been little or no pressure— no heartbeat—to pump blood into the injured area after the blow was delivered. JonBenet Ramsey had been in shock and near death—literally dying—when her skull was fractured. She was most likely already in what pathologists called the "agonal" stage of death—the moments just before clinical death arrives. Death is not a single moment; it is a process. It takes time—varying amounts of time from person to person, depending on the cause—for death to occur.

Seven or eight c.c.'s of blood was roughly what would have been present in the capillaries after the heart had stopped—"residual blood," Wecht called it. If the blow to the head had released only that amount of blood, that meant JonBenet's heart had already stopped, or was about to stop, when she was struck. She was clinically alive but at death's door. Pathologists use the term "peri-mortem"—around the time of death. It was the only possible explanation for this unexpected twist in the medical evidence.

Wecht found an implied support for his conclusions as he again checked Dr. Meyer's diagnosis of the cause of death, listed on the first page of the autopsy report. Meyer had written "asphyxia by strangulation associated with craniocerebral trauma." To Wecht, that meant the coroner in Boulder had set the garrote around the neck as the cause, with the skull fracture as a contributing factor—just as Wecht had concluded. In fact, the list of injuries cited by Meyer placed "ligature strangulation" first and "craniocerebral injuries" after that.

All of this provided a new factor to be introduced into the equation of JonBenet's death. As Wecht considered its import, he remained comfortable with his conclusion about the actual cause of death—the interruption of electronic messages to the heart and lungs from the vagus nerves in the neck as they were pinched by the garrote. In fact, this new evidence strengthened that diagnosis. Something had slowed and nearly stopped JonBenet's heart before the blow crushed her skull. The blow would have soon been fatal—even if she had received immediate and expert medical attention. But it had come as she was already dying from another cause, and the evidence told Wecht that he was correct about that previous fatal factor.

Wecht now faced a new investigative quandary. If this child had already been at death's door—certainly appearing dead to the layman lacking a stethoscope—why was such a cruel, devastating, unnecessary blow delivered? He went back to his theory about the perverted sex game gone awry. She had died unexpectedly amid her molester's sick mistreatment, instilling sudden panic in the person now holding her limp body. Even shaking her had not restored her to consciousness—although it inflicted the bruises to the sides of her brain. How could this child's death be explained now? She hadn't fallen down the steps and broken her neck. She hadn't slipped and fallen in the bathtub, knocking herself unconscious and causing her to drown. So what was the innocent explanation? What was there to incriminate someone other than the person now looking at her lifeless body?

The best evidence Wecht could find in this document and media reports led directly to the conclusion that the killer had been someone close to the family, someone with a comfortable knowledge of the large house, someone with essentially no fear of discovery by anyone else. With that as an assumption, Wecht began to look for evidence to explain what had happened in the moments between JonBenet's apparent death and the horrible blow to her head. He was left with the conclusion that this terrible predicament had brought an amazingly cold, calculated response, and the hatching of a somewhat unlikely, clumsy scenario born of desperation.

To point the authorities away from the truth—away from the identity of the person who was kneeling over JonBenet's body—a bogeyman had to be invented. An intruder, a homicidal interloper, had to be introduced. A kidnapper perhaps? Yes, a kidnapping that had gone bad—as terribly bad as the real events that night. The molester then was faced with creating a cause of death to explain the inexplicable reality. As the last moments of JonBenet's life were about to drain away, someone decided to provide a dramatic and obvious reason for her death—and a massive blow to the side of her head became the answer. What, Wecht wondered with a shudder, must that moment have been like?

The horror of that act was the only explanation that worked. What about the reverse? Why couldn't someone have inflicted the head injury—perhaps even accidentally—and then staged the scene with the garrote and the cord around JonBenet's hand to confuse the truth and misdirect those who would look for the answers later? Wecht studied on that, only to realize that it made no sense at all. If the skull fracture had caused the death of an otherwise uninjured, unmolested child, who would hope to throw off the police and medical examiners with a garrote? It would never work, and even the most inept, panicked bungler would have realized that.

Plus, there was the overwhelming evidence of sexual molestation. How could that fit into this alternative scenario? Some would suggest that JonBenet had been suffering the sexual abuse by one person when another blundered in, flew into a rage, and began flailing about with the blunt instrument, only to hit the child by mistake. One theory would argue that a wife had lost control upon finding her husband molesting their daughter, and had tried to protect the child in an effort that went terribly wrong. A variation was that the woman had actually struck JonBenet in misguided resentment of the child's usurpation of the husband's sexual attentions. Whatever the explanation for that scenario, it seemed to fail the test of the medical report that Wecht had read. JonBenet had been molested and was near death when the blow was struck. It was nearly impossible to fit her into that other scenario.

The ransom note remained a significant supplement to the medical evidence. To Wecht, it appeared there had been a decision to create a bogeyman who was not a stranger, but one with a grudge against the Ramseys—one close enough to be familiar with the details of their lives and their daughter and their home. The note seized upon dangerous facts, however, claiming the amount of John Ramsey's yearly bonus as ransom and making the apparent reference to Subic Bay, his naval assignment. But here, too, the scheme had fallen apart. Would this evil kidnapper have arrived at the house without a ransom note prepared and ready to be delivered? Would he take the time necessary to compose and print out two and a half pages of diatribe?

No, Wecht concluded, there was only one likely scenario that could fit all the criteria established by the autopsy report and the crime-scene facts as publicly available so far. Someone from inside that family had used JonBenet for a perverted sex game, caused her death, delivered the skull fracture to try to cover up the truth, left the note to misdirect the police, and then set into motion all of the events that were to follow.

* * *

Wecht turned back to the other new information in the autopsy report. Meyer had reported that the brain had swollen to a weight of 1,450 grams. That was fifteen percent larger than the 1,200 to 1,250 grams that would be normal for a child of JonBenet's age and description. Some would argue later that the swelling resulted directly from the blow to the head, and that this evidence contradicted Wecht's conclusion that JonBenet was about to die when the blow was delivered. According to the other scenario, she had to have lived longer than Wecht would allow for the brain to swell that much. Wecht disagreed with that proposition. First, the brain would have swollen as it reacted to the deprivation of oxygen from the effects of the garrote. Decreasing the oxygen flow to the brain is, after all, the direct intent of this vicarious auto-erotic asphyxiation. The brain would have reacted quickly, and swelling from hypoxia would have begun within seconds. There was no way to define just how long JonBenet had suffered the torturous effects of the strangulation, or how long her brain had battled the hypoxia. But if she had been struck on the head first, that blow would have caused her death within moments, before she could have been strangled.

Meyer concluded his examination of the brain by noting two predictable reactions. There was a thin film of subarachnoid hemorrhage—a little blood collecting under the spider-like membrane that lies below the dura membrane. Under the area of the skull damaged from the blow, Meyer also found a purplish contusion—a bruise—that was about seven inches long and an inch and three-quarters wide.

Wecht now turned to the other long section of new information—eighteen lines about the vaginal

examination that elaborated on the information that
had been released before. What Wecht would find here
would only reinforce his earlier conclusions about the
sexual abuse endured by JonBenet.

Meyer reported a small amount of dried blood located at the bottom of the labia majora—the outer lips
of the vagina. The blood was at the top of the tissue between the vagina and the rectum—called the perineum.
Likewise, there was a small amount of dried and semifluid blood on the membranous tissue between the
outer and inner lips—called the fourchette—as well as
in the entrance to the vagina, the vestibule.

Inside the vestibule Meyer found areas of reddish
hyperemia—congestion of the vagina and vaginal wall.
Congestion was the engorgement of more than the normal amount of blood in the vessels there, the result
of some pressure or injury. The congestion was "circumferential," Meyer found, meaning the object that
inflicted the injury had moved in a circular pattern—
around the vagina and vaginal wall. Wecht thought
again about the action of a finger inserted into the
vagina and manipulated—exactly a circular motion.

A small "red-purple area of abrasion"—a scratched
and bruised area—was present on the lower side of
the opening of the hymen, the membrane over the
entrance to the vagina. Meyer listed the location at
the seven o'clock position—another affirmation of
Wecht's analysis of the manipulation by someone's
right finger to the lower left side of the vagina. To
Wecht, that abrasion was a significant injury for a girl
of this age—not in severity but in location. How could
she have suffered that injury at that spot but by sexual
abuse?

Meyer's next observation was just as critical. He re-

ported that all that was left of the hymen was a rim of
tissue between the two o'clock and ten o'clock positions. That meant the hymen covering the vaginal
opening and the rest of the hymen's rim were gone—
missing in a six-year-old girl. JonBenet's hymen should
have been intact and undamaged. Certain strenuous
athletic activities could have caused some damage to
the hymen. But at her age and given the rest of the evidence, Wecht knew this finding strongly supported a
diagnosis of some extended history of sexual penetration. That, when considered with the earlier reference
by Meyer to "chronic inflammation" of the vaginal
wall, convinced Wecht his conclusions about a pattern
of repeated sexual abuse were inescapable. What other
story could be told by the fresh blood in the vagina,
the injuries inside the vagina, the missing hymen, and
the older inflammation?

But there was more evidence from the vaginal exam.
Meyer found a very faint area of violet discoloration
on the right, outer lip of the vagina. A superficial
bruise, Wecht assumed, probably inflicted during the
sexual abuse. And inside the vagina—in the vaginal
vault—Meyer found a small amount of what he described as "semifluid, thin, watery, red fluid." Wecht
read that as referring to the liquid part of blood with
some mucus mixed in—not as thick as whole blood.
The fluid was another indication of a fresh insult to
the vagina of this little girl.

Wecht finally turned his attention to new information about the rest of JonBenet's body. On the previously omitted page three, the report described the
"deep ligature furrow" pressed into the skin of Jon-
Benet's neck by the cord of the garrote. The width

varied from an eighth of an inch to five-sixteenths, and
the furrow was horizontal. There was no upward deviation, which proved she had not been suspended—
hanged—by the noose; that would have caused it to
sweep upward at the back of her neck. The skin on her
neck also showed scratching and petechial hemorrhages, those pinpoint ruptures of tiny blood vessels
classically associated with strangulation.

As the description of injuries carried over to page
four, Meyer offered more detailed observations about
the marks on the body: a scratch below and behind her
right ear; a small one on the right side of her chin and
scratches on her right shoulder, lower left back, and
four inches above the heel on the back of her left leg.
Wecht thought again that the marks on her back could
have come as she lay face up, squirming against her
molester's advances.

One more area of new information held a surprise
for Wecht. On page two, amid several areas still whited
out of the report, was part of the coroner's narrative
describing his arrival at the Ramsey house. Meyer
wrote that he had arrived at 8:00 P.M. That struck
Wecht as odd, since he was aware that JonBenet's body
had been discovered a few minutes after one. What explained the seven-hour delay? Had Meyer dispatched
some of his deputies and investigators earlier? That
was plausible and acceptable, and some reports later
would suggest that deputy coroners were on the scene
by 1:45 P.M.

The autopsy report did not tell Wecht if valuable
medical evidence had been collected from the body at
the scene. The coroner or his deputy could use a probe
to check liver temperature or a needle to withdraw eye
fluid to check potassium levels—both significant pieces

of scientific data that can help establish an approximate time of death.

Rigor mortis, the stiffening of the tissues and joints, begins about two hours after death and becomes fixed between eight and ten hours—quicker in some violent deaths. The same could be said for livor mortis, the settling of the blood and the resulting formation of a dark red color on the skin. The blood settles in about two hours and becomes fixed at eight to ten. Any of those facts could have provided valuable information shortly after one o'clock.

The last of the new disclosures may have added support for reports that possibly valuable DNA evidence had been obtained through skin scrapings taken from under JonBenet's fingernails. Meyer listed "fingernail clippings" among the standard evidence from the body that he had turned over to the police. The list included another possible reference to material that could contain DNA—Meyer had taken swabs of samples from her right and left thighs, and her right cheek. The other evidence he submitted to police included hairs and fibers from her clothing and body, samples of her hair and blood, the garrote, her clothing, and standard vaginal smears.

Wecht studied the full contents of the report as now disclosed to the public, and concluded that the few portions still under court seal probably included more details of the scene Meyer found at the house, the condition of JonBenet's body there, and a description of JonBenet's clothing.

What other surprising particulars did those portions of Dr. Meyer's report hold? Wecht could only wonder.

CHAPTER 28

The reaction of some experts to the new details of the autopsy would shock Cyril Wecht almost as much as anything he had read in the document itself.

On July 15, news accounts of the pages released the day before focused on the comments and analysis from several expert sources, including a doctor now advising District Attorney Alex Hunter on the case. Dr. Richard Krugman, dean of the University of Colorado School of Medicine and a nationally recognized expert on child abuse, read the same report that Wecht had read. But Krugman arrived at a completely different conclusion; he found the information insufficient to offer a diagnosis of sexual abuse.

"I know nothing that I have seen that would make me think the primary finding is sexual abuse," he told the *Rocky Mountain News*. He added, "I look at this and see a child who was physically abused and is dead. I don't believe it's possible to tell whether any child is sexually abused based on physical findings alone."

He said the various descriptions of "mild trauma" listed in the report—the dried and fresh blood in and around her vagina, the abrasions and inflammation inside her vagina, the bruise outside her vagina, and the abrasion and damage to her hymen—were not enough for him to diagnose sexual abuse. Those conditions could have been caused by many things other than sexual abuse, Krugman said, including irritation from bubble bath or an infection.

He said sexual abuse usually was confirmed by the presence of semen, evidence of a sexually transmitted disease, or a study of the child's medical history. There was nothing in the report that indicated a history of sexual abuse, he concluded.

The skull fracture had convinced him, he told the *Denver Post*, that JonBenet had suffered from an "explosion of rage." But Krugman said he was unable to tell whether JonBenet died from strangulation by the garrote or the blow to the head.

The problem was, Krugman added, that there was no way to tell from an autopsy who killed a child in the middle of the night while several adults were present in a house.

Dr. Todd Grey, chief medical examiner for the state of Utah, told the *Post* that he believed the strangulation had occurred last. "This wasn't a gentle killing; this kid was fighting." He noted that the injuries to her neck and the petechial hemorrhages there proved she had been alive when she was strangled.

The Ramseys' lawyers issued a statement saying they had not read the new information. "But credible experts who have, confirm what we have been saying all along—that there is no evidence of abuse or molestation prior to the night of her murder."

"Flabbergasted" was the first word that came to Dr. Cyril Wecht's mind as he tried to understand what Krugman and others had said. No evidence of sexual abuse? What was Krugman talking about? A six-year-old girl's hymen had been destroyed and the area around it showed abrasions. How did that happen except by penetration of the vagina? There was blood inside the vagina and around the outside. Where did the blood come from? A nose bleed? There shouldn't have been any blood there at all! The vaginal wall showed chronic and acute inflammation. Again, what other cause but penetration could explain that? Wasn't forced penetration of a six-year-old girl a definition of sexual abuse?

Wecht also found it surprising that Dr. Grey had concluded the strangulation came after the skull fracture, but that the strangulation had been accompanied by a struggle from JonBenet. The evidence was more than clear to Wecht that the blow to the head had come just as JonBenet was dying from another cause—the strangulation. Moreover, if she had suffered the massive head and brain injury first, she would have been unconscious, near death, and unable to struggle if she were then strangled. Wecht certainly agreed with Grey that JonBenet had been alive at the beginning of the strangulation, but Wecht believed that was because the strangulation had come before the head injury.

Finally, Wecht found the statement by the Ramseys to be nothing more than self-serving spin doctoring.

Wecht was glad to see more support for his conclusion of sexual abuse arrive the next day from other colleagues. The *News* quoted Dr. Ronald Wright, director of forensic pathology at the University of Miami School of Medicine and former medical examiner for Broward County, as saying JonBenet obviously had been penetrated and sexually abused. Wright—who had handled the famous, unsolved murder of six-year-old Adam Walsh—was surprised to hear that some experts had doubts about sexual abuse. "Somebody's injured her vagina, and she's tied up. Doesn't that make it involuntary sexual battery?" he asked.

Wright also concluded that the "birefringent foreign material" located in the vagina was consistent with penetration by someone wearing rubber gloves. That, and the evidence that JonBenet's body had been wiped after the attack, argued against her killer being a typical child molester. Wright said people who liked having sex with young girls were not usually so painstaking as to don rubber gloves before and wipe off their victims after.

But Wright's conclusions about the rest of the evidence departed from Wecht's. Wright believed the swelling and hemorrhaging in the brain indicated she had been struck on the head twenty to sixty minutes before she was strangled and died.

The *News* also added support for the sexual-abuse conclusions from another doctor—Robert Kirschner, a clinical associate in pathology and pediatrics at the University of Chicago and the former deputy chief medical examiner for Cook County. There was evidence of acute vaginal injury, he agreed, and that indicated "some kind of sexual assault." Some reports quoted him as saying there was evidence that JonBenet's vaginal opening was twice the normal size for a girl her age.

As he had so often, columnist Chuck Green served as the Greek chorus to this tragedy, as the spoken conscience of those who prayed for justice. He hoped the blow to the head had indeed come first. "We can only hope she didn't know about the rest," he said. But that scenario, he realized, meant someone had "toyed" with her corpse after delivering that crushing blow to the head. He could find no sense in that, and he feared that there had been more to the night's events.

Only D.A. Hunter and Chief Koby had the power to solve this riddle, Green said. They could charge someone and let the justice system do its duty, or they could "turn their back on JonBenet's grave and walk away, shrugging their shoulders in official frustration.

"In the meantime, the rest of us can only pray that JonBenet's final moments were brief.

"And that in the final judgment, her killer is afforded no mercy.

"Otherwise, her lonely night of terror continues."

On July 16, the *News* reported that John and Patsy Ramsey had submitted to an interview by Lou Smit, the retired homicide detective working for Alex Hunter. Sources said that on July 12, the Ramseys had slipped into the D.A.'s offices with no fanfare to talk to Smit about their daughter's death.

The next day, the *Post* responded with a story quoting its sources as saying Smit had not interrogated the Ramseys, but had discussed with them other leads in the case, including suspects other than John and Patsy. The husband and wife were together when they met with Smit for less than an hour, the sources said.

Alex Hunter said only, "We had specific questions about a number of narrow subjects."

The same story in the *Post* offered another bit of news. Testing of the ransom note was complete, and the Ramseys' fingerprints had not been found on it or the legal pad from which the pages had been torn.

Other experts told the *News* that there was no significance to the absence of the Ramseys' fingerprints on an object that admittedly came from their home. Finding their fingerprints on it would have been just as insignificant.

While all of that news was breaking, John Ramsey was attending a business conference sponsored by Access Graphics at a ski resort in Keystone, Colorado, and he granted an interview to a reporter from a magazine called *VARBusiness*.

He complained of harassment by the media and photographers for supermarket tabloids, and said he had been forced to hire a former cop as a personal bodyguard.

"We didn't choose to be a topic of conversation," he lamented. "The media, being the sharks they are, saw an opportunity to profit. . . . We became a way for the talk shows and the Geraldo Riveras to make a lot of money. One [tabloid] said their revenue went up thirty percent when they started putting our stories on the first page."

He said the coverage of JonBenet's death had interfered with Access Graphics' plans for global expansion, but his recent move to Atlanta should revive those efforts. In the days ahead, Access Graphics would reveal that Ramsey was moving his personal offices and several staff members to Atlanta, where he would supervise the North American and European operations.

John repeated his denial of any role in his daughter's death.

"We're normal human beings and a good family that loved our children more than anything in the world," he said. And then he posed his own query to the media:

"The question I would like to ask some of these people is, 'Would you kill your daughter or child?' No. Then why would you think I would?"

CHAPTER 29

Dr. Cyril Wecht would not have to wait long for the release of the final portions of the autopsy report, and more intriguing revelations.

A judge ordered the release of the rest of Coroner John Meyer's document on August 13—six days after JonBenet's seventh birthday was observed with a prayer at the family's former church in Boulder, and a padlock on the gates to the cemetery that held her grave in Georgia. Media reports noted that no one had seen John and Patsy visit their daughter's grave that day.

Despite the report's clinical language, the new information drew a heartrending portrait of what Meyer had found when he entered the Ramseys' house on the evening after Christmas. JonBenet's body was "covered by a blanket and a Colorado Avalanche sweatshirt. On removing these two items from the top of the body, the decedent was found to be lying on her back with her arms extended up over her head. The head was turned to the right. A brief examination of the body disclosed a ligature around the neck and a ligature around the right wrist. . . . The decedent is clothed in a long-sleeved white knit collarless shirt, the mid anterior chest area of which contains an embroidered silver star decorated with silver sequins. . . . There are long white underwear with an elastic waistband containing a red and blue stripe. The long underwear are urine stained. . . . Beneath the long underwear are white panties with printed rose buds and the word 'Wednesday' on the elastic band. The underwear is urine stained . . ."

The next phrase about JonBenet's Christmas night panties would rock Wecht one more time and convince him that his original analysis had been right on target.

". . . and in the inner aspect of the crotch are several red areas of staining measuring up to 0.5 inch in maximum dimension."

Meyer had found what Wecht could assume were blood stains in JonBenet's panties, just as there had been blood on the outside of her vagina. To Wecht that meant that her molester-killer had undressed her—or at least pulled down her underwear—sexually abused her, and then redressed her. That did not fit the pattern Wecht had ever seen in a random sexual assault. What kind of crazed sexual predator—capable of breaking into a family's house, ravaging and killing the little girl inside in the dark without awakening anyone else, and writing a bogus ransom note—would then redress his victim? Would that kind of monster really care about the final dignity of the little girl whose innocence and life he had just ripped from her? Or was that more likely the action of someone who cared for the girl, but whose perverse sexual appetite had led inexplicably to her sudden and unintended death? Some adult who could neither explain nor bear what had happened, and who could not leave her to suffer the final indignity of death in that exposed and vulnerable condition? Didn't all of that confirm the schizophrenic nature of this event? A rather gentle sexual abuse and then a brutal blow to the head? A sex game gone bad and then a desperate cover-up?

Although some sources would argue that—lacking the results of tests on the stains—no one should assume they were blood, Wecht would learn later from police affidavits that Meyer had told Detective Arndt that the stains "appeared to be consistent with blood." More support for Wecht's analysis.

There was still more to be gleaned from this final disclosure. Meyer's report turned toward the similar white cords around JonBenet's neck and right wrist. The garrote was double-knotted at the back of her neck and tied in several loops around a section of a tan wooden stick, four and a half inches long. The stick was irregularly shaped—apparently broken—on both ends. It bore several colors of paint, and part of it glistened with what Meyer assumed was varnish. Gold letters on one end of the stick said KOREA. Strands of JonBenet's blond hair were entwined in the knot and wrapped around the stick.

JonBenet had not gone to her death without some pieces of childish jewelry and other endearing little markings. A gold chain with a cross was around her neck, and she wore a gold ring on the middle finger of her right hand—just as the photograph Wecht had seen months ago revealed. On her right wrist—the same one bearing the white cord—was what obviously had been a Christmas present: a gold identification bracelet with her name and the date, "12/25/96." And someone—probably JonBenet herself—had drawn a little heart in red ink on the palm of her left hand. Such childish innocence, abused so horribly. Her hair was pulled back into two ponytails—one on the top of her head, secured with a cloth tie and a blue elastic band; the other, lower on the back of her head, also held by a blue elastic band.

The Ramsey team issued another statement after these disclosures, saying the information again supported the family's contention that the crime had been carefully planned by an intruder who had brought the garrote into the house with him.

But shortly after the final report was released, the *Rocky Mountain News* disclosed that the broken stick used for the garrote had been part of a long-handled artist's brush taken from Patsy's painting supplies in the basement. Police had matched the broken sections of the brush—still in Patsy's art kit—to the garrote handle, sources reported.

Although that really proved little—and certainly not who had applied an innocent artist's brush to such a heinous, evil purpose—it was another straw piled upon a camel's back. Anyone—even an elusive intruder—could have taken the brush from Patsy's supplies and twisted it into the cord around Jon-Benet's neck. But so far, Wecht observed, the significant evidence disclosed publicly had come only from inside that house—the paper for the ransom note, the pad itself. There was no proof yet of a criminal's kit bag brought along to facilitate this ill-conceived plan.

There were many questions, of course. What was the source of the white cord used in the garrote? What about the duct tape that had covered JonBenet's mouth? Where had they come from? That list certainly was lengthy. But Wecht was struck by the fact that everything he could list from the evidence so far argued that this killing was indeed an inside job.

CHAPTER 30

A new war of words was about to erupt, and all sides in the increasingly tense investigation would become combatants. This time the issue would be the release of the full text of the ransom note—previously one of the tightly held secrets of the police, the prosecutors, and the Ramseys. But in early September reporters for *Vanity Fair* and *Newsweek* magazines obtained copies of the note and announced that they would publish the full text. The three sides mired in the case each had copies, but they all passed this hot potato. The Ramseys, the cops, and the D.A.'s office all condemned the leak and denied being the source.

Hal Haddon immediately attacked the police, calling them cowards for slipping the note to the press and compromising the integrity of the investigation and their own department. He demanded an independent criminal investigation to determine who had committed "this extraordinary and unprofessional misconduct" that deserved disciplinary and criminal action. If the police leadership hadn't authorized the leak, Haddon charged, it had lost control of the department. To him it was clear that a cop had provided the note to *Vanity Fair* in return for a story that flattered the police and smeared the Ramseys.

Chief Koby was out of town on vacation, but Commander John Eller offered his typically succinct response when asked if the police had leaked the document: "You must be kidding." Spokeswoman Leslie Aaholm would say later that there would be no investigation into the leak; that would be "extremely disruptive" to the investigation.

Alex Hunter said his office certainly was not the sieve that let the note slip. Despite being displeased by the leak, he said there was a possibility that someone would recognize the phrasing used by the killer and provide important clues to the authorities. His spokeswoman, Suzanne Laurion, added later that the downside was losing the ability to corroborate witness statements with undisclosed details from the note.

The flap led John Ramsey to write a fiery letter to the *Boulder Daily Camera* from his home in Atlanta, blasting the police department.

"The leadership of the investigation into the murder of my daughter is flawed," he charged. "The people of Boulder should be asking for a change. As the father of a precious child who was murdered in the city of Boulder, and where the murderer still walks free, I beg for it."

Ramsey also responded to a *Camera* story that said the police had been rebuffed by Hunter's office when they asked for warrants to search Ramsey's airplane hangar and his company offices in Boulder. Ramsey said in his letter that he would have given the police permission to conduct the searches if they had come to him. He believed they didn't ask so they could imply that he wasn't cooperating with the investigation. He told the *Camera*, "I can only assume your 'unnamed sources' are from within the Boulder police department, who are trying to blame others for their mistakes."

The new conflagration broke as the prosecutors and police prepared to make a trip to Quantico, Virginia, to discuss the investigation with the FBI's Child Abduction Serial Killer Unit. Such consultations are common by the elite members of the unit, and the FBI had been working with the Ramsey team since the case began. In twelve hours of meetings on September 8 and 9, most of the fourteen agents in the unit and its chief, William Hagmaier, gathered around a conference table with some FBI crime-lab specialists, five Boulder police detectives, two assistant district attorneys, and D.A. investigator Lou Smit.

Notable by their absence were D.A. Alex Hunter, Chief Tom Koby, and Commander John Eller. Little was revealed about the sessions then, but Hagmaier said his team hoped to provide the Boulder task force with guidance to cover all aspects of the case, from the crime scene to the courtroom.

Later, the *Rocky Mountain News* would report that the detectives had discussed three theories with the FBI experts: JonBenet had been murdered by an intruder; she had been killed by her mother, with her father as an accomplice; or she had been killed by her father, with her mother as accomplice. None of the scenarios suggested any culpability for her brother, Burke, and none of them broke any new ground.

The comings and goings around the sessions got full coverage. The Boulder officials left Denver International Airport under the watchful lenses of several TV news crews, and were met by another one when they landed at Washington/Dulles International Airport.

At Quantico, a bureau spokesman said he had never seen so much media coverage of a consultation with the CASKU group.

Alex Hunter had already cast somewhat of a cloud over the sessions by bowing out at the last minute. In a decision that hinted at continuing tension between the cops and the prosecutors, he said he had changed his mind after learning that the briefing the detectives had planned for him and his staff before the trip wouldn't include a review of all the physical evidence gathered so far. That, he said, made his participation at Quantico premature.

Eller expressed his regret at Hunter's decision. "This was Alex's trip," he told the *News.* "He scheduled this. I think it would have been helpful if he had followed through."

But after the meetings Hunter said Hagmaier had filled him in. "Hagmaier was struck by the extent to which everybody around the table in Quantico had their eyes on JonBenet," Hunter said. He said the FBI had provided valuable insights into investigative approaches and directions.

While the meetings at FBI headquarters were underway, Hunter surprised many sources by releasing copies of the ransom note to the media in Boulder. He said it already had been quoted in *Vanity Fair* and reproduced in *Newsweek.*

A few days later, Ramsey private eye H. Ellis Armistead sent out a mass mailing of fliers to Boulder residents, and it included a reproduction of the note. "Who talks like this? Who writes like this?" the flier asked.

In the flurry of stories about the note, the *Vanity Fair* article had stung the most. Chief Koby had actually planned to put his top brass and his Ramsey detectives on polygraphs to see if any of them was the source of the leaks that provided writer Ann Louise Bardach's story with the first copy of the note and details from some police reports never disclosed before. Koby's plan was scotched, however, after the police union pointed out the contractual prohibition against requiring lie-detector tests for officers.

Bardach's story delved deeply into the complex relationships between everyone touched by the case. While she focused on the cops' handling of the investigation, she also struck at the allegedly cozy relationship between the two sides of a supposedly adversarial system—Hunter and his staff on one side, and the lawyers on the Ramsey team on the other. She repeated what she said were accounts of regular breakfast meetings between Hunter assistant Peter Hofstrom and his old friend, Ramsey lawyer Bryan Morgan. She said one of Patsy's lawyers, Patrick Burke, was often seen chatting with Hofstrom and prosecutor Tripp DeMuth in the doorway of the off-limits "war room." DeMuth was the assistant, claimed Bardach, who advised the Ramseys to include in their ad the suggestion that a mystery man had been approaching children. When the police got a set of handwriting samples from the Ramseys, Bardach reported, the session was held at Hofstrom's home. She said a later review of the handwriting had been conducted at the office of Ramsey friend Mike Bynum, and Ramsey attorney Lee Foreman had been seen giving DeMuth a backrub during a break. After the demonstration, a source told Bardach, Hunter was heard asking Hal Haddon, "Well, where should we go from here?"

Bardach charged that the police were convinced that

the Ramseys should be charged in their daughter's
death, while Hofstrom's prosecutors resisted that
view. When the police had suggested polygraph tests
for John and Patsy, Hofstrom immediately had shot
down the idea. He also refused police requests to sub-
poena the records of the Ramseys' toll calls and credit-
card purchases. Bardach said Hofstrom was the man
who argued that the Ramsey team should be given
copies of the original statements by John and Patsy as
a condition for getting their formal interviews in May.
The detectives chafed as Hofstrom gave credence to
the intruder theory and dismissed their carefully collected evidence. They were frustrated by investigator
Lou Smit's serious consideration of the idea that a
grown man had slipped through the Ramseys' basement window, even though Bardach quoted Hunter as
saying, "No one came through that window." To some
detectives—and in stark contrast to the opinion of
Smit's colleagues—he came to be viewed as "a delu-
sional old man" who had decided the Ramseys were
good Christians who could not have harmed their
daughter, according to Bardach. The source also called
the meeting between the Ramseys and Smit in July a
joke, with Smit asking John and Patsy for their
thoughts about the intruder. The police later accused
Smit of contaminating the case file by putting in reports exculpatory of the Ramseys; his response was
that he would write his reports as he saw fit.

Bardach cited sources close to the investigation as
saying the police, supported by the FBI and CBI, finally had decided they could not share information
with the prosecutors because it was being disclosed
to the Ramsey team. Prosecutors provided Ramsey
lawyers with copies of sensitive police reports, gave

them copies of the ransom note and the so-called practice note from the same pad, and even allowed them to see the garrote found around JonBenet's neck, Bardach said.

After *Vanity Fair* hit the newsstands, Hal Haddon called the story "glossy tabloid trash."

But that didn't end the reports about disturbing links between the lawyers on both sides of the Ramsey table. A few days after Haddon's comment, more reports surfaced. The *Rocky Mountain News* said Hunter and the Ramseys' civil attorney, William Gray, had been limited partners in the same commercial complex in Boulder since 1969. The general partner in the ownership group was Hunter's top man, First Assistant D.A. Bill Wise.

Hunter called the partnership irrelevant and said the men had never even conversed about the building, let alone the Ramsey case.

The story also resurrected the news of the verdict that connected Haddon to one of the cops' new legal advisers, Robert Miller, and a split of some $15 million in fees. Former Denver prosecutor Craig Silverman said he was surprised to see Miller show up in the Ramsey case, since people who had helped each other earn $15 million would be likely to favor each other a month or two later.

The *News* then found a link between another of the police department's counselors, Daniel Hoffman, and Ramsey attorney Lee Foreman. It seemed that Foreman had defended Hoffman against a legal-malpractice suit filed by one of Hoffman's former clients.

The third legal adviser for the cops came to his colleagues' defense. Richard Baer noted that all three lawyers were donating their time to the police, and he described his two associates as among the most ethical lawyers in the country.

Haddon complained to the *Post* that although the police had sought out the lawyers for help, he was now being accused of planting them as moles inside the investigation to funnel information to him. He called that suggestion "totally phony."

One former newspaper editor and ethics teacher suggested those stories were the result of slow news days on major cases. "Desperation time" for reporters, another professor called it.

Before long, Haddon also issued another statement blasting the police, just as a judge released to the public some of the search warrants filed in the case. He charged that the police had gathered evidence that could have cleared the Ramseys of suspicion in their daughter's death, but chose not to make it public. He cited three items: what appeared to be recent pry marks on the handle of a locked back door; the broken basement window under an iron grate in the backyard, in an area under the balcony at JonBenet's bedroom; and a blue suitcase removed from the basement floor under the broken window. Haddon suggested the public had not heard about those items because they did not support the cops' theory of the Ramseys' guilt.

"It is significant that while the defamatory contents of the search warrant affidavits and inventories have previously been leaked to the media by police sources, those 'sources close to the investigation' did not leak information which is exculpatory to the Ramsey family," Haddon said. He said the items he cited "demonstrates substantial evidence of an intruder."

The media's repeated reports that there was no evidence of forced entry seemed to be contradicted by the pry marks on the door handle. But the *Rocky Mountain News* found Tom Johnston, the owner of the company that had changed the locks at the Ramsey house, and he said flatly, "There was no forcible entry." His serviceman had seen the pry marks, but Johnston said he remained unconvinced that they were evidence that an intruder entered the Ramsey house that night.

Gregg McCrary wondered if the marks could be just another element of what he believed was some fairly extensive staging of the crime scene.

Other sources said Haddon's short list could actually turn out to be more potent than what the police had accomplished in so many months. An unidentified pubic hair on JonBenet's bedding. A broken basement window not far from the room where her body was found. Pry marks on a door. John Ramsey eliminated as the writer of the note. Patsy ranking low as a possible author. Disputed evidence of previous sexual abuse.

How would these elements play in the face of the D.A.'s burden of proving guilt beyond a reasonable doubt?

CHAPTER 31

"It is accurate to say that if we had to do it all over again, we would do it differently."

Those words, spoken by Chief Tom Koby about the JonBenet Ramsey investigation, were the first official break in the monolithic insistence that the police department had done everything just right in this fractured case. The introspective look backward by the beleaguered chief was not a full about-face, however. He still insisted, "At the same time we responded the best we could. . . . There are few, if any, agencies that would have done it differently than we did in those first few hours."

That, of course, was widely open to serious debate.

But Koby's primary focus on October 10, 1997—his first news conference in eight months—was the road ahead, and he turned the investigation to a new course. He removed Commander John Eller as the head of the case and replaced him with Commander Mark Beckner, a forty-one-year-old veteran of several major assignments within the department and a recognized leader known for handling the pressure and demands of administrative duties.

The chief also announced that he was pulling his troops out of the D.A.'s "war room," returning them to their department offices, and restoring a more conventional relationship between the police and the prosecutors. Alex Hunter's staff would be available for consultation and advice, but would not be involved in the daily work of the police investigation, Koby explained. He admitted there had been some friction between the two camps—"disagreements between investigators and prosecutors," he described it bluntly—over how to approach "all of the possible suspects." A hard line on one side, a "less antagonistic approach" on the other. Both strategies were legitimate, he said; the prosecutors had traditionally followed the second course, and that had served Boulder well. He did not have to plant the department's flag on the other peak to call attention to the obvious, but he added, "In this case there was, and still is, a difference of opinion about which is more appropriate."

Koby acknowledged that personalities had played a role in the conflict. He mentioned Eller directly, noting his "very intense personality." Beckner would be more "low-key." And the chief said Beckner would have the help of three more detectives just assigned to the team, bringing it to eight.

Another source of friction was Hunter's recent decision to talk more to the media; Koby opposed that, and complained again about the intense coverage of the case around the world. Too often, he believed, the media had looked for a "bad guy" in this case, and too often they had cast the cops in that role. Koby even whipped out a pocket edition of the U.S. Constitution from his suit coat, read from the First Amendment, and lectured the reporters on their responsibilities. "You know," he explained, "I get one chance to present my side of the story in this case, and that's in a court of law, not in the media. I'm not mad at you; I'm disappointed in you. I can't help that."

But when a reporter asked a question that Koby apparently didn't like, he abruptly snapped, "Next question," without offering a response. Some reporters found it difficult to tell disappointment from anger.

Koby was no longer promising, let alone vowing, that an arrest would be made. "We will know that when we get the work done. We have not finished the work." He had a timetable in his head, but he wasn't about to share it with the world. He denied reports that detectives had already tried to get an arrest warrant from prosecutors.

Just the same, his earlier pledge that "our guy won't walk" seemed to be coming back to haunt him regularly now.

Hunter's spokeswoman, Suzanne Laurion, agreed that there was a strain between the authorities on the case and that Hunter had recognized the need for reorganization. He did not oppose Koby's decision to withdraw from the "war room." But Hunter stressed that the change did not affect Lou Smit's participation in the investigation.

The refocused and perhaps rejuvenated Ramsey investigation—now with expenses reaching $300,000 for cops and prosecutors—would truck along without major eruptions for some weeks. The media learned that Lou Smit was looking for a convicted sex offender who had lived in the Ramseys' neighborhood at the time of the killing but moved away soon after. The man, now fifty-four, had been arrested for a crime against a child in 1965 in Oceanside, California, and ended up convicted of misdemeanor indecent exposure. It was "just normal business," Smit said, to ask the police there to check around for the man. A sergeant in Oceanside told the *Denver Post* that detectives in Boulder had run the man's name through a computer and discovered his police record in California. Smit told the *North County Times* in San Diego County, "It's a small lead and I don't know if it means anything. It's just somebody to look at. We're looking at everyone whose name is connected to the case."

Hal Haddon was encouraged that an investigator, especially the experienced Smit, was willing to consider the possibility that someone had broken into the home, willing to look at someone besides the Ramseys.

The police apparently were looking at a lot of other people. Detectives were tracking down known pedophiles and sex offenders in the Boulder area, working from a list or three dozen or so. The police had as many as seventy-one registered as sex offenders, as required by state law, and there were another thirty-two listed with the sheriff for the unincorporated areas of the county.

Although some wondered if this effort signaled a shift in the focus away from the Ramseys, other sources suggested the police were simply answering all of the questions that could be asked later. They just wanted to know what to say about anyone who could be a suspect—including known sex offenders—by the time the investigation was complete.

Patsy Ramsey weighed back into the fray when she told a tabloid TV show that she suspected JonBenet might have been killed by a student from the nearby University of Colorado who had seen her riding her bicycle.

Chuck Green could not resist that column fodder.

"In a single swoop, there's suddenly another 25,000 suspects whose alibis need to be checked."

Meanwhile, the police had turned to a new and different kind of expert for a consultation. Corporal John Van Tassel of the Royal Canadian Mounted Police spent six days in Boulder to examine the knots and the cord used in the garrote. One of the few forensic knot analysts in the world, Van Tassel told the *News* he would try to determine if the knots were linked to a job or a hobby such as fishing, or were similar to other knots in a suspect's belongings. He would ask if anyone had ever seen a suspect tie similar knots. He said he had conducted such investigations in more than fifty cases, mostly involving deaths; some had been homicides, some suicides, and some had involved sadomasochistic activities.

There was a major development for the Ramseys in November as well; Lockheed Martin announced the sale of Access Graphics to a division of General Electric Company. Access Graphics and its six hundred employees would remain in Boulder. But President John Ramsey would leave the company when the sale closed, about the end of the year.

The Ramseys' houses in Michigan and Boulder generated more news in November, too. A judge in Michigan released the affidavit that Boulder Detective Jane Harmer had signed in January to get a search warrant for the summer home in Charlevoix. Harmer wrote that the police believed the killer might have conducted surveillance on that house, or even broken into it; checking the Ramseys' mail and answering machine might tell the cops if anyone had studied the family's activities by sending mail or making calls.

Without citing the ransom note, the affidavit referred to mail or documents "from any person, group or faction containing or alluding to threats to any members of the Ramsey family."

The Ramseys' spokeswoman said the police had seized nothing after the search.

But an edited version of another police affidavit—filed in Michigan in March and released there in November—shed a little more light on the ransom note and Patsy. "There is evidence which indicates the ransom note may have been written by Patricia Ramsey," the affidavit said, "but the evidence falls short of that necessary to support a definite conclusion." The police hoped to find samples of her handwriting that "might not contain any elements of distortion, attempts to disguise handwriting, or nervousness," according to the affidavit. With that search warrant the police took some of Patsy's recipe cards, an address book, a legal pad, a table from a bedside table, and other samples of her handwriting from the house in Charlevoix.

In Boulder, a source told the *Rocky Mountain News* in November that police had found six windows and a door unlocked when they arrived at the Ramsey house that first morning—and that was in addition to the broken basement window. The unlocked door near the kitchen was the same one where an officer reportedly had found pry marks. A defense attorney said that kind of evidence was welcome to the Ramseys, providing additional likelihood that someone had slipped into their house.

The biggest news of the fall broke in mid-November when Chief Tom Koby announced his retirement. But he delayed his final day for some thirteen months to give himself time to see the Ramsey case through to completion before stepping down at the end of 1998. He was not leaving to take another job, he explained; he was just ready—at forty-eight and after a difficult year—to retire for a while. He would decide what to do with the rest of his life after that.

He predicted being able to make the final call on the Ramsey case within three to six months—perhaps as early as February 1998 or by that May. "If it needs to go forward, I'll make sure it goes forward. If it is not going to go forward, I need to be the one to make that call. . . . I need to resolve it. I have to be the one to bless it, I guess."

The police union responded to the chief's retirement with something of a rebuke—an affirmation of the officers' no-confidence vote from earlier in the year.

Three days after Koby's announcement, Commander John Eller said he, too, would be retiring, but his departure would come at the end of February 1998. "It's been a tough year," the fifty-year-old officer told the *Denver Post.* "I'd like to take some time and reflect."

As November drew to a close, the possibility that Alex Hunter could convene a grand jury to investigate the Ramsey case took another turn at center stage—mostly as a topic of discussion on television and radio talk shows. *Newsweek* reported that Hunter had all but decided to take the case to a grand jury; he immediately denied that. But he would say later that it always remained an option, and he had discussed it with aides more frequently than before. Troubling aspects of the procedure, however, were the question of granting immunity to reluctant witnesses in exchange for their testimony, and the possibility that a runaway grand jury would return a popular indictment on thin evidence. That in turn could lead to a difficult and perhaps unsuccessful trial that would do nothing but frustrate everyone.

Questions flew about whether John, Patsy, and Burke Ramsey could be brought back from Georgia to appear before a Colorado grand jury; experts said yes, there was a legal process for getting court orders to compel witnesses to go to another state to testify. Others wondered whether there was any reason to go before a grand jury at all. More experts said a grand jury would help only if witnesses had refused to cooperate with investigators or a prosecutor had decided to see if the citizens' panel would agree with his decision on whether to file charges.

What about calling on Colorado attorney general Gale Norton, a Republican, to take over the case that many sources believed was irretrievably stalled somewhere between the cops and the local prosecutors? Norton said she could assist a local prosecutor only if he had filed murder charges and was seeking the death penalty; then she could send in her special unit on capital crimes.

For days Peter Boyles focused much of his KHOW radio show on the idea that a little-known Colorado court case from 1912 could apply in the Ramsey case. Boyles said he found the case establishing the legal principle that the governor could use an executive order to send the attorney general into a community to take over a case with the same authority as the county D.A. Norton said that was an extremely rare situation, and she didn't believe it applied here because Hunter was still performing his statutory duties.

Another flap arose over JonBenet's big brother,

ten-year-old Burke. Had he ever been interviewed by the police? Critics of the Ramseys and the police said no, he had never been asked what he knew about what happened to his little sister that night. Defenders disagreed; Burke had been interviewed by the police on December 26, and he had given a lengthy interview to a social worker in January. But many sources said that was not enough, not in this case.

CHAPTER 32

John and Patsy Ramsey remained under "an umbrella of suspicion" in the killing of their daughter, the new leader of the police investigation said calmly as he faced the media for the first time. In the city council chambers in Boulder on December 5, Commander Mark Beckner riveted the press corps as he took the stage, flanked by a semicircle of his team of eight young, eager-looking detectives. Six men and two women. The oldest was forty-four, the youngest thirty-one.

Beckner, just forty-one and already a twenty-year veteran of the department, looked as fresh-faced as his team. As he graciously answered the questions that he could about the famous case that now rested in his hands, he could easily have been mistaken for a young corporate exec. In reality he was a seasoned officer whose experience ranged from the detective bureau, to patrol, undercover investigations, narcotics, internal affairs, bank robberies, tactical planning and training. In case his boyish face suggested otherwise, it was explained that he also had served as the SWAT commander. He had earned a master's degree in criminal justice and was described as a quick study, intelligent, and focused. No-nonsense. By the book. Task oriented.

Opening with a prepared statement, Beckner

announced that he was pleased with the progress since he had taken over nine weeks earlier. He had assembled a list of seventy-two items that detectives needed to complete: twenty-eight had been finished; about a dozen more were in progress; others awaited action. Each detective had a list of tasks assigned directly to him or her. They had re-interviewed some significant witnesses, consulted with more forensic experts, reviewed almost two hundred videotapes seized in the Ramsey house, and checked computer files also taken there. They were arranging additional laboratory testing on some of the trace evidence.

The tasks yet to be completed included re-interviewing some other witnesses, collecting and analyzing more evidence, and finishing other forensic tests.

And then, without warning or even a change in the inflection in his voice, he added, "One of the most important tasks yet to do is the re-interviewing of some family members, specifically Mr. and Mrs. Ramsey and their son, Burke. We have made a formal request for these interviews and expect this to be completed in the near future."

He provided that news as if it were just another item on the list, to be tossed off without any special attention. He offered no acknowledgment of the nasty months of bare-knuckled negotiations needed to arrange those first interviews last May. He just said coolly that he expected these interviews to be done soon. An optimist with a badge.

He also caused a stir with his list of options once the investigation was completed: "We could seek an arrest warrant and prosecution, we could ask for a grand jury investigation, or we could inactivate the case until such time that additional information becomes available."

Some sources were certain Beckner had become the first figure in authority to acknowledge that the last year of heartache and work, and all that lay ahead, could lead to a dusty shelf—waiting for some unforeseen, fortuitous break that might not ever materialize.

Beckner promised a "focused and aggressive investigation," and then turned his attention to the other cloud hanging over his head: the relationship between the police and prosecutors. He called his experience with them positive and professional, adding, "I have had regular contact and conversations with Peter Hofstrom. They continue to provide counsel and advice in this investigation that has been very helpful."

Before opening the session for questions, Beckner added that the police had not yet sought an arrest warrant because the investigation was incomplete.

The first query was whether the Ramseys were just "a focus" of the investigation, or had been elevated to the status of suspects.

"We have an umbrella of suspicion," Beckner explained as his hands rose in front of him to mold the image, "and people have come and gone under that umbrella. They do remain under an umbrella of suspicion, but we're not ready to name any suspects."

Beckner had just delivered the kind of phrase the reporters had hoped to hear. Nearly every one there would make those words—umbrella of suspicion— the lead of the story.

What about Burke Ramsey? "At this time we're treating him as a witness."

Why did they need new family interviews? "It's been approximately six months since we last interviewed the Ramseys. During that time there's been a lot of investigation. We've uncovered a lot of new information. We have a lot of new questions, and they can help us answer those questions. They are significant in this case, and they have information that's important to us."

Any response from the Ramseys yet? "We made our formal request last week, and we have not heard back from them. But they have indicated every willingness to cooperate and have done so—during my nine weeks, anyway. So I expect we'll get that done in the near future."

Will there ever be an arrest? "I'm confident it will be solved, yes."

Were Beckner and his team starting the investigation all over again? No, there had been a lot of quality work done before, and this team was taking that and moving forward. He felt no pressure to make an arrest and would not offer a timetable. He understood the frustration of the public and the family and his own officers, but he was not going to rush. It remained a circumstantial case, and he was confident his team would collect more evidence before this case was closed.

The press was impressed with this new commander. No lecturing on the First Amendment. No waving pocket Constitutions. No snapping, "Next question." Actually introducing his investigative team to the media. Trying to answer questions as directly as possible. Was Beckner trying to establish a new relationship with the media and the American public?

"I'm being myself. This is me," he said with a genuine air. "You either like it or you don't. You know, I'm not Tom Koby; I'm not anybody else. This is how I interact when I interact with the media."

Could Beckner offer any observations about the decisions in the early hours of the investigation and how they affected the outcome?

"I haven't gone back and tried to use hindsight and twenty-twenty vision, and analyze why and how everything was done. Nine weeks ago, I came onto this case and I took what was on the plate, and my focus has been forward. Let's go forward. This is what we have today. How do we get to where we want to be tomorrow? And that's what I'm focusing on."

Among miscellaneous questions, he wouldn't discuss the kinds of suspects they were or weren't looking at. A question asking if police could eliminate the possibility of an uninvited intruder required discussing details he was not comfortable doing. He wasn't concerned about old rumors that the Ramseys and their attorneys were somehow getting too much inside information about the investigation.

And then Commander Beckner went back to work, with his eight investigators following him.

CHAPTER 33

On a frigid December 26, 1997, Judith Phillips brought some fifty people together in the street in front of the forsaken Ramsey mansion for a vigil to mark the first anniversary of JonBenet's death. Judith wanted to ensure that no one would forget the sweet little girl whom she missed so much amid all of the other trappings of this ghastly crime and this unending media feast—the little girl whose body had been wheeled out of that house exactly a year before. "She will have justice," Judith vowed on this candlelit night.

The lonely lamppost that stood sentry at the walk leading to the Ramseys' front door had become a memorial to JonBenet. The *Globe*—the tabloid that had broken many JonBenet stories and published the troubling photos that had drawn Dr. Cyril Wecht into the case—had helped arrange the displays at the lamppost. Holiday poinsettias, an empty Christmas stocking, and a small cross bearing the initials JB. Judith added one of her photographs of JonBenet, hanging it above two golden angels.

Many of those who came really were mourners, and they wept for JonBenet. They sang songs, including "Amazing Grace." Ten-year-old Melody Secord of

Broomfield brought a sparkling tiara, offering it at the memorial for the girl who had won so many crowns.

But a reporter who attended for the *Denver Post* found an undercurrent of anger at this sad event—anger that no one had been brought to justice. One retired businessman said he was disgusted by the performance of officials in charge of the case.

Judith Phillips's efforts were not the only attempts to remember JonBenet. On Christmas night fifteen people braved the Rockies' bitter winds and temperatures to stand vigil in front of the Boulder County Courthouse. Organizer Pat Walsh said she wanted the world to know that Boulder would not accept the death of any child—JonBenet, who died a year ago, or Susannah Chase, the University of Colorado student who had been beaten beyond recognition in an alley near her home five days before this vigil, and died the day after the attack. Some of the detectives from the Ramsey investigation had been assigned to the new homicide.

Walsh, a retired nurse, complained that JonBenet's death had been turned into "a parlor game like Clue," while the agony of the real child who had been tortured and killed was forgotten. On this Christmas night the *Post* called the Ramsey case "an outlandish mystery ogled by the nation and the world."

JonBenet's older brother, John Andrew, had attended a special memorial service on December 14 at the First United Methodist Church in Boulder; her parents' absence drew some comments, including a note in the *Globe*. But John and Patsy had sent a special message that was printed in the program for the service.

The Ramseys also broadcast a Christmas message on the Internet: "On one hand, we feel like Christmas should be canceled. Where is there joy? Our Christmas is forever tainted with the tragedy of her death, and yet the message rings clear. Had there been no birth of Christ, there would be no hope for eternal life and hence, no hope of ever being with our loved ones again."

What obviously was meant as a message of hope was soon turned against the Ramseys. Sources began noting the use of the stilted, seldom used phrase—"and hence"—in this message, just as it had been in the ransom note. Hunter had already turned to linguistics experts to analyze the note and look for clues leading back to an author with similar speech and writing traits.

In the weeks after Commander Mark Beckner demonstrated a firm grip on the investigation, several new disclosures had kept the story bubbling as it neared the anniversary date.

First came the reports that the police had been reinterviewing the Ramseys' friends and neighbors, asking intriguing questions. Had they or the Ramseys owned shoes made by companies called SAS or Hi-Tech? Sources reported that the police believed footprints in the house, including the basement, might have been made by the distinctive soles of SAS walking shoes and Hi-Tech hiking boots. The *Rocky Mountain News* said the footprints had been discovered the first day of the investigation, but overlooked until Beckner's team had reviewed the evidence. A source close to the Ramseys denied that any of them had ever owned shoes of either make.

The other question being asked of friends and neighbors was really a surprise. Did they know of the Ramseys or anyone else owning a so-called "stun gun?" Some detectives had wondered if the pair of marks noted on JonBenet's lower left back during the autopsy could have been the physical results of the electrodes on a two-pronged stun gun—a device that delivers a disabling electrical shock to its human target. Coroner Meyer had described "two dried rust-colored to slightly purple abrasions." One measured an eighth by a sixteenth of an inch, and the other was an eighth by three-sixteenths.

The police had investigated the stun-gun angle more than six months earlier, but had charged it up again during new questioning of neighbors and family. Store owners said they had talked to detectives about stun guns, and some of the police had tested the weapons, which leave two marks on the skin, between one and two inches apart. Coroner Michael Dobersen of Arapahoe County, who had exhumed a body to test for stun-gun marks that helped win a murder conviction, told the *Post* that the police had shown him photographs of the pair of red abrasions on JonBenet's back. They could have been from a stun gun, but they also could have been just scratches, he told the police; the only way to be sure was to exhume her body and look at the tissue under a microscope.

In a comment to the *Post*, Hal Haddon said the police had told him "affirmatively" that a stun gun had been used on JonBenet. That was the mark of a psychopath—not a parent, not even a parent inflicting sexual abuse on a child or caught in a fit of rage at the child, Haddon insisted. "This is the kind of thing an outsider does—a predator."

His associate Patrick Furman fired off some impressive hyperbole by proclaiming, "It must now be clear to any open-minded person that this vicious crime was committed by an outsider."

The *News* reported later, however, that a videotape about corporate security that was among the two hundred seized in the Ramsey house contained a reference to stun guns.

Alex Hunter was dismayed when the stun-gun angle hit the papers; if anyone close to the case had had one, they would have soon disposed of it. Hunter added that he would be willing to exhume JonBenet's body if it became necessary to clear up this question.

Haddon called the suggestion of an exhumation "just monstrous," and Commander Beckner said it was not under serious consideration at that time.

Cyril Wecht agreed with Dobersen and Hunter. An exhumation could be emotionally difficult and distasteful for the family and the public, but it could provide the answer to an important question. Wecht saw that as the greater good, as he had when he recommended exhuming Mary Jo Kopechne's body to look for answers in the Chappaquiddick incident. Finding the truth in the pursuit of justice had to be the best course, Wecht felt, and an exhumation could provide a more fitting and just outcome for JonBenet than an unsolved murder and an unpunished killer.

The police had collected at least four pieces of physical evidence that could solve the case, the *News* reported just before Christmas. The items had been recovered at the Ramseys' house, and although the paper's sources wouldn't be specific, the story suggested they could include "tools, utensils and clothing found in the home, hair or fiber samples, and footprints." A glimmer of hope for a solution to the mystery existed now because of that, the *News* said, and an invigorated police investigation that had returned to "old-fashioned police work—chasing a long list of leads and re-interviewing witnesses." The police also were following the advice from the session with the FBI in September—eliminate all potential suspects, no matter how remote their link to the case.

The approach of Christmas had brought a plea for peace from an unsuspected source—Fleet White. In a letter to the *New York Times,* the man who had watched as John Ramsey carried his daughter's body from that basement room begged the media for restraint, in the spirit of the season. "We request that Boulder be given the opportunity to enjoy this sacred season in peace without interruption from anyone who intends to further erode our community's privacy and exploit our misfortunes for the purpose of profit or personal gain," he wrote.

That, of course, did not happen. There were a number of media accounts of the anniversary of JonBenet's death; it remained, after all, a made-for-the-media story by its very nature. But on the whole, Boulder officials were surprised that there were not more TV trucks roaming the city streets, and that the reports were not more bombastic.

A month would pass before another dramatic overture by Fleet White was disclosed. Reports in January would describe a meeting on December 19 among White, his wife, and Colorado governor Roy Romer in which the Whites sought appointment of a special prosecutor to take over the Ramsey case. Actions by Alex Hunter, the Whites charged, had created "the strong appearance of impropriety, professional incompetence, and a lack of objectivity." They accused him of sharing evidence with the Ramsey team and others not officially involved in the case. "There appears to be an atmosphere of distrust and non-cooperation between the Boulder County district attorney and the Boulder Police Department regarding the investigation. This relationship appears to be irreparably damaged with respect to the Ramsey case," the Whites wrote in a letter they subsequently released publicly.

Romer turned down their request. He said he had conferred with Chief Tom Koby—not with Hunter—and Koby had told him that removing Hunter was unnecessary; the investigation was proceeding and hadn't even been turned over to the D.A. for consideration. Romer decided it was improper for him to intervene "at this time."

Hunter said he understood the frustration of people who were "so closely linked to an investigation of such complexity and duration. Unfortunately, because of Mr. and Mrs. White's status as witnesses in the case, we are unable to share with them information and insights that might provide them with the reassurance they seek."

Stories about evidence sparked the beginning of the new year. *Time* magazine offered a supposed scoop on the fate of the heavy flashlight rumored to have disappeared from the Ramseys' kitchen counter that first day. The flashlight had surfaced, according to *Time*, right in the police department's evidence vault. The crime lab was now testing it for any links to the case—such as evidence that it was the weapon that had crushed JonBenet's head.

Unfortunately for *Time*, the story seemed to be inaccurate. Leslie Aaholm announced that the flashlight had never been missing at all. It had been bagged as evidence, sent to the crime lab for tests, and returned to the evidence vault when the work was finished. Now some more tests were underway. No mystery. No story.

Peter Boyles added an interesting twist to the web of evidence in the case by getting into real webs—spider webs—on his talk show on KHOW Radio. Boyles said sources had told him that the police had found intact spider webs in the well of the basement window where the Ramsey team believed an intruder could have gained entry. The police had even consulted an entomologist—an insect expert—to ask if spiders could have spun new webs between the times someone would have climbed through the window that night and the webs were photographed by police the next day. The expert's answer, according to Boyles' report, was no.

New Yorker magazine also weighed in with a report that DNA material recovered from JonBenet's body did not match either of her parents—returning to the possibility of an unidentified intruder. Alex Hunter confirmed that there was such a sample, and that the police were taking swab samples from the insides of the mouths of family, friends, and neighbors to try to locate the source of the DNA.

If there was such a DNA sample, Wecht found it curious that the two internationally recognized experts drafted for Hunter's dream team knew nothing about it yet. Lawyer and DNA expert Barry Scheck and criminalist Dr. Henry Lee said they were unaware of any such samples. But they also said they had not been deeply involved in the case, unlike the implication offered when their participation was announced by Hunter.

Scheck said he had agreed to serve as an unpaid DNA consultant, although he would not participate in any trial that might result. He said in January that he had not been asked to review any evidence; essentially, he had not been used in the investigation.

Lee said his involvement in the case had been minimal. But he had met with Hunter and detectives three times to review the evidence and offer some conclusions and advice about what he called "an extremely difficult case." There had indeed been problems with police decisions at the crime scene, but it was apparent to him that they had been working very hard since then. He was not going to engage now in "Monday morning quarterbacking" about the investigation.

Although he had not been consulted about the new DNA report, he said such material found on a body obviously could be an important clue. But the existence of such a sample did not necessarily prove a particular theory of the crime, and could often turn out to mean nothing. In some six thousand homicide investigations, he had been able to identify the source of barely half of the DNA material collected. Such samples—hair, skin scrapings, saliva, and other bodily fluids—were transferred easily from person to person, clothing to clothing, as easily and innocently as a guest using a bathroom before a resident of the house did. As a scientist, he needed to know the "mechanism of transfer" to provide a complete analysis. Even in this science, he said, it could be easy to make something out of nothing.

There were other disclosures in *The New Yorker* that some feared would do nothing but cause more damage inside the renewed investigation. Hunter was quoted as calling the case as it stood then "unfilable"—meaning he did not see a case he could prove beyond a reasonable doubt to a jury. He said essentially that the police had developed tunnel vision early on and had refused to investigate leads that led away from the Ramseys. At the beginning, he said, the police were sure they had a "slam-dunk" case against the parents. "The cops became so convinced that the Ramseys did it that they've never been able to look at the evidence objectively," the magazine quoted Hunter as saying.

His first assistant, Bill Wise, also told *The New Yorker* that his earlier optimism of perhaps an eighty-five percent chance of making a case against the Ramseys had tumbled: "I'm not at a forty, but I'm down in the sixties," he said now. Hunter added, "The public may be seeing the Ramseys more as prime suspects than we are. I've never before seen anything like the battery upon these people who, wealthy or not, are not receiving the presumption of innocence. And I am troubled by that."

Hunter also was disturbed by publicized questions about his direction and performance in the Ramsey case. "In all my political life, these kinds of allegations have never been raised before. There is a shadow hanging over me. People are taking shots at what I think may be one of the best, if not the best, effort at the very difficult goal of getting as close to justice as you can."

In mid-January, the word came down on Beckner's formal request for new interviews with the Ramseys. The commander had indeed been too optimistic; there would be no interviews. Beckner said the Ramseys again had loaded the issue with conditions that were too burdensome for the police, including the demand to review all of the evidence before answering only

written questions. The police would have to show
their "good faith" by meeting the conditions. "I expected the Ramseys to agree to another interview because I believed their public and private statements
about their desire to do whatever was necessary to
help resolve the case," Beckner said.

He later revealed that the Ramseys had offered to
meet privately with him in Atlanta—an offer apparently made without their attorneys' knowledge. Beckner told the *News* that he had to refuse the offer,
however, because the Ramseys wanted to limit the
scope of his questions too severely. He stressed that
the door to the police department remained open any-
time the Ramseys wanted to reconsider.

The question of an interview with young Burke also
was unanswered. But in February the Ramseys disclosed that they had added another lawyer to their
team; this one, in Atlanta, would represent Burke in the
discussions with police about interviewing their son.
Two weeks later, the *Denver Post* reported that the conditions set by police on such an interview were among
the impediments. They wanted the interview at a neutral site, conducted by a detective, and videotaped. But
a fourth condition was said to be the most difficult:
John and Patsy could not be told the contents of the interview with their son. Experts consulted by the *Post*
said that proviso would be almost impossible to en-
force. In late February, Burke's attorney in Atlanta said
the sides had been ninety-five percent in agreement on
terms, but negotiations failed because the conditions
were leaked to the *Post*; there would be no interview
with Burke, the lawyer now said. He blamed the cops,
and said the leak proved that they were not really interested in an interview, just in using the boy as a weapon

in their publicity war against his parents. Beckner denied that the police were the source of the leak.

The Ramseys had decided to cooperate, however, with a request on a different topic. In late January they turned over the clothes they had been wearing Christmas night. Sources told the *Post* that the Ramseys submitted two shirts, a pair of pants, and a sweater. The police obviously wanted to check those articles for trace evidence such as hair, fibers, blood, and other bodily fluids, as well as to compare those fabrics to fibers that had been found on JonBenet's body or other parts of the crime scene.

While the conflict raged between the Ramseys and the authorities, Chuck Green weighed in again with a provocative observation about John and Patsy, and their decisions about cooperating with the police.

"Yes, they have the legal right to remain silent. But they also have a moral obligation to do all they can to help find the monster who killed their daughter. They have chosen to place legality above morality, while complaining that the public just doesn't understand. Yet all the lawyers in the world, and all the public-relations experts on the planet, cannot change the perception that the Ramseys are hiding something. . . .

"Not until the whole truth is known can JonBenet begin to rest in peace."

February became the month for Ramsey–related lawsuits, and one of them was a shocker. Linda Arndt filed a notice of intent to sue her chief and city for "outrageous conduct," alleging that Koby had defamed her by not correcting inaccurate and damaging media reports about her performance as the first detective at the house. She sought $150,000 for emotional distress, a sullied reputation, violation of her right to free speech, and a "nearly intolerable work environment." Her attorney said Koby's gag order on officers kept Arndt from defending herself against what she said were false charges that she had disturbed evidence by covering JonBenet's body with a sheet, that she failed to seize as evidence a flashlight and hammer, that she refused to allow the FBI into the house, that she later gave the Ramsey team a photocopy of the ransom note, and that she had taken a medical leave because of exhaustion and guilt over her handling of the case. Her attorney said Koby's silence had helped make Arndt a "scapegoat," but a city attorney argued that the chief and police department had a right to impose a gag order on its officers during the active investigation of a crime.

Two other suits were remarkable in their own ways. A photographer in Boulder, Stephen Miles, sued John Ramsey and the *National Enquirer* for libel and slander, claiming that John and the tabloid had falsely implicated Miles in JonBenet's death. The suit said the October 21 and November 11 issues of the *Enquirer* quoted sources as saying John had told police that he believed Miles, who lives about six blocks from the Ramseys' house, could be a suspect. (Miles was not to be confused with a man who moved from the neighborhood and was being sought for questioning by Lou Smit.) In March, lawyers for John and the *Enquirer* filed a motion asking that Miles's suit be removed from state court to the federal court in Denver because it was a case involving residents of different states and sought damages above $75,000.

The other suit, by a man in Louisiana, named several of the national tabloid television shows and some local

TV stations, claiming they had falsely linked him to the JonBenet case after he was arrested on charges of showing pornographic videos to two teenagers. The man's work with some beauty pageants in that state had led the TV shows to ask people who knew him about any potential link to JonBenet, and the man charged that such questions were unfounded and improper.

The famous house in Boulder also returned to the news in February when a group of Ramsey friends announced they had bought it for $650,000 from a relocation company that had purchased it from the Ramseys after they left town. Mike Bynum told the *Post* that the "investor group" hoped to sell the house for more, and donate the profit to the JonBenet Ramsey Children's Foundation, the organization set up by the family to administer the $100,000 reward fund. The price paid the Ramseys by the relocation company was not disclosed, but Hal Haddon said it was less than they thought it was worth. "John and Patsy took a bath on it financially," he said.

The end of the month focused sharply on the evidence in the case, and some new leads came to light. The *Rocky Mountain News* disclosed that family friends were being asked to provide their palm prints to police, leading to new reports that such a print had been found on the ransom note. The *News* reported later that police had lost some evidence, including notes of two interviews the first day and some palm prints provided by friends. Commander Beckner was being forced to retrace some of the investigative steps to repair damage done before he took over, the paper said.

Despite those disclosures, the cops generated some good press in February. Koby demonstrated his confidence in the man now leading the JonBenet investiga-

tion by promoting Beckner to chief of the detective
division. But more important, Dr. Henry Lee spent
about five hours meeting with officers and prosecutors
at the Denver airport on February 13. Lee said he had
gone into that session estimating the chances of solving the case at a lowly two in ten. But after talking
to the cops in this fourth meeting—his first with
Beckner—Lee dramatically upped his assessment to
fifty-fifty. He called the case "extremely difficult" and
said solving it would require "a little luck," but he was
impressed with the tremendous amount of work performed so far. He would take some documents and
evidence back to Connecticut for more analysis.

And Lee offered some defense of the cops' approach
to the case: "I don't think the police have tunnel vision
and are just looking at one person. I think they are
open-minded. . . . Everybody is a suspect."

Beckner announced that Lee had given the police
some "very helpful" suggestions, and that had increased the number of points on their investigative
punch list to eighty-four. Forty-five were complete,
and ninety percent of the others were in progress.

Alex Hunter made his own news after the session
with Lee. Hunter said he was disappointed that the
Ramseys had not been more cooperative in the investigation's search for the truth. That amounted to Hunter's
first plea for more help from the Ramseys. But Haddon
rejected that as another "public-relations attempt to
smear the Ramseys." They had provided all of the information requested from them, but would continue to
refuse to cooperate with the police because they were
"hopelessly biased," Haddon told the newspapers.

His associate on the Ramsey team, Patrick Furman,
went even further, turning the situation around on

Hunter and using his own words against him by quoting his comment to *The New Yorker*: "The cops became so convinced that the Ramseys did it that they've never been able to look at the evidence objectively." How could it be surprising that the Ramseys would refuse to cooperate with the police when the prosecutor had perceived that mindset? Furman asked.

Chuck Green added an intriguing detail to Lee's reappearance by quoting sources as saying police had consulted him about the duct tape John Ramsey said he pulled from his daughter's mouth. Green said the police had earlier tested the tape for fingerprints and manufacturing information, but had just recently decided to test it for DNA evidence. After all the other testing and handling by investigators, Green suggested, it might be too late to look for DNA now. He wondered whether DNA would prove that the tape had ever really been on JonBenet's mouth in the hours after she died—hours he said could be as few as six and as many as sixteen. He noted that Coroner Meyer's autopsy report had not mentioned any discovery of tape residue around JonBenet's mouth or damage to that tender skin from ripping off that famously sticky tape. Despite all of those questions, Green reported a week later that DNA had been found on the tape, and he said that tended to support John's account.

Green also concluded that it was becoming increasingly likely that Hunter would impanel a grand jury to investigate the case, particularly in light of the Ramseys' refusal to grant additional interviews with them and their son. With its power to compel testimony, he said, the grand jury could be the last hope for solving the killing of JonBenet.

* * *

Henry Lee had made his visit to Denver on his way home from the national conference of the American Academy of Forensic Sciences in San Francisco—an event also attended by Cyril Wecht. The JonBenet Ramsey case was the talk of the conference, and that inspired more national coverage in a special episode of *America's Most Wanted* on the Fox Network on February 21. The show featured a compelling exchange of analysis and information among four experts seated in the now empty conference hall in San Francisco. Cyril Wecht was joined for the session by retired FBI profiler Robert Ressler, defense attorney David Kaplan, and Carol McKinley, the radio reporter whose coverage of the case had propelled her to a new job for the Fox News Channel in Denver.

McKinley provided a series of intriguing new details. She said the unmatched DNA in recent reports was scraped from under JonBenet's fingernails, but she disclosed that the samples were cracked and hardened; that meant it was old—not fresh skin scraped by her nails as she fought for her life that night. It therefore had little value to the investigation, the experts agreed; Wecht added that he had heard from very reliable sources that no DNA evidence was currently being examined by the authorities.

But McKinley said a new line of inquiry by police that could prove valuable focused on the seemingly unimportant fact of JonBenet's last snack—the bits of pineapple found in her stomach. McKinley had learned that none of the Christmas parties attended by the Ramseys that day had served pineapple. The police now wondered if, contrary to the Ramseys' account of their arrival at home that night, JonBenet had been awake and had eaten pineapple before going to bed. If so, why had the Ramseys said they had put a sleeping JonBenet to bed as soon as they arrived at home?

McKinley also said that the ransom note had been written left-handed, and that it took about thirty-five minutes for a right-handed person to print out that text—and that did not allow for the time needed to compose the carefully worded epistle. The police also were compiling a profile of Patsy, McKinley said, and they were finding her to be a strong and caring but controlling woman. She was "not some withering magnolia," McKinley said.

Ressler offered his profile of the writer: college-educated, articulate, bright—and female. He said the note was one of the many contradictions in the criminal patterns exhibited at that house. A criminal usually shows consistent patterns of behavior, but a staged crime scene might offer the kind of discrepancies that existed in the dynamics in this house.

McKinley also said that the Ramseys' recently surrendered clothing was being checked to see if it could account for the dark blue fibers found on their daughter's vaginal area. The fibers had been left behind, the police believed, when JonBenet's body was wiped off following the sexual assault.

John Walsh, the intense host of *America's Most Wanted*, closed the episode with a personal note. As the parent of a murdered child, he knew too well what the Ramseys were enduring now. But he also knew that, no matter how difficult for them, they had to co-operate with the police—and the police had to cooperate with the district attorney.

"That is the way to get justice, so little JonBenet can rest in peace," he said in the sad voice of experience.

* * *

On March 12, 1998, almost fifteen months after Jon-
Benet's death, the police confirmed what many others
had feared—that their investigation had not produced
enough evidence to prove a charge against anyone beyond a reasonable doubt in a trial. Chief Tom Koby and
Commander Mark Beckner met for ninety minutes with
prosecutors Alex Hunter and Peter Hofstrom to ask officially for the district attorney's office to convene a grand
jury to investigate the case. Koby admitted to the *Rocky
Mountain News*, "We are not comfortable at this time
that we have a case that has a high enough percentage of
being a successful prosecution for us to file charges. We
feel a grand jury at this point will help the investigation." Beckner called turning to the grand jury the next
logical step, a move the police believed would advance
the investigation. And for those awaiting some promise
of justice for JonBenet, that development could open a
new chapter sparked by drama and tension and more
fascinating legal strategies.

When asked about suspects at that late date, Beckner
returned to an earlier theme and said only, "The umbrella has gotten smaller." The number of to-do items on
the cops' list had grown to ninety, he said, and sixty-four
were complete. Koby said the volumes of reports had
expanded to more than twenty-five thousand pages,
and hundreds of pieces of evidence had been collected.

Hunter acknowledged that he had been giving serious consideration for some time to taking the case to a
grand jury. But he called that a difficult decision about
a complex and expensive effort, and he did not expect
to make a decision for months. By late March, however, he was seeking advice from grand-jury experts
around the area, and the county courts were beginning to make arrangements to handle a media crush

when the next grand jury was impaneled in late April to begin an eighteen-month term.

Chuck Green told *Denver Post* readers that there was no doubt that Hunter would go to a grand jury, and that investigators had no choice but to try to compel John and Patsy Ramsey to appear. They could claim the Fifth Amendment right against self-incrimination, Green noted, and that would push Hunter into what the columnist called "the ultimate dilemma": which Ramsey would be given immunity from prosecution to provide testimony against the other? Green explained that a prosecutor can bestow immunity, stripping a witness of the right to remain silent because he or she is no longer a target of the investigation. An immunized witness who refuses to testify then can be jailed for six months for contempt of the grand jury—a powerful weapon. (As the potential for such a drama developed in Boulder, the Ramseys had only to look southeast to see what could happen. After refusing to testify against President Bill Clinton before the Whitewater grand jury under a grant of immunity, Susan McDougal remained in jail in Arkansas in a standoff with special prosecutor Kenneth Starr.)

But Green said uncooperative parents in the Ramsey case might find six months in jail for contempt "an acceptable price to pay for continued silence."

Cyril Wecht studied the alternatives for the Ramseys, and predicted disaster for them if they took refuge behind the Fifth. Although grand jurors would not be officially informed that the Ramseys had refused to testify, the parents' absence before the panel investigating their daughter's death would be painfully obvious. Surely that would have an impact on the grand jurors and their deliberations. How could jurors eager to hear from these grieving parents deal with their conspicuous absence? Guiding the case through the grand jury without the Ramseys would have to affect the prosecutors as well, and the bombastic news reports about the Ramseys' decision would fall hard on an already suspicious public. Wecht wondered how a grand jury could find itself with any alternative but to indict. Everyone had the right not to incriminate themselves. But in the real world of the JonBenet Ramsey case—and before a group of average citizens—was silence perhaps the most damning evidence?

One law professor offered a different analysis, however, suggesting that a grand jury would find no lighted path to justice in this case no matter what happened there; convening the panel would not solve the crime or even advance the investigation. And if the Ramseys refused to testify, that would shut down the case flatly, without a prosecution.

But Beckner saw it differently and, for the newspapers, he gladly listed the advantages that a grand jury investigation had over basic police work. First, the grand jury had the authority to compel sworn testimony from reluctant witnesses through subpoenas and threats of jail for contempt. Second, subpoenas also could be issued for physical evidence or documents that the police had not been able to acquire. And third, the grand jury could perform a final review of the case and decide independently whether to issue an indictment.

Alex Hunter had rarely used grand juries during his twenty-six years in office, but they are a common tool for prosecutors across the country. In Colorado, grand juries are made up of twelve jurors and four alternates who, as is standard everywhere, meet in absolute, sacred secrecy. Anyone violating the veil of secrecy is subject to harsh penalties. A witness may be accompanied by a lawyer for advice, but the lawyer cannot participate or even object to questions from the prosecutor or grand jurors. After the evidence is in, votes by at least nine of the twelve jurors are needed to return an indictment. The standard for evidence sufficient to indict is "probable cause," requiring only that the jurors find it more likely than not that the defendant committed the crime. That is far less than the burden that must be met for a conviction in court—proof beyond a reasonable doubt.

In the Ramsey case, many sources speculated that Hunter was concerned that a panel of average citizens would be eager to indict on charges that he would find difficult to prove beyond a reasonable doubt in court—a rare situation known to terrified prosecutors as a "runaway grand jury." No prosecutor—especially the one responsible for finding justice for JonBenet—would want to find himself afflicted with the O.J. Simpson syndrome—losing a high-profile case many Americans thought he should have won.

The Ramseys remained silent on the question of a grand jury investigation for several days, finally speaking through a letter signed by their four lead attorneys—Hal Haddon, Bryan Morgan, Patrick Burke, and Patrick Furman. Without disclosing whether the Ramseys would agree to testify, the attorneys said they welcomed the investigation now that it had been turned over to "objective and competent professionals," and as long as the conduct of the police would be subject to review by the grand jury as well. The letter renewed charges of police leaks to the media as part of a campaign of "outright smears of the Ramseys." The letter called that "serious misconduct" by "a police department bent on scapegoating" the Ramseys.

There were more intriguing questions associated with a grand jury investigation. Would John and Patsy be able to invoke "spousal privilege," the protection against a husband and wife testifying against each other? Some sources said the spousal protection could be canceled by a judge in a case that involved a felony or, in a first-degree murder, if the victim was younger than twelve and the killer was a person in a position of trust.

Could eleven-year-old Burke be compelled to testify? Experts told the *Post* that a witness older than ten could be subpoenaed as an adult, although such a child surely would be accompanied by a lawyer and guardian.

Just what would the Ramseys do if process servers arrived at their Georgia home with subpoenas for John, Patsy, and Burke? Would that force a protracted battle testing Colorado's power to drag the family back to Boulder?

As the second spring arrived in the Rockies since JonBenet's death, Commander Beckner still was warning that a decision on the grand jury could be months away. And he added that, grand jury or no, there were no "magic bullets" that would offer a quick solution to this case.

Reports about a critical piece of evidence also sparked new interest in March. Newpapers and TV stations reported that police had bought the entire stock of white Stansport Nylon Utility Cord found at the Boulder Army Store, and had sent samples to the CBI lab for comparison to the cord used in the garrote around JonBenet's neck and the loop around her wrist.

Reports said the police were almost certain the cord from the store would match what was used in the grisly crime. That was not a surprise to Boulder journalist Frank Coffman. He had learned months earlier that the army surplus store just a block from John Ramsey's office at Access Graphics sold the cord so similar to what had appeared in the photographs published by the *Globe*. In fact, the *Globe* had printed a story about the cord and the store as early as July 1997.

At the end of March, Chuck Green reported in the *Post* that the Ramseys had cooperated with a British TV crew to produce a documentary to be broadcast in the summer. Green said a journalism professor at the University of Colorado who had befriended Patsy had arranged the interview—a major coup in the hotly competitive TV world. According to Green's sources, the Ramseys sat with two reporters from *Newsweek* magazine to tape hours of interviews to be used in the documentary. Green said he was told that there were no restrictions on the questions, and that the Ramseys covered topics from the night of their daughter's death to their views on the police investigation. Green also offered his spin on this latest media development, noting that the broadcast was planned during the same period when a grand jury would be hearing evidence.

On April 1, 1998, the end of Tom Koby's tumultuous seven-year reign as police chief appeared on the horizon—somewhat sooner than had been expected. Acting city manager Dave Rhodes announced that he had asked Koby to step aside early—probably in May—so that his successor could be named long before Koby's official retirement date arrived at the end of the year. He would finish his days working on selected projects in a "transitional post" inside the city manager's office, still drawing his $100,000 salary.

Rhodes said Koby's replacement would be named from within the department, ending twenty years of chiefs brought in from the outside. Rhodes said the city wanted to develop its future leaders internally, adding that the new official would be known as the director of police services, not as chief. Among the officers known to be interested in the job was Commander Mark Beckner.

Mayor Bob Greenlee said he had been encouraging Rhodes for several weeks to move Koby out of the chief's job early. Rhodes said he had waited until Koby officially requested a grand jury investigation, relieving him of some of the responsibility for making the final call on the Ramsey case that had kept him at the heart of an amazing firestorm. Rhodes acknowledged that Koby's announced retirement had left the department without much confidence in who was steering its course, and said choosing a successor soon would restore some stability.

Koby said the change had not been his idea, but he respected the decision. He said he still had no plans after leaving office—except to take some needed time off.

CHAPTER 34

As Dr. Cyril Wecht evaluated the evidence before him in the JonBenet Ramsey case, he could find no absolute and unequivocal answer to what had happened in that house that night. If the police had evidence that clearly solved the mystery, they had hidden it remarkably well despite an atmosphere of news leaks, interdepartmental conflicts, and intriguing machinations that surpassed by far anything in Wecht's considerable experience. There were, of course, reports that the cops had managed to hold back at least four pieces of evidence that could solve the case. Wecht hoped that was true, for the sake of JonBenet's memory and the public's confidence in its justice system.

But what could Wecht conclude from what he had seen in the public record?

First, JonBenet's death was almost certainly an inside job. Wecht's own analysis was buttressed by experts—such as former FBI profilers Gregg McCrary and Robert Ressler—with the experience and qualifications to reach logical, scientific conclusions based on the materials at hand and reasonable inferences that could be drawn from them.

The reasons why Wecht could disprove the intruder theory were almost too obvious: He could find no valid evidence to support the suggestion that a sexually motivated, homicidal kidnapper had slipped into the darkened Ramsey mansion on Christmas night, carried out this long list of incredible activities undiscovered, and then disappeared into the night once again. Perhaps the lack of footprints in the snow around the entrances to the house suggested an alternative, rooftop point of entry. Wecht found the very idea almost laughable, were it not for the tragic circumstances that spawned it.

Wecht could not even find a motive for an intruder that would fit all the facts. He wasn't a sexual predator or a pedophile, because they don't leave phony kidnapping notes. He wasn't a kidnapper, because they don't sexually torture and kill their victims and leave their bodies behind. He wasn't someone with a grudge against the Ramseys, because he tried to hide the killing that would have been the message of revenge. He wasn't a member of some ridiculous band of foreign terrorists, because he had no motive, he spoke perfect English, he asked for only $118,000 from a multimillionaire, and he was never heard from again. He wasn't an intruder in the house at all, because he spent too much time doing too many things that he was too comfortable doing; he wasn't the least bit worried that he was going to awaken protective parents who would charge in and rescue their daughter.

Still, Wecht looked at the evidence that the Ramseys argued would support their theory; he found it wanting. The report of unmatched DNA evidence was unconvincing—so far. Even if it was true, there were too many possible explanations on acceptable scientific grounds. Wecht also was struck by the facts that neither of his colleagues who had been introduced with such fanfare as members of Hunter's team—Barry Scheck and Henry Lee—had even been consulted about this DNA evidence. Were they really just window dressing? Just political cover for the prosecutor?

What about the unidentified pubic hair from Jon-Benet's bedding? That proved little to Wecht because there were too many innocent explanations for how that could have gotten there, even as simple as some-one changing clothes in JonBenet's bedroom during a party or using her bathroom. Although hardly the de-finitive word, the *Globe* had quoted an unnamed source as saying the hair belonged to John's surviving daughter, Melinda.

The shoe prints? Possibly useful evidence, but Wecht expected them to be explained eventually as the footwear of patrol officers, detectives, or others with legitimate reasons to be in the Ramsey house.

Pry marks on an unlocked door? Even the locksmith said they were insufficient to be evidence of forced en-try. And besides, there was no way to know who put the marks there or when.

A stun gun? This struck Wecht as perhaps the most far-fetched, but intriguing, report. Only an exhuma-tion and new tests offered any chance of an answer, but that still might fail because of changes in tissue more than a year after death. Even a microscopic ex-amination could prove fruitless. And even if the use of a stun gun was proven, how could the person behind the gun be identified?

The suitcase under the broken basement window? An interesting combination that could suggest an en-trance point and an assisted exit. John Ramsey claimed to have broken the window himself. Who knows who put the suitcase there? According to reports, there were no footprints in the snow around the heavy iron grate that covered that recessed window well on the outside. Wecht also had no indication that police had found fibers, threads, fingerprints, or any other evidence of a person wiggling through that fairly small opening. To him it remained an unlikely point of entry, but a convenient ruse.

Besides, he wondered, even if this phantom intruder had somehow gained entrance into the house, how did he manage to leave so little evidence that he was there? One unidentified DNA sample and some footprints in a house that had been filled with cops and friends and observers for the better part of a day—only three days after a party for a hundred guests—didn't carry the argument for Wecht. He found all of that unpersuasive as support for the intruder theory.

And there was another factor. John Ramsey had hired an expensive team of lawyers and investigators and profilers and handwriting analysts. If they had come up with something solid—a credible suspect— wouldn't they have announced that with a great flourish? Where had the Ramseys' investigation really led?

On the other side, Wecht would point out that the major pieces of evidence had come from within the house. The ransom note and the legal pad. The broken handle of Patsy's paint brush twisted into the garrote. An intruder would have wasted untold time searching the house for those materials used in the crime, but someone who lived there would find them readily available.

Next, Wecht found the ransom note almost insultingly phony. It worked on not a single level of reasonable analysis. After all, the girl had not been kidnapped; that fact alone made the note—as so many loved to call it—bogus. As Ressler told the *Denver Post*, "When there's a note at the Ramsey residence, there shouldn't have been a dead child. When there's a dead child at the residence, you shouldn't find a note. It's totally stupid."

From everything anyone had learned, JonBenet already lay dead when the note was carefully composed and hand-printed at length on the Ramseys' own legal pad, after the false start on a separate page. Getting past the idiocy of a kidnapper who forgot to bring a ransom note or at least the paper on which to write one, penning the note was a time-consuming act marked by great comfort and confidence. No criminal—not even members of an audacious, fanatical, suicidal "small foreign faction"—would gamble that long on being caught. And no one who had investigated a genuine kidnapping had ever seen a ransom note so lengthy or so revealing about the identity of the supposed kidnappers. It simply made no sense—except perhaps to panic-stricken people who found themselves in a crisis they had never expected and weren't prepared to handle.

The text of the note was ludicrous on its face. Here, Wecht agreed with the Ramseys' analysis that it reflected nothing so much as popular crime movies. As McCrary and Ressler said, the note was written by someone who was not a criminal but was trying to sound like one. It was an amateurish effort by someone who McCrary said was well educated and comfortable giving orders, but woefully ignorant about the mind and motive and method of a true kidnapper.

The use of John Ramsey's yearly bonus as the

ransom figure also was an effort that had boomeranged. It appeared to be designed to channel suspicion toward a fictional disgruntled employee of John's company, someone with a grudge so deep and vicious that it would justify the killing of John's daughter. But the transparency of the note as a whole simply made it clear that it had really come from someone who just knew much too much about the Ramseys, and not enough about kidnapping.

The state's experts reportedly had eliminated John Ramsey as the writer of the note, but the results on Patsy were inconclusive. She had not been ruled out or in; the scientific evidence here remained a puzzle.

McCrary and the others were absolutely sure the crime scene had been "staged," the term they used to describe a criminal's attempt to rearrange reality into something he hopes will deflect suspicion away from him. The note was most certainly part of that. There was some disagreement among public analysts about the garrote and the cord around JonBenet's wrist; some thought those were part of the staging as well. The autopsy report pointed strongly away from that proposition, Wecht insisted.

Next in his analysis was the crime itself. This hybrid of sexual predator and kidnapper was unprecedented, and incredibly unlikely. Those two very divergent sets of characteristics just don't intersect in the same person. People who kidnap for ransom or for revenge don't exhibit such blatantly sexual conduct toward the victims. Sexual abusers care only for the sex; they have no interest in kidnapping for profit or staging a phony kidnapping. Wecht had never encountered a crime with that mix of characteristics in his decades of investigating thousands of homicides.

He was left with what his experienced analysis could find in the cold facts of JonBenet's physical death, and what he could interpret about the conduct of those who caused that death.

JonBenet had died during a sex game that went fatally wrong, Wecht was sure. As the garrote was tightened— intentionally short of complete strangulation—the noose pinched the vagus nerve and shut down her cardio-pulmonary system. As he had explained many times, the medical evidence told him that her killer had not intended to end her life, or even to harm her seriously. The perverse sexual pleasure of her abuser— apparently fueled by this sick torture of the victim—had been the only goal. All of the medical evidence presented by JonBenet's body proved that.

Her death was accidental—probably a voluntary manslaughter under most criminal codes. Wecht's experience as a prosecutor suggested that an aggressive district attorney might argue for a murder charge, claiming that anyone who tied a sophisticated garrote around a six-year-old girl's neck and tightened it while sexually molesting her had indeed intended her harm, and should have known death was a great probability. The medical evidence would support an allegation that the skull fracture certainly had been an intentional act inflicted on a living child. Perhaps a jury should sort out whether JonBenet had died from the garrote or the blow, and whether that made the crime voluntary manslaughter or first-degree murder.

As Wecht thought about what had happened after the garrote left a limp and dying JonBenet, he was faced with a crime that chilled his blood—a cover-up so violent that it was hard to imagine, even for those in the business of sorting through the aftermath of such acts. In a panic, amid a frantic search for a way to explain this child's unforeseen death, there had been a cold, cruel decision to hide the truth under the violence of a staged kidnapping and murder. To turn fatal sex abuse into a failed abduction and a grisly killing, someone had delivered a vicious blow to the little head under those tinted blond locks.

But who could do such a thing? There was no indisputable evidence—no semen or anything else—that pointed specifically at one person, or even a gender.

A man? Statistics on sex abuse would make a man the more likely offender. And the violence of that final act could be argued to be too severe for a woman. Could a sex abuser invoke such violence to cover up his crimes? Marilyn Van Derbur Atler—who had suffered sexually at the hands of her father—was convinced he would have inflicted a violent death on her to save himself.

That all pointed toward the only adult male in the house—John Ramsey.

What about a woman? Wecht had encountered cases of sexual abuse of girls by women. And he had seen terrible violence committed by women. Could a woman with emotional problems and other brewing crises in her life find the resolve for such acts? Certainly.

That all could point at Patsy Ramsey.

Another child? Wecht could not eliminate that possibility entirely. But the police specifically referred to Burke only as a witness—apparently excluding him from the "umbrella of suspicion" they said still covered his parents. The police wanted to interview him, but they did not seem to be approaching that with the intensity of their efforts to talk to John and Patsy. The involvement of another child in this tragedy would not shock Wecht, but it was improbable and did not fit with his analysis.

One of Wecht's favorite quotations was from Sherlock Holmes, and it was perfect for analyzing the suspect list in the Ramsey case: "Once you eliminate the impossible, what remains—no matter how improbable—must be the answer."

After Wecht eliminated the pedophile, the sexual predator, the revenge-driven kidnapper, and the small foreign faction, he was left with the two adults in that house on that night—John and Patsy.

And a long list of questions he could not answer with certainty.

Had JonBenet's father been the molester who accidentally twisted the switch that turned off her life? Had he resorted to the violent act, the desperate ransom note, and the continuing cover-up? Had JonBenet's mother known about any of that? Had she been cowed into cooperating after the fatal damage was done? Had she agreed to preserve what was left of their wealthy life by doing what had to be done?

Or had JonBenet's mother been the abuser and the accidental killer? Had a life battered by fading glory of past beauty titles and a cataclysmic battle with cancer set her on some inexplicable course? Had she offered her daughter to her sexually frustrated husband as a surrogate, or perhaps looked the other way until the supposedly secret abuse of her daughter by her husband finally sent her into a rage that somehow claimed her daughter's life? Had chronic bed wetting become an issue that pushed a troubled mother beyond control?

The questions and scenarios were almost endless.

Wecht could not determine precisely which had led to the death of JonBenet Ramsey, but he could cite circumstantial evidence supporting the view that both of her parents were involved in a cover-up of the truth. And Wecht knew that many arrests and prosecutions were based solely on circumstantial evidence.

Wecht believed the evidence appeared to support charges against both John and Patsy—one perhaps the accomplice to the other. Legally, ethically, and morally—Wecht could find no separation between the responsibilities of those who had led JonBenet to her grave and subsequently led the rest of the country to this unsolved mystery. He believed an aggressive prosecutor could establish probable cause for criminal charges and a prima facie case against John and Patsy worthy of presentation to a jury.

Once charged, if one of them wanted to talk about the actions of the other, so much the better for the authorities. Outside of romance novels and movies, Wecht had never heard of two people walking hand in hand to the gallows if one of them had something to offer in exchange for leniency. Lover to lover, husband and wife, best friends, whatever the relationship: when the executioner, or even a prison cell, awaits, loyalty deteriorates rapidly.

After all, why had John and Patsy hired separate lawyers from the very beginning if not to assure that their individual interests would be protected? One lawyer would be unable to represent two clients whose interests diverged, or perhaps conflicted directly with each other. Wecht had no problem with people of means hiring as many lawyers as they wanted to. But he also knew how to draw an inference from the evidence—in this case, separate attorneys for a husband and wife whose daughter had been murdered in their home. If they were both innocent and knew nothing about the crime, why would they need separate counsel?

With all of those considerations, why had no criminal charges been filed?

First, the investigation had been horribly botched by the police in the first hours and days. The crime scene was not cleared, secured, and thoroughly searched, and valuable evidence probably was lost. There were no prompt separate and intense interviews of the Ramseys as possible suspects, losing the chance to lock them into detailed and unrehearsed statements. Boulder police did not request or take advantage of help from more sophisticated police departments, leaving inexperienced detectives to flounder amid one of the most difficult cases anyone had ever seen.

Second, wealthy and intelligent people had taken very good advice about getting legal representation, and then letting the attorneys make all the decisions after that. The result was an impenetrable wall that shielded the Ramseys. This case would have been entirely different if the victim was a girl from a poor or even middle-class home.

Third, a district attorney's office that might have been overwhelmed by the opposition from familiar, agile defense attorneys seemed indecisive. Wecht disagreed with Alex Hunter's contention that he could only file a case that he knew he could win. In Wecht's experience, that was not the standard for criminal prosecution. If it was, defense attorneys would never win, plea bargains would be obsolete, charges would never be dismissed before trial, and appellate courts would be superfluous. Justice, Wecht insisted, was not a scientific pursuit.

There were troubling aspects to the relationship between Hunter's office and the Ramsey legal team, such as reports of prosecutors sharing police reports and investigative information with the Haddon group, and Hunter and a Ramsey lawyer linked by a limited partnership in a building. Hunter had even acknowledged that the legal profession in Boulder was characterized by a certain familiarity among the participants. Wecht knew that was true in most small communities. The courts bred a certain incestuous intimacy. Judges and lawyers lunched together; defense attorneys and prosecutors drank together. But in Boulder, those ordinary relationships seemed to add to public confusion about progress on the case.

Wecht also had learned that the conflict between the police and prosecutors ran deep, and there seemed to be little chance of bridging the gap.

Just what was Alex Hunter waiting for? Wecht could find little chance that new scientific evidence would be found to break open the case. After more than a year, what was left to be learned? How cold was the trail? How many more interviews could be conducted? How much more evidence could be analyzed by the crime labs?

Didn't it boil down to making a move and giving this case the best shot versus turning and walking away? To Wecht, the latter was unacceptable, and he believed most of the people in Boulder and the rest of the country agreed.

Given all the circumstances, Wecht found it appropriate to call on Colorado attorney general Gale Norton or governor Roy Romer to appoint a special prosecutor—one totally independent, certainly from outside the Denver-Boulder area and perhaps even from outside the state—to review the massive case and come to a final determination free from political baggage and influence. If the state's officials won't act—and Romer already had rejected a similar call from Fleet White—perhaps the U.S. Department of Justice could find grounds for an investigation and a special prosecutor.

If the officials in Boulder are unable to determine who killed JonBenet Ramsey, then Cyril Wecht and so many others believe that everyone owes it to the little girl they all feel as if they know—the little blonde they all mourn, the beauty queen with the baby teeth—to do whatever has to be done to answer that solitary, haunting question:

Who killed JonBenet Ramsey?

APPENDIX A
The JonBenet Ramsey Ransom Note

Mr. Ramsey,

Listen carefully! We are a group of individuals that represent a small foreign faction. We ~~do~~ respect your bussiness but not the country that it serves. At this time we have your daughter in our pozession. She is safe and unharmed and if you want her to see 1997, you must follow our instructions to the letter.

You will withdraw $118,000.00 from your account. $100,000 will be in $100 bills and the remaining $18,000 in $20 bills. Make sure that you bring an adequate size attache to the bank. When you get home you will put the money in a brown paper bag. I will call you between 8 and 10 am tomorrow to instruct you on delivery. The delivery will be exhausting so I advise you to be rested. If we monitor you getting the money early, we might call you early to arrange an earlier delivery of the money and hence, a cashier ~~delivery~~ pick-up of your daughter.

Any deviation of my instructions will result in the immediate execution of your daughter. You will also be denied her remains for proper burial. The two gentlemen watching over your daughter do ^we particularly like you so I advise you not to provoke them. Speaking to anyone about your situation, such as Police, F.B.I., etc., will result in your daughter being beheaded. If we catch you talking to a stray dog, she dies. If you alert bank authorities, she dies. If the money is in any way marked or ~~tampered~~ with, she dies. You will be scanned for electronic devices and if any are found, she dies. You can try to deceive us but be warned that we are familiar with law enforcement countermeasures and tactics. You stand a 99% chance of killing your daughter if you try to out smart us. Follow our instructions

and you stand a 100% chance
of getting her back. You and
your family are under constant
scrutiny as well as the authorities.
Don't try to grow a brain
John. You are not the only
fat cat around so don't think
that killing will be difficult.
Don't underestimate us John.
Use that good southern common
sense of yours. It is up to
you now John!

Victory!

S.B.T.C

APPENDIX B

Complete text of the JonBenet Ramsey

Autopsy Report Issued by

John E. Meyer, M.D., Boulder County

Coroner, on August 13, 1997

OFFICE OF THE BOULDER COUNTY CORONER

PRESS RELEASE   August 13, 1997

This press release is in conjunction with the release of the complete JonBenet Ramsey autopsy report.

The remaining portions of the autopsy to be released on August 13th include additional portions of the "external examination" and the "external evidence of injury" sections. Contrary to several media reports over the past few days, the autopsy report on JonBenet Ramsey does not and has never contained information on the estimated time of death. I have not been able to determine the original source of the statement that the report contained the estimated time of death, but it certainly did not come from this office.

The time of an "unwitnessed" death is very difficult to determine with any precision, and at best is an estimate based not only on autopsy findings but also on investigative information.

I consider estimation of time of death to be an interpretive finding rather than a factual statement, and it is not this Office's practice to include this estimate as part of any autopsy report. As has been stated in the past, it would also be inappropriate for me, as a potential expert and material witness, to make interpretive statements prior to testifying in court.

Office of the Boulder County Coroner

AUTOPSY REPORT

NAME:	RAMSEY, JONBENET	AUTOPSY NO:	96A-155
DOB:	08/06/90	DEATH D/T:	12/26/96 @ 1323
AGE:	6Y	AUTOPSY D/T:	12/27/96 @ 0815
SEX:	F	ID NO:	137712
PATH MD:	MEYER	COR/MEDREC#:	1714-96-A
TYPE:	COR		

FINAL DIAGNOSIS:

I. Ligature strangulation
  A. Circumferential ligature with associated ligature furrow of neck
  B. Abrasions and petechial hemorrhages, neck
  C. Petechial hemorrhages, conjunctival surfaces of eyes and skin of face

II. Craniocerebral injuries
  A. Scalp contusion
  B. Linear, comminuted fracture of right side of skull
  C. Linear, pattern of contusions of right cerebral hemisphere
  D. Subarachnoid and subdural hemorrhage
  E. Small contusions, tips of temporal lobes

III. Abrasion of right cheek
IV. Abrasion/contusion, posterior right shoulder
V. Abrasions of left lower back and posterior left lower leg
VI. Abrasion and vascular congestion of vaginal mucosa
VII. Ligature of right wrist

Toxicologic Studies

blood ethanol - none detected
blood drug screen - no drugs detected

CLINICOPATHOLOGIC CORRELATION: Cause of death of this six year old female is asphyxia by strangulation associated with craniocerebral trauma.

The body of this six year old female was first seen by me after I was called to an address identified as 755 - 15th street in Boulder, Colorado, on 12/26/96. I arrived at the scene approximately 8 PM on 12/26 and entered the house where the decedent's body was located at approximately 8:20 PM. I initially viewed the body in the living room of the house. The decedent was laying on her back on the floor; covered by a blanket and a Colorado Avalanche sweatshirt. On removing these two items from the top of the body the decedent was found to be lying on her back with her arms extended up over her head. The head was turned to the right. A brief examination of the body disclosed a ligature around the neck and a ligature around the right wrist. Also noted was a small area of abrasion or contusion below the right ear on the lateral aspect of the right cheek. A prominent dried abrasion was present on the lower left neck. After examining the body, I left the residence at approximately 8:30 PM.

EXTERNAL EXAM:
The decedent is clothed in a long sleeved white knit collarless shirt, the mid anterior chest area of which contains an embroidered silver star decorated with silver sequins. Tied loosely around the right wrist, overlying the sleeve of the

shirt is a white cord. At the knot there is one tail end which measures 5.5 inches in length with a frayed end. The other tail of the knot measures 15.5 inches in length and ends in a double loop knot. This end of the cord is also frayed. There are no defects noted in the shirt but the upper anterior right sleeve contains a dried brown-tan stain measuring 2.5 × 1.5 inches, consistent with mucous from the nose or mouth. There are long white underwear with an elastic waist band containing a red and blue stripe. The long underwear are urine stained anteriorly over the crotch area and anterior legs. No defects are identified. Beneath the long underwear are white panties with printed rose buds and the words "Wednesday" on the elastic waist band. The underwear is urine stained and in the inner aspect of the crotch are several red areas of staining measuring up to 0.5 inch in maximum dimension.

EXTERNAL EVIDENCE OF INJURY: Located just below the right ear at the right angle of the mandible, 1.5 inches below the right external auditory canal is a $3/8 × 1/4$ inch area of rust colored abrasion. In the lateral aspect of the left lower eyelid on the inner conjunctival surface is a 1 mm in maximum dimension petechial hemorrhage. Very fine, less than 1 mm petechial hemorrhages are present on the skin of the upper eyelids bilaterally as well as on the lateral left cheek. On everting the left upper eyelid there are much smaller, less than 1 mm petechial hemorrhages located on the conjunctival surface. Possible petechial hemorrhages are also seen on the conjunctival surfaces of the right upper and lower eyelids, but livor mortis on this side of the face makes definite identification difficult.

Wrapped around the neck with a double knot in the midline of the posterior neck is a length of white cord similar to that described as being tied around the right wrist. This ligature cord is cut on the right side of the neck and removed. A single black ink mark is placed on the left side of the cut and a double black ink mark on the right side of the cut. The posterior knot is left intact. Extending from the knot on the posterior aspect of the neck are two tails of the knot, one measuring 4 inches in length and having a frayed end, and the other measuring 17 inches in length with the end tied in multiple loops around a length of a round tan-brown wooden stick which measures 4.5 inches in length. This wooden stick is irregularly broken at both ends and there are several colors of paint and apparent glistening varnish on the surface. Printed in gold letters on one end of the wooden stick is the word "Korea". The tail end of another word extends from beneath the loops of the cord tied around the stick and is not able to be interpreted. Blonde hair is entwined in the knot on the posterior aspect of the neck as well as in the cord wrapped around the wooden stick. The white cord is flattened and measures approximately $1/4$ inch in width. It appears to be made of a white synthetic material. Also secured around the neck is a gold chain with a single charm in the form of a cross.

A deep ligature furrow encircles the entire neck. The width of the furrow varies from one-eighth of an inch to five/sixteenths of an inch and is horizontal in orientation, with little upward deviation. The skin of the anterior neck above and below the ligature furrow contains areas of petechial hemorrhage and abrasion encompassing an area measuring approximately 3×2 inches. The ligature furrow crosses the anterior midline of the neck just below the laryngeal prominence, approximately at the level of the cricoid cartilage. It is almost completely horizontal with slight upward deviation from the horizontal towards the back of the neck. The midline of the furrow mark on the anterior neck is 8 inches below the top of the head. The midline of the furrow mark on the posterior neck is 6.75 inches below the top of the head.

The area of abrasion and petechial hemorrhage of the skin of the anterior neck includes on the lower left neck, just to the left of the midline, a roughly triangular, parchment-like rust colored abrasion which measures 1.5 inches in length with a maximum width of 0.75 inches. This roughly triangular shaped abrasion is obliquely oriented with the apex superior and lateral. The remainder of the abrasions and petechial hemorrhages of the skin above and below the anterior projection of the ligature furrow are nonpatterned, purple to rust colored, and present in the midline, right, and left areas of the anterior neck. The skin just above the ligature furrow along the right side of the neck contains petechial hemorrhage composed of multiple confluent very small petechial hemorrhages as well as several larger petechial hemorrhages measuring up to one-sixteenth and one-eighth of an inch in maximum dimension. Similar smaller petechial hemorrhages are present on the skin below the ligature furrow on the left lateral aspect of the neck. Located on the right side of the chin is a three-sixteenths by one-eighth of an inch area of superficial abrasion. On the posterior aspect of the right shoulder is a poorly demarcated, very superficial focus of abrasion/contusion which is pale purple in color and measures up to three-quarters by one-half inch in maximum dimension. Several linear aggregates of petechial hemorrhages are present in the anterior left shoulder just above deltopectoral groove. These measure up to one inch in length by one-sixteenth to one-eighth of an inch in width. On the left lateral aspect of the lower back, approximately sixteen and one-quarter inches and seventeen and one-half inches below the level of the top of the head are two dried rust colored to slightly purple abrasions. The more superior of the two measures one-eighth by one-sixteenth of an inch and the more inferior measures three-sixteenths by one-eighth of an inch. There is no surrounding contusion identified. On the posterior aspect of the left lower leg, almost in the midline, approximately 4 inches above the level of the heel are two small scratch-like abrasions which are dried and rust colored. They measure one-sixteenth by less than one-sixteenth of an inch and one-eighth by less than one-sixteenth of an inch respectively.

On the anterior aspect of the perineum, along the edges of closure of the labia majora, is a small amount of dried blood. A similar small amount of dried and semifluid blood is present on the skin of the fourchette and in the vestibule. Inside the vestibule of the vagina and along the distal vaginal wall is reddish hyperemia. This hyperemia is circumferential and perhaps more noticeable on the right side and posteriorly. The hyperemia also appears to extend just inside the vaginal orifice. A 1 cm red-purple area of abrasion is located on the right posterolateral area of the 1 × 1 cm hymenal orifice. The hymen itself is represented by a rim of mucosal tissue extending clockwise between the 2 and 10:00 positions. The area of abrasion is present at approximately the 7:00 position and appears to involve the hymen and distal right lateral vaginal wall and possibly the area anterior to the hymen. On the right labia majora is a very faint area of violent discoloration measuring approximately one inch by three-eighths of an inch. Incision into the underlying subcutaneous tissue discloses no hemorrhage. A minimal amount of semiliquid thin watery red fluid is present in the vaginal vault. No recent or remote anal or other perineal trauma is identified.

REMAINDER OF EXTERNAL EXAMINATION: The unembalmed, well developed and well nourished caucasian female body measures 47 inches in length and weighs an estimated 45 pounds. The scalp is covered by long blonde hair which is fixed in two ponytails, one on top of the head secured by a cloth hair tie and blue elastic band, and one in the lower back of the head secured by a blue elastic band. No scalp trauma is identified. The external auditory canals are patent and free of blood. The eyes are green and the pupils equally dilated. The sclerae are white. The nostrils are both patent and contain a small amount of tan mucous material. The teeth are native and in good repair. The tongue is smooth, pink-tan and granu-

lar. No buccal mucosal trauma is seen. The frenulum is intact.
There is slight drying artifact of the tip of the tongue. On the
right cheek is a pattern of dried saliva and mucous material
which does not appear to be hemorrhagic. The neck contains
no palpable udenopathy or masses and the trachea and larynx are midline. The chest is symmetrical. Breasts are prepubescent. The abdomen is flat and contains no scars. No
palpable organomegaly or masses are identified. The external
genitalia are that of a prepubescent female. No pubic hair is
present. The anus is patent. Examination of the extremities is
unremarkable. On the middle finger of the right hand is a yellow metal band. Around the right wrist is a yellow metal
identification bracelet with the name "JonBenet" on one side
and the date "12/25/96" on the other side. A red ink line
drawing in the form of a heart is located on the palm of the
left hand. The fingernails of both hands are of sufficient length
for clipping. Examination of the back is unremarkable. There
is dorsal 3+ to 4+ livor mortis which is nonblanching. Livor
mortis is also present on the right side of the face. At the time
of the initiation of the autopsy there is mild 1 to 2+ rigor mortis of the elbows and shoulders with more advanced 2 to 3+
rigor mortis of the joints of the lower extremities.

INTERNAL EXAM: The anterior chest musculature is well
developed. No sternal or rib fractures are identified.

Mediastinum: The mediastinal contents are normally distributed. The 21 gm thymus gland has a normal external appearance. The cut sections are finely lobular and pink-tan.
No petechial hemorrhages are seen. The sorta and remainder of the mediastinal structures are unremarkable.

Body Cavities: The right and left thoracic cavities contain approximately 5 cc of straw colored fluid. The pleural surfaces
are smooth and glistening. The pericardial sac contains 3-4 cc
of straw colored fluid and the epicardium and pericardium
are unremarkable. The abdominal contents are normally dis-

tributed and covered by a smooth glistening serosa. No intra-abdominal accumulation of fluid or blood is seen.

Lungs: The 200 gm right lung and 175 gm left lung have a normal lobar configuration. An occasional scattered subpleural petechial hemorrhage is seen on the surface of each lung. The cut sections of the lungs disclose an intact alveolar architecture with a small amount of watery fluid exuding from the cut surfaces with mild pressure. The intrapulmonary bronchi and vasculature are unremarkable. No evidence of consolidation is seen.

Heart: The 100 gm heart has a normal external configuration. There are scattered subepicardial petechial hemorrhages over the anterior surface of the heart. The coronary arteries are normal in their distribution and contain no evidence of atherosclerosis. The tan-pink myocardium is homogeneous and contains no areas of fibrosis or infarction. The endocardium is unremarkable. The valve cusps are thin, delicate and pliable and contain no vegetation or thrombosis. The major vessels enter and leave the heart in the normal fashion. The foramex ovale is closed.

Aorta and Vena Cava: The aorta is patent throughout its course as are its major branches. No atherosclerosis is seen. The vena cava is unremarkable.

Spleen: The 61 gm spleen has a finely wrinkled purple capsule. Cut sections are homogeneous and disclose readily identifiable red and white pulp. No intrinsic abnormalities are identified.

Adrenals: The adrenal glands are of normal size and shape. A golden yellow cortex surmounts a thin brown-tan medullary area. No intrinsic abnormalities are identified.

Kidneys: The 40 gm right kidney and 40 gm left kidney have a normal external appearance. The surfaces are smooth and glistening. Cut sections disclose an intact corticomedullary architecture. The renal papillae are sharply demarcated. The pelvocaliceal system is lined by gray-white mucosa which is unremarkable. Both ureters are patent throughout their course to the bladder.

Liver: The 625 gm liver has a normal external appearance. The capsule is smooth and glistening. Cut sections disclose an intact lobular architecture with no intrinsic abnormalities identified.

Pancreas: The pancreas is of normal size and shape. Cut sections are finely lobular and tan. No intrinsic abnormalities are identified.

Bladder: The bladder is contracted and contains no urine. The bladder mucosa is smooth and tan-gray. No intrinsic abnormalities are seen.

Genitalia: The upper portions of the vaginal vault contain no abnormalities. The prepubescent uterus measures 3 × 1 × 0.8 cm and is unremarkable. The cervical os contains no abnormalities. Both fallopian tubes and ovaries are prepubescent and unremarkable by gross examination.

Gallbladder: The gallbladder contains 2–3 cc of amber bile. No stones are identified and the mucosa is smooth and velvety. The cystic duct, right and left hepatic duct and common bile duct are patent throughout their course to the duodenum.

G.I. Tract: The esophagus is empty. It is lined by gray-white mucosa. The stomach contains a small amount (8–10 cc) of viscous to green to tan colored thick mucous material without particulate matter identified. The gastric mucosa is autolyzed but contains no areas of hemorrhage or ulceration. The proximal portion of the small intestine contains fragmented pieces of yellow to light green-tan apparent vegetable or fruit material which may represent fragments of pineapple. No hemorrhage is identified. The remainder of the small intestine is unremarkable. The large intestine contains soft green fecal material. The appendix is present.

Lymphatic System: Unremarkable.

Musculoskeletal System: Unremarkable.

Skull and Brain: Upon reflection of the scalp there is found to be an extensive area of scalp hemorrhage along the right temporoparietal area extending from the orbital ridge, posteriorly all the way to the occipital area. This encompasses an area measuring approximately 7 × 4 inches. This grossly appears to be fresh hemorrhage with no evidence of organization. At the superior extension of this area of hemorrhage is a linear to comminuted skull fracture which extends from the right occipital to posteroparietal area forward to the right frontal area across the parietal portion of the skull. In the posteroparietal area of this fracture is a roughly rectangular shaped displaced fragment of skull measuring one and three-quarters by one-half inch. The hemorrhage and the fracture extend posteriorly just past the midline of the occipital area of the skull. This fracture measures approximately 8.5 inches in length. On removal of the skull cap there is found to be a thin film of subdural hemorrhage measuring approximately 7–8 cc over the surface of the right cerebral hemisphere and extending to the base of the cerebral hemisphere. The 1450 gm brain has a normal overall architecture. Mild narrowing of the sulci and flattening of the gyri are seen. No inflammation is identified. There is a thin film of subarachnoid hemorrhage overlying the entire right cerebral hemisphere. On the right cerebral hemisphere underlying the previously mentioned linear skull fracture is an extensive linear area of purple contusion extending from the right frontal area, posteriorly along the lateral aspect of the parietal region and into the occipital area. This area of contusion measures 8 inches in length with a width of up to 1.75 inches. At the tip of the right temporal lobe is a one-quarter by one-quarter inch similar appearing purple contusion. Only very minimal contusion is present at the tip of the left temporal lobe. This area of contusion measures only one-half inch in maximum dimension. The cerebral vasculature contains no evidence of atherosclerosis. Multiple coronal sections of the cerebral hemispheres, brain stem and cerebellum disclose no additional abnormalities. The areas of previously described contusion are characterized by purple linear streak-like discolorations of the gray matter perpendicular to the surface of the cerebral cortex. These extend approximately 5 mm into the cerebral cortex. Examination of the base of the brain discloses no additional fractures.

Neck: Dissection of the neck is performed after removal of the thoracoabdominal organs and the brain. The anterior strap musculature of the neck is serially dissected. Multiple sections of the sternocleidomastoid muscle disclose no hemorrhages. Sections of the remainder of the strap musculature of the neck disclose no evidence of hemorrhage. Examination of the thyroid cartilage, cricoid cartilage and hyoid bone disclose no evidence of fracture or hemorrhage. Multiple cross sections of the tongue disclose no hemorrhage or traumatic injury. The thyroid gland weighs 2 gm and is normal in appearance. Cut sections are finely lobular and red-tan. The trachea and larynx are lined by smooth pink-tan mucosa without intrinsic abnormalities.

MICROSCOPIC DESCRIPTION: (All Sections Stained with HAE)

(Slide key) - (A) - scalp hemorrhage, (B) - sections of vaginal mucosa with smallest fragment representing area of abrasion at 7:00 position, (C) - heart, (D–F) - lungs, (G) - liver and spleen, (H) - pancreas and kidney, (I) - thyroid and bladder,

(J) - thymus and adrenals, (K–L) - reproductive organs, (M) - larynx, (N–T) - brain.

Myocardium: Sections of the ventricular mycoardium are composed of interlacing bundles of cardiac muscle fibers. No fibrosis or inflammation are identified.

Lungs: The alveolar architecture of the lungs is well preserved. Pulmonary vascular congestion is identified. No intrinsic abnormalities are seen.

Spleen: There is mild autolysis of the spleen. Both red and white pulp are identifiable.

Thyroid: The thyroid gland is composed of normal-appearing follicles. An occasional isolated area of chronic interstitial inflammatory infiltrate is seen. There is also a small fragment of parathyroid tissue.

Thymus: The thymus gland retains the usual architecture. The lymphoid material is intact and scattered Hassall's corpuscles are identified. Mild vascular congestion is identified.

Trachea: There is mild chronic inflammation in the submucosa of the trachea.

Liver: The lobular architecture of the liver is well preserved. No inflammation or intrinsic abnormality are identified.

Pancreas: There is autolysis of the pancreas which is otherwise unremarkable.

Kidney: The overall architecture of the kidney is well preserved. There is perhaps mild vascular congestion in the cortex but no inflammation is identified.

* * *

Bladder: The transitional epithelium of the bladder is autolyzed. No significant intrinsic abnormalities are seen.

Reproductive Organs: Sections of the uterus are consistent with the prepubescent age. The ovary is unremarkable.

Adrenal: The architecture of the adrenal is well preserved and no intrinsic abnormalities are seen.

Brain: Sections from the areas of contusion disclose disrupted blood vessels of the cortex with surrounding hemorrhage. There is no evidence of inflammatory infiltrate or organization of the hemorrhage. Subarachnoid hemorrhage is also identified. Cortical neurons are surrounded by clear halos, as are glial cells.

Vaginal Mucosa: All of the sections contain vascular congestion and focal interstitial chronic inflammation. The smallest piece of tissue, from the 7:00 position of the vaginal wall/ hymen, contains epithelial erosion with underlying capillary congestion. A small number of red blood cells is present on the eroded surface, as is birefringent foreign material. Acute inflammatory infiltrate is not seen.

EVIDENCE: Items turned over to the Boulder Police Department as evidence include: Fibers and hair from clothing and body surfaces; ligatures; clothing; vaginal swabs and smears; rectal swabs and smears; oral swabs and smears; paper bags from hands; fingernail clippings; jewelry; paper bags from feet; white body bags; samples of head hair, eyelashes and eyebrows; swabs from right and left thighs and right cheek; red top and purple top tubes of blood.

END OF REPORT